FAMOUS REGIMENTS

Britain's Brigade of Gurkhas

For a list of the other titles in this series
please write to the publishers.

FAMOUS REGIMENTS

Edited by
Lt-General Sir Brian Horrocks

Britain's Brigade of Gurkhas

The 2nd K.E.O. Goorkha Rifles
The 6th Q.E.O. Gurkha Rifles
The 7th D.E.O.Gurkha Rifles and
The 10th P.M.O. Gurkha Rifles
The Queen's Gurkha Engineers, Signals
and Transport Regiments

by E. D. Smith

A Leo Cooper Book
Secker & Warburg, London

First published in Great Britain, 1973
by Leo Cooper. Now reissued in 1982
by Leo Cooper in association with
Martin Secker & Warburg Limited
54 Poland Street, London W1V 3DF

Reprinted 1984, 1994

ISBN 0 436 47510 3

Printed and bound in Great Britain at
The Camelot Press Ltd, Southampton

Acknowledgements

THIS is in no way an official history of the four Regiments of 'Britain's Brigade of Gurkhas'. Mistakes and opinions are mine alone.

It is important to stress that no reference is made to the exploits of the other six Gurkha regiments who, until 1947, were part of the Gurkha Brigade in the Indian Army. It would have been impossible to have included them without doubling the size of the book. Throughout the period 1817 to 1947, one or other of those fine regiments shared the ordeals and triumphs of their fellow Gurkhas whose sons and grandsons now serve in the British Army. The reputation of the Gurkha regiments now serving in the modern Army of India is as high as ever.

My problem in attempting to cover the story of the four famous regiments has been to decide what to include from the many battles and actions fought over the years. I am conscious that the 'Confrontation' in Borneo has been but sketchily dealt with. Alas, current security rules will not allow the full story to be told for many years to come.

The book could not have been written without generous help and advice from many friends. The list is too long to enumerate but I thank them all with sincerity. If I single out Lt-Col H. C. S. Gregory, it is to show my gratitude for giving up so much of his time to read the manuscript and give me the benefit of his advice on many points.

Finally, I would like to thank the four Regimental and three Corps Associations for so kindly giving me permission to use material and quote passages from their Histories.

E. D. Smith,
1972

Illustrations

The author and publishers are grateful to the following for per-
mission to reproduce copyright photographs: The India Office
Library, Nos 1, 2, 7, 9; The National Army Museum, Nos 3, 4, 5,
8, 11, 16, 24; The Imperial War Museum, Nos 6, 12, 13, 14, 15;
Robin Adshead Esq 22, 26; Lt-Col Humphreys, No 10; Soldier
Magazine, No 18; British Army Public Relations Service, No 17;
Central Press Photos, No 25; Associated Press, No 27

Britain's Brigade of Gurkhas

INTRODUCTION
by Lt-General Sir Brian Horrocks

I understand that while I am writing this Introduction, the author, Brigadier 'Birdie' Smith is on a tour of duty in Nepal – so no more need be said about his having the right background for the job! He has certainly paid a worthy and well-deserved tribute to the men he has served and commanded and while his loyalty to and affection for them is ever-apparent he is to be warmly congratulated on this objective and highly readable book.

It is longer than most of the books in the Famous Regiments Series because it covers the histories of the four Gurkha regiments which became part of the British Army in January, 1948, after the partition of India. These were the 2nd, 6th, 7th and 10th Gurkha Rifles. But although their history does not go back as far as that of the home-raised Infantry regiments of the British Army, in nearly 160 years of service with the Indian and British Armies, they have won as much glory and acquired as splendid a reputation as the oldest and proudest Regiment of the Line.

It was in 1814 that Lieutenant Frederick Young first obtained permission to enrol a corps of Gurkha soldiers and the following year saw the formation of the Sirmoor Rifles, later to become the 2nd King Edward VII's Own Gurkha Rifles. Young served as their commandant for 28 years, thereby setting from the start an example of single-mindedness and continuity of purpose which distinguishes the Gurkhas to this day.

The British soldier has always got on exceptionally well with and, perhaps even more important, has had absolute confidence in the fighting quality of, 'Johnny Gurkha', as he is affectionately known, and in making him what he is today Johnny Gurkha owes not a little to his British officers. Before the First World War they skimmed the cream from the officer potential at Sandhurst. When I arrived there in 1912 and suggested that I might be considered for a commission in the Indian Army my request was received with hoots of laughter. It was pointed out to me that to be considered at all I would have to pass out in the top quarter and I had passed in three from bottom. Moreover British Gurkha officers were selected from the best in this top quarter.

One of their finest and most famous officers transferred to the 6th Gurkha Rifles from a British Infantry Regiment and later commanded the 2/7th. He was of course, Field-Marshal Viscount Slim, Bill Slim, in my opinion the greatest leader of men in the Second World War. The Gurkha officer whom I knew best was 'Gertie' Tuker who commanded the 1/2nd Goorkhas (the only Regiment to spell it that way!) who later became Lieutenant-General Sir Francis Tuker and commanded the famous 4th Indian Division – a brilliant, if unorthodox, leader and a man of rare intellect.

For a brief period I had the privilege of having the 1/2nd Goorkhas and 1/9th Gurkhas, both in the 4th Indian Division, under my command in the Western Desert and in North Africa. They had just succeeded brilliantly in the Battle of Wadi Akarit. The two Gurkha units were given the leading role in the attack to capture the heights which dominated the surrounding country. The final peak was captured, thanks to the gallantry of Subedar Lalbahadur Thapa, the Second-in-Command of D Company: at the head of his men, he dealt with enemy post after enemy post on the steep path leading up the cliff. Just below the crest he had only two riflemen left with him, but he never hesitated and killed several more enemy before the remainder fled. He thus secured and held the one feature which was vital to the success of the operation. His bravery was recognized with the immediate award of the Victoria Cross – the first to be won by a Gurkha in the desert.

On one occasion after this success we were suffering from an intermittent long range enemy artillery bombardment which

The Gurkhas of Nepal

O N a map of the world the small mountain state of Nepal is sandwiched between giant neighbours, India and China. This is something that the Nepalese have learnt to live with over the years, but it is nearly two centuries since they bent their knees to foes from across the border. Within the confines of the capital, Kathmandu, great Powers have sought to influence the rulers of Nepal by gifts, cajolery and threats, but the fact is that Nepal has continued to be a completely independent State, friendly indeed with the British when they ruled India but never part of the old Empire.

It is difficult for the many tourists who now pay fleeting visits to Kathmandu to understand how the people they see in the none too clean bazaars of the city have maintained their independence. It is true that the plain of Kathmandu is ringed by mountains including some of the famous giants of the Himalayas. But mountains alone can deter but not defeat invaders. The peace-loving Newars, the town dwellers of Kathmandu, have never claimed or demonstrated martial qualities; they are craftsmen, keepers of shops and tiny street stalls, with a few of their number aspiring to the title of merchants or businessmen during the last few years. These are the Nepalese – in the surrounding hills live the Gurkhas.

Not all who claim to be Gurkhas live as hillmen, although the majority still cling to their traditional way of life in the small mountain villages. Here are houses often sturdily built and attractive from the outside. To reach a village means walking, although a few ponies exist and can be hired. But for the Gurkhas themselves the winding tracks, up the ridges and down to the steep valleys, over frighteningly slender bridges swaying above ice-cold roaring rivers, are their lifeline and many of their songs are about them, sung as they toil up the hillside or as relaxation when the day's walking is over.

Everyone and everything goes up and down these tracks. The soldier returning to his village after three years in the hot plains of India wears the Indian Army badge on his cap. With him may well be a fellow villager in a mixture of uniform and mountain garb from a British Army Gurkha unit in Hong Kong. Porters tread slowly but surely with heavy loads on their backs, balanced by a band around their foreheads which takes a lot of the strain. Other travellers pass, sometimes on long journeys, or possibly going to their fields nearby to reap the harvest and cut down trees for fuel. The world has changed and the Gurkha soldiers have become more sophisticated but the mode and speed of their travel remains as slow and tough in 1971 as it was three hundred years ago.

Such a life produces a strong, sturdy race; a people who have bodies that can endure the back-breaking loads that are carried by women and children as well as young boys and old men. To balance on and climb the steep slopes, Nature has made the Gurkha villagers short and stocky with thigh and leg muscles that are exaggerated in size and shape. Added to this physique there is a simple and strong sense of humour, deep pride in race, village and family, a people asking little but the right to cultivate their little plot of land, build their own house and when the work is done, to enjoy the occasional village party. Such a hardy and independent people have remained masters in their mountain villages and have sent thousands of first class soldiers to the many parts of the world visited by the British and Indian Armies.

Food and shelter there is for all these hill folk with clear cold streams running near their villages and tiny hamlets. Some years are good, others indifferent, whilst natural disasters like avalanches, swollen river torrents, droughts in the summer and bitter winters are frequent hazards in the hills. Nevertheless there are few cases of dire poverty and starvation is virtually unknown. It is true that medical facilities as enjoyed by western nations are non-existent so that only the strong survive if any serious illness or accident should befall. On such occasions the stoical and fatalistic qualities of the Gurkha come to the fore. Pain is endured with a smile and the sorrow of others viewed with a cool indifference.

All live as farmers on the land and depend completely on the land for work, food, fuel and the basic necessities of life. The word 'farm' is not a very accurate description of the small plots of land or few animals carefully watched on the mountainside. On these smallholdings there is invariably work for one son of the family but rarely for two. It is the 'surplus' young men who leave their homes, usually with the blessing and often with the encouragement of their parents to seek employment as soldiers. Over the years the majority of families have sent many of their young men to enlist so that a tradition of military service has grown up and is added to by successive generations. The exploits of their soldiers are respected by all and sundry. Of such ingredients are soldiers made, the professional soldiers of Nepal.

A soldier returning to his village after a period of service abroad is welcomed as a father or husband, son or brother. The joy in reunion is genuine and natural. Added to this, however, are the savings he brings back, the gifts he has brought and hands to grateful relations. The economy not only of his immediate family and village but also of the nation of Nepal relies to a large extent on the money brought back by the professional soldier. The Left Wing politicians down in the plains of Kathmandu resent the fact that their countrymen serve the foreign armies of India and Britain but, to date, they cannot suggest an alternative solution. Nepal needs the money earned by her Gurkha soldiers and, just as important, these fairly sophisticated and much travelled young men would require alternative employment and equivalent salaries if employment in the British or Indian Armies was terminated by events in Nepal. Nepal, even in 1973, can neither employ nor pay such a large body of men so that the protests of irresponsible students encouraged by unfriendly Powers are ineffectual – so far.

As a young soldier climbs up the track to his village, his mind goes back to the day he left his friends and loved ones, possibly about three years before, to enlist into the 'paltan' (regiment). He would have been one of a group of young men, some from his village, others certainly from the surrounding district, who left still dressed in mountain costume to walk for anything up to ten days to the nearest British or Indian Recruiting Centre. Shepherding the party would be a recruiter, invariably a retired NCO who had settled in the district and is known by repute, if not personally, by the youngsters in his charge. For them all it would be a gamble: the recruiter would only be paid for those who were accepted, with a bonus for outstanding volunteers, whilst the young men would suffer bitter disappointment if not selected by the Recruiting Officer or rejected by the Medical Officer thereafter. For the failures, the alternatives are the weary walk home or possibly a continued journey to seek employment on the Plains of India.

The Recruiting Depots are now on Nepalese soil, but this is a fairly recent innovation. Prior to the mid-nineteen fifties the recruiter and his little band of hopeful youngsters had to cross the border into India before their long walk could be rewarded. In the modern Depots, the young hillmen, hopefully claiming to be at least seventeen years old, see the outward signs of the Army they have come to join. British officers, possibly the first white men the young Gurkha has ever seen, study their physique, judge their intelligence and speak to them in something akin to their language, fluently but at first incomprehensibly because of their accent and strange pronunciation. No matter, if they are accepted and if possible can join the same 'paltan' as their eldest brother is serving in or continue where their fathers had served before them. Acceptance means money to the recruiter and joy to the new recruit. Life is strange as new clothing is given him and the intricacies of wearing army boots are explained by a patient but slightly blasé serving soldier.

Service in the Army is beginning and within days the recruits are on an aeroplane bound for Hong Kong to start their basic training. The mountains of Nepal are left behind but after two years have passed, the Gurkha Rifleman's thoughts turn to the anticipation of his first leave of six months which will soon be due.

As he re-enters his village he does so as an experienced traveller. No trace of the timid recruit remains. He has now become one of the many Gurkha soldiers from Nepal.

The story of four of these Gurkha Regiments and soldiers follows.

Chapter 1

'I went there one man and I came out three thousand'

FREDERICK YOUNG

THE seeds of the long-lasting friendship between Britain and Nepal were not sown in times of peace but in a short and bloody war. The war was not sought by the Honourable East India Company who, in the person of the Governor-General of India, showed remarkable patience and restraint in the face of deliberate and planned Nepalese forays into the low-lying district of the Terai which separates the mountains of Nepal from the adjoining plains of India. The British were not keen to start an open war with Nepal. In the Nepalese capital of Kathmandu there was little desire to appease, chiefly because the rulers had to keep their army busy in order to avoid disbanding large numbers of men for whom there was no employment. And as most of the upper classes held rank in the army, it was very much in their interests to see that the reserves of trained soldiers were recalled at regular intervals.

The beginning of the nineteenth century saw the tiny state of Nepal holding sway over her neighbours to the north-east and west. From Sikkim to the borders of Kashmir and into the Dogra country, all came within her domain. A direct confrontation with the British led to the first words of caution from the leading Nepalese general, Amarsing, to his prime minister, Bhimsen: 'We have hitherto but hunted deer; if we engage in this war we must prepare to fight tigers.' His words prompted an arrogant reply: 'If the English wanted war against the Gurkha conquerors, they could have it.' So war became inevitable. Hostilities began after three British police posts had been attacked by Nepalese soldiers at the end of May, 1814.

Although the British-Indian Army heavily outnumbered its

opponents the Gurkha soldiers were fighting in mountains they knew well and under commanders who added ruthlessness and cruelty to bravery and toughness. Fortunately for Britain the campaign produced a first class commander and tactician in the person of David Ochterlony and, in a series of engagements, he outmanœuvered his opponents, forcing them to retreat from well-prepared strongholds. All this took time and a heavy toll of lives on both sides. Mutual respect grew and by the end of 1814 an assessment of the Gurkha soldier included the remark: 'They are hardy, endure privation and are very obedient. Under our Government they would make excellent soldiers.' After a particularly fierce battle at Kalunga, in which the Gurkha force lost some 520 men out of 600, the inscription on a small white obelisk paid a British tribute to their gallant foes: 'They fought in their conflict like men and, in the intervals of actual conflict, showed us a liberal courtesy.'

But courage alone was not enough to defeat the superior forces available to the British, and Nepal was forced to accept a cease-fire, to cede the Terai and to accept, with great reluctance, the presence of a British Resident in Kathmandu. Ochterlony on his part had already recommended that Gurkhas should be enlisted in the Company's army and one of the officers selected to raise a corps was a Lt Frederick Young. No man could have had more dramatic meetings with the soldiers he was to lead, command and love than Frederick Young.

His first encounter with the Gurkhas was at Kalunga where his commanding general, Gillespie, died in his arms. At the height of the battle a Gurkha appeared waving his hand, as a sign that he wished to enter the British lines. A shot had shattered his lower jaw and he sought and received treatment from a British surgeon. After being discharged, the Gurkha asked permission to return to his own army to continue fighting the British! Young's next meeting in the autumn of 1814 was even more memorable. The party of irregulars he was commanding fled when attacked by a Gurkha force, leaving Young and a handful of officers at bay. When asked why he had not run away as well, Young replied: 'I have not come so far in order to run away. I came to stay.' And he sat down. Such a reply made a big impression on his captors who replied: 'We could serve under men like you.' The seeds of a long and successful partnership were sown, and after the Nepal war was over Frederick Young obtained permission to enrol a corps of Gurkha soldiers. As he described it afterwards: 'I went there one man and came out three thousand.'

The formal agreement between Britain and Nepal on the enlistment of Gurkha soldiers reads: 'All the troops in the service of Nepal, with the exception of those granted to the personal honour of Kagjees Ummersing and Rangor Sing, will be at liberty to enter into the services of the British Government if agreeable to themselves and the British Government choose to accept their services.' Such permission was tardily given and did not hide the ill feeling that existed in Kathmandu towards the British for another thirty or forty years. However, the intrigues at the Royal Court and the feelings of the upper classes in Kathmandu were of little concern to the Gurkha hillmen in their mountain villages. Volunteers flocked down to the plains to enlist in the new corps. For over 150 years the Gurkhas' desire to serve as soldiers has transcended the whims of politicians.

In this, the story of the present-day British Brigade of Gurkhas, the first Corps whose fortunes we follow from the early days of 1815 is the one raised by Frederick Young, the Sirmoor Rifles. For the first time Gurkhas were enlisted under the British flag. Already a high degree of mutual respect existed between the two races; the highest praise the Gurkhas could give to their new comrades in arms was: 'The English are as brave as lions; they are splendid sepoys, very nearly equal to us'. (After the storming of Bhurtpore in 1826).

The incredible keenness of the newly enrolled soldiers of the Sirmoor Battalion made Frederick Young's task a long but rewarding one. He served as their commandant for twenty-eight years, handing over in 1843; truly the father figure of the Sirmoor Rifles, a title used with pride by the 2nd KEO Goorkha Rifles to this day. Young had such confidence in his new soldiers that within six months he had reported them as being fit for active service, but two years were to elapse before his wish was granted. During this time his men discarded various forms of mountain dress and received uniforms more appropriate to their status as soldiers in the Company's employment. Young's determination to test his men in action was to be rewarded in October, 1817 by a summons from his old commander, Sir David Ochterlony.

By that time the second regiment of the present-day British Brigade of Gurkhas had been raised in haste to meet the threat of a rebellion in East India in the State of Cuttack. The Corps was originally called the Cuttack Legion but changed its title several times during the nineteenth century before it eventually emerged as the 6th Gurkha Rifles.

Meanwhile, the Sirmoor hillmen joined General Sir David Ochterlony's Grand Army for their first experience of active service. In the campaign against the Maharattas and Pindaris, Sir David's forces, expertly handled in a series of rapid moves, induced the rebels to come to terms. Only at a village called Sambhar was there any opposition and the Sirmoor Battalion as part of the Reserve Division, helped to take the place without difficulty. As a reward the Battalion was nominated to escort to Delhi the 300 guns surrendered by the Maharatta Army.

Frederick Young's desire to give his Gurkhas another bout of active service 'before the spirit of his men had evaporated' was not fulfilled until 1824, when the Magistrate of Saharanpore sent an urgent cry for help to Dehra Doon, where the Sirmoor Battalion was based. With some 200 Gurkhas under his command, Young moved against a force of about 800 Goojars, who had seized a place called Koonja in the Eastern Doon. Within twenty-four hours an enemy force outside a mud fort had been dispersed. This was done by men who had that day marched over thirty-six miles before they assaulted and was a clear indication that the Sirmoor Rifles had trained hard in the six years of peace.

There was to be no respite, however, as the rebels temporarily withdrew behind the high walls of the mud fort, and it was appreciated that any delay would allow them to disperse and later reunite elsewhere. The problem that faced Capt Young and his men was not easy. It was impossible to climb the walls without ladders, and the defenders, outnumbering their opponents by about three to one, were desperate ruffians. There was, moreover, a massive wooden door which, without guns or gunpowder, could only be forced by a battering ram. Consequently, a large tree was cut down and the branches lopped off by the Gurkhas' kukris. Volunteers carried the battering ram on both sides by ropes while a simple plan was made invclving a covering fire party, with a third group poised to rush the entrance once it was forced.

Under furious fire from the walls, which wounded many Gurkhas, the party with the ram reached the door; after five blows, an entrance was made and, led by Young, the men poured in. Heavy hand-to-hand fighting resulted in over 150 of the Goojars being killed before they were routed. Two small iron cannon taken from the fort walls have ever since had an honoured place outside the Sirmoor Battalion Quarter Guard, as has a wooden Roman battering ram, suitably inscribed, which was presented by the residents of Saharanpore. The final honour was that the Sirmoor Rifles were allowed to wear the Ram's Head on all Regimental accoutrements. Young, in his official report on the action, not only praised the excellent fighting qualities of his men but their control and self-discipline after the attack was over. Captives, men as well as women and children, were all treated with respect and dignity.

Barely a year later, three companies of the Battalion joined the army sent by the Government against the usurper of the throne of the State of Bhurtpore, one Doorjan Sal. A series of long forced marches took them from Dehra Doon to Bhurtpore, where they were attached to the 59th Foot. Within tall walls of solid mud, Bhurtpore was defended by some 25,000 Jats, Pathans and Rajputs. A swift move in the early skirmishings had prevented the enemy from filling up the moat around the city and the British cordon was tightened to within 600 yards of the wall. However, the strong earth walls resisted the heaviest siege guns so that mining had to be resorted to. In this, men of the Battalion played their full part until two huge mines were ready for blowing, on the morning of 18 January, 1826.

At dawn the mines were blown and the attack launched. Fighting was fierce but the enemy never recovered from the shock of the two huge explosions. The Sirmoor casualties appear to have been very light; the commander, Capt Fisher, implies that the 59th bore the brunt: 'I am thankful to say we were in with the 59th, who covered themselves with glory – it was the most glorious sight eyes ever beheld'. Nevertheless, the Gurkha contingent was singled out for praise by the divisional commander, General Nichols, and a General Order later gave Bhurtpore as the first of the many battle-honours that were to follow.

The longest period of peaceful inactivity in the whole history of the Second Goorkhas (Sirmoor Rifles) then followed. Old records from Dehra Doon show that the Battalion helped to open up the district by improving communications and assisting in other useful projects. Although in those days there were rarely more than five British officers present in the Regiment, nevertheless they found little to do as the native officers conducted most of the drill parades and field training was rarely, if ever, carried out. As a result Capt Young and his fellow officers turned their attention to other matters – for example, Capt Young became the Political Agent and the Super-intendent of the Doon district, while his Adjutant devoted much of his time to canal construction. Old records in Dehra Doon pay testimony to the industry and resourceful efforts of Young and his men in opening up the district around the town.

During the 1830s the Regiment gradually obtained more land and set up permanent lines in Dehra Doon. By 1833 their uniform was virtually the same as the Rifle regiments in the British Army, green with black facings and black belts, while the old musket had been replaced by the fusil. The pay of the sepoy was a mere pittance of five rupees eight annas a month, but in spite of this discipline and morale during the peaceful interlude was of high order. Capt Young recorded that in a period of over five years there was only one court martial.

1846 saw the end of this inactivity when the Sutlej Campaign and Sikh War started. By 1846 the Sikh Army had not only taken over power in their own land, the Punjab, but had moved down to cross the Sutlej into East India Company territory. Pillage, looting and destruction followed until General Sir Hugh Gough succeeded in sending detachments to safeguard outlying towns and cantonments. To a place called Loodianah went the Sirmoor Battalion, with a small contingent of Patiala cavalry, and for six hours they faced a large body of Sikhs on the other side of the parade ground; their steadiness so impressed the Sikhs that the latter decided to withdraw without a shot being fired.

This was to prove but a brief respite, as a large force under a Sikh leader, Sirdar Ranjore Singh, threatened the whole area of Loodianah and only after a period of move and counter-move was Sir Hugh Gough able to take firm control of the town. Ranjore Singh withdrew to a position near the village of Aliwal, his army arranged in a semi-circle with the River Sutlej guarding his flanks and an impressive array of heavy guns and mortars to protect his front. Thus ensconced, the Sikh leader awaited his immediate opposite number, General Sir Harry Smith.

On this day, 28 January, 1846, Capt Fisher was commanding the Sirmoor Battalion who together with the 50th Foot and 43rd Native Infantry were in General Wheeler's Brigade, on the left of the British force. The Sikh artillery took a toll of the attackers but could not delay or hold up the assault. 'Wheeler's Irresistible Brigade', as Sir Harry Smith called it, was heavily engaged on the left. The Sirmoor Colours were almost shot to pieces, the Gurkha officer carrying them was killed and the black regimental colour was, for a few moments, in the hands of the enemy. Havildar Badalsing Thapa, an NCO destined to distinguish himself again during the Mutiny, led a party to recover the Colours and then he personally captured a Sikh standard. The Sikhs wavered and, losing cohesion, were put into dire confusion by cavalry charges made by, among others, the 16th Lancers and 3rd Light Cavalry. The day was won. Capt Fisher was mentioned in despatches and the Battalion lost just under fifty killed and wounded, out of the army's total of some 590 men.

Meanwhile, the main Sikh Army, although disheartened by this reverse, remained further up the River Sutlej at Sobraon. Their position was in many ways similar to that adopted by their comrades at Aliwal; the river protected both flanks, a triple line of breastworks to the fore was bristling with guns and there were some 35,000 Sikh soldiers ready to fight to the death. But, as at Aliwal, the river behind them was to be a doubtful ally. It curtailed movement and, in the end, this factor assisted the attacking force.

On 10 February, 1846, General Gough's guns began the bombardment that heralded a battle destined to rage fiercely from early morning until late in the day. On this occasion, the Sirmoor Gurkhas found themselves in the centre in General Gilbert's division. Initially, openings had to be made through the entrenchments and this was done by the sappers. Through the breaches field guns and cavalry entered to throw the defenders off balance before the infantry closed on the Sikhs in fierce hand-to-hand conflict. Three divisions of infantry hurled the Sikhs back into the river, where hundreds were to die from drowning or from the British fire. Sobraon, called 'a brutal bulldog fight' by Sir Harry Smith, was over, but the part played by Capt Fisher's force needs to be recorded.

Being in the centre, their task was probably the severest. Their Commandant, Capt Fisher, was killed at the head of his troops, a sad but gallant end to many years with the Battalion. Over a hundred of his troops were killed or wounded, nearly a quarter of the casualties lost by Sir Hubert Gough's whole army. The General, writing of his troops, stated: 'I especially noticed the two Gurkha Corps employed under me, viz the Sirmoor Battalion and the Nassira Battalion (later 1st Gurkhas). . . . Soldiers of small stature, but indomitable spirit, they vied in ardent courage with the Grenadiers of our own nation and armed with a short weapon of their country, were a terror to the Sikhs throughout this great conflict'. At a lower level, a British NCO commented, 'The Gurkhas are dressed in dark green. They kept time and pace with out English regiments. The Sikhs were fighting bravely for their guns and camp. . . . But, oh, to tell the loss'.

The Sikh War was over, and under a new Commandant the Battalion marched back to Dehra Doon in the knowledge that their great services had been recognized and promulgated in the Governor-General's own Order of the Day. For eight years after 1846 the Battalion was not called on to participate in any warlike activities and this period was used to the full in reorganization; it saw re-armament, with the old two-grooved Brunswick rifles being replaced by the smooth bore fusil, and another change of uniform. But it is now time to trace the exploits of the Cuttack Legion from their early days until the Indian Mutiny.

Unlike the Sirmoor Rifles the Cuttack Legion did not contain any Gurkhas from Nepal until 1828, and even then, hillmen from Nepal formed but two of the ten companies in the Regiment. Such a policy was to continue until as late as 1886 when the Regiment finally became completely Gurkha. The fact that it changed titles several times has been mentioned before but its primary role throughout the nineteenth century was to keep the peace in the Eastern provinces of India. For such a reason it was particularly appropriate when the Regiment became 'light infantry' in 1823, a title which matched its role during this period. Small mobile detachments sought out bands of tribesmen who refused to accept encroachments by the East India Company into their territories, and these soldiers by their very presence encouraged peaceful citizens to go about lawful pursuits in a normal manner.

In the Cuttack district elements of the Regiment saw their first active service in an expedition against a rebellious tribe called the Kols. Little is recorded of the part played by the Regiment in this campaign but the Kols fought 'with a degree of rashness and hardihood scarcely credible' – and as a result suffered heavy casualties. They pressed home attacks on the mounted troops with their axes and continued to do so until many of their own men had been sabred to death. The Corps at this time consisted of cavalry and artillery, as well as three companies of infantry, so that the first commander of the Regiment, Capt Simon Fraser, had about 650 men under his command. After the successful outcome of these clashes with the Kols tribesmen, the Regiment moved back to the province of Rangpur in Bengal.

Soldiers in the Indian Army in those days were paid pittances by modern standards. The total monthly pay for a company of ninety-four infantry soldiers in the Cuttack Legion is recorded as having been Rs549 – approximately £30 at the current rate of exchange. The instruction which gives details of the pay and allowances at the same time disbanded the cavalry element in the Legion and led to a further re-organization and another change in title, to the Eighth Rangpur Light Infantry. Bearing this name the Regiment took part in its first big campaign during the Burma War from 1824 to 1826.

The port of Chittagong was the objective sought by the invading Burmese armies, including the one whose advance from Assam was attacked by a British force which contained four companies of the 8th Rangpur Light Infantry. The Burmese were defeated and forced to retreat after a series of attacks made with great spirit by the small British forces. Nevertheless, it is worth recording that the Burmese tactics were well in advance of those adopted by other armies. 'It was with astonishment that our men saw the Burmese advance and then leading lines would disappear; we saw them advancing in a regular line, but presently the men forming that line were prostrate on the ground and in a very short time, very comfortably ensconced in small excavations made with a tool they carried, from which they fired until a further forward move was decided'. The Burmese were successful at a place called Ramu, but thereafter suffered many defeats and eventually decided to evacuate all the ground they had won. The difficult country, grave lack of transport and the long monsoons curtailed operations for many months and the campaign dragged on until February, 1826, when a British force within striking distance of Ava, the capital of Burma, induced the Burmese to negotiate peace. The Regiment had lost a few men in action and many more from sickness. At the same time the first official note of appreciation was received from the column commanders. 'The conduct of the Rangpur Light Infantry merits my warmest approbation. . . . To their OC Capt McCleod, my best thanks are especially due.'

A new era began when the Regiment moved to Assam, where it was to be stationed for the next thirty-four years. Appropriately, the title was changed in 1827 to the Assam Light Infantry and, as mentioned before, the strength of the unit was increased by an extra two companies composed entirely of Gurkhas. All these changes took place against a background of turbulence, as the Nagas and other tribes in Assam were continually causing trouble. The Singpohs, a tribe of the Kachins, were the most recalcitrant as they resented the efforts of the British to stop slavery. Small outposts were attacked with regularity, but when commanded by British officers they were usually able to hold out until relieving forces arrived from the main Regimental base.

One tragedy which upset all ranks of the Regiment occurred in 1839 at the regimental base in Sadiya. For the first time the Regiment was commanded by an officer above the rank of major. Lt-Col White, recently promoted to that rank, had taken great pains to establish a good personal relationship with the Kampti tribe who lived around Sadiya. The Regiment's Subedar Major had told his CO about rumours of an impending attack against the cantonment, but Col White chose to disregard the warning. Just before daylight on 28 January, 1839 the cantonment was suddenly attacked from three directions by a large force of tribesmen. Regardless of age or sex, everyone whom the tribesmen met was massacred; the magazine was taken; Col White was cut to pieces on his way to the lines and the Subedar Major died after a gallant fight in which he killed seven of the enemy.

Retribution was swift and the enemy was counter-attacked by the other companies of the Regiment. After suffering heavy casualties, the tribesmen broke into small parties and sought cover in the jungle. The majority of them were overtaken and cornered near the banks of the River Brahmaputra, where few escaped death or captivity. Later, the Kampti tribes were broken up and large numbers were deported to various parts of India, and thereafter they ceased to play an active part in the provinces near the North-East Frontier.

The next Commanding Officer, Capt J. F. Hannay, was to hold the appointment for twenty-two years. Long periods of command were not unusual in the early days of the Indian Army and Hannay's tenure almost coincided with Charles Reid's eventful days as CO of the Sirmoor Rifles. Men like Hannay and Reid assumed a great responsibility at an early age, an important factor when the ardours of the Indian climate had to be endured without modern conveniences like air conditioning and refrigerators. In compensation, however, those youthful commanding officers were not burdened by twentieth-century bureaucratic methods of administration, nor were their actions scrutinized and examined by news-hungry reporters and television cameramen.

Hannay's command began quietly, but the task of outpost detachments and patrols continued throughout the eighteen-forties. In most cases the presence of these small military parties acted as a deterrent to the local tribesmen, but every now and again the temptation to attack a group of soldiers became too difficult to resist. Two examples can be quoted. A truly gallant stand by a tiny garrison on detachment at Mingri in 1843 beat off four determined attacks by over 300 Singpoh tribesmen who eventually retired to their homes. In contrast to this successful outcome, another party at Pisa, forty miles south of the regimental base at Sadiya, was besieged for over a week until food, water and ammunition were exhausted. Beguiled by promises of safe conduct given by the Singpohs, the Subedar in command of the twenty-three man detachment opened the gates. The tribesmen then slaughtered every man. Full retribution for any reverse was always quick to follow and in this particular instance the whole Regiment, after a thorough and meticulously planned operation, crushed the Singpoh tribesmen. Villages and crops were burnt and the leaders were either killed or captured; the will to resist soon disappeared and the power of the Singpohs was completely broken.

In the years that immediately preceded the Indian Mutiny the 1st Assam Light Infantry, as they were now called, continued to be tested by one tribe or another on the north-east border of Assam. Junior officers were given ample opportunities to use their initiative and to tackle situations without first seeking advice from their superiors. One such officer was Lt Eden, who was sent to capture a chief of the Mishmi tribe, Kishi Gohon, a man wanted for the murder of some French missionaries. Eden set off with his company but soon realised that such a force going into the Mishmi Hills would be noticed and thus raise the alarm. He selected twenty men, and after eight days of forced marching, swinging over dangerous torrents on bridges of single canes, experiencing bitter cold in the high ranges, and showing a wonderful endurance of great harships, Eden's party reached the village on the banks of a river in the grey dawn of a misty morning. As dawn was breaking Eden and his selected party of men moved into the Chief's house and captured him in bed. The second half of the task was to get their captive back without the alarm being raised, but this was achieved by the cool leadership of the young Eden and Kishi Gohon was hanged after a trial in Dibrugarh.

Actions like these showed the local population that the Regiment was to be respected. When the Indian Mutiny broke out in 1857 the number of incidents in the north-east area around Dibrugarh did not increase. This was due to the work put in by Hannay's men, and their efforts had not been in vain.

Chapter 2

'Without such men I never could have held the position entrusted to me'

CHARLES REID

WITH the passing of the years misconceptions about the Indian Mutiny have grown, especially in the minds of many Indian historians. The temptation to present it as a part of the struggle against the British, starting in 1857 and culminating in 1947, has proved difficult to resist. Nevertheless, definitive and authentic accounts written during and after the Mutiny show that it was indeed a mutiny by parts of the Native army as opposed to a national uprising. Only in Oudh did a great rising assume anything like the appearance of a national movement; affairs there had been brought to a head by tactless handling of much-needed land reform by the British officials concerned. Elsewhere the outbreak remained a military mutiny by sepoys, supported by despotic rulers eager for more power, merchants seeking further wealth and malcontents ready to spread anarchy for their own twisted satisfaction and gain.

The conspirators knew not where, when or how the Mutiny would start. None of the grievances was serious enough to change the grumbling into a rising with bloodshed and violence. Eventually a spark was found to ignite the tinder of unrest when the new greased cartridge was taken into service in the army. It was coated in animal fat. To both Hindu and Muslim soldier, who had to bite off the end of the cartridge to release the powder, it was an outrage to their religious feelings as the grease was alleged to be a mixture of pig and cow fat. Stories spread around that the British were deliberately trying to convert the sepoys to Christianity by making them lose caste; thereafter feelings were easily roused. Although the Mutiny began without a definite timetable, nevertheless it was not spontaneous; many had planned for it even though they were surprised at the timing and intensity of the first outbreak of violence.

May, 1857, found the Sirmoor Battalion in their lines at Dehra Doon and the First Assam Light Infantry at Dibrugarh in Assam. The Sirmoor Battalion was about to face one of the most momentous periods in its history. The Assam Light Infantry had a watching brief in the east where the only trouble occurred near Chittagong. The 34th Native Infantry mutinied and moved northwards in an attempt to raise the district against the British, but they were not successful. Eventually they broke into small groups which were harried to death or captivity. In these operations the future 6th Gurkha Rifles played a notable part; otherwise their role of pacifying Assam tribesmen continued without any other distractions throughout the Mutiny.

On Sunday, 11 May, 1857, the rumbling burst into the open at Meerut. The Commandant of the Sirmoor Battalion, Major Charles Reid, had his men in a state of immediate readiness; on 14 May a tired camel sowar arrived in Dehra Doon with instructions that the Regiment was to move with the greatest possible urgency to Meerut where the Europeans were already in dire trouble. Four hours later, Reid, two British officers and six companies of Gurkha soldiers were on the move.

The march to Meerut, even without opposition and the general chaos that existed in the countryside, was a test of endurance. Distances of up to thirty miles a day were covered in the heat of the mid-May Indian summer. The first brush with mutineers came on the fifth day of their march near the Ganges Canal. The ringleaders were seized, tried and shot that night and although five of them were Brahmins, none of the Gurkha Brahmins serving in the battalion were swayed by the plight of the Indian mutineers, even though they were of the same high caste.

As the distance to Meerut lessened, so did the skirmishes with the rebels increase. On 30 May Reid was told to move to a place called Ghaziabad and reinforce Brigadier-General Wilson's force, which was being hard-pressed by the mutineers. Starting at six p.m. and moving through a night of terrific heat, the Sirmoor Battalion covered twenty-seven miles before dawn the next day. After a short rest the exhausted men continued until they reached Wilson's camp on 1 June. It was here that the Sirmoor Battalion met the 60th Rifles for the first time and began an association that has lasted for over a hundred years. The initial greeting by the British was understandably suspicious as their faith in the native regiments had been badly shattered by events in Meerut. The Gurkhas' tents were pitched on the left, next to the artillery who, it was afterwards learnt, had been told to pound them if any signs of mutiny were detected. Events in the next few days were to dispel such mistrust and the highest degree of mutual admiration was attained.

After one successful encounter with the Sepoys, General Wilson's small force was ordered to move toward Delhi. The capital city of the old Mogul empire, Delhi was a symbol to the native insurgents and its recapture was the most urgent need as far as the British were concerned. As long as it was in the hands of the mutineers the rising would continue and more and more of India be encouraged to take up arms.

The city circumference was over seven miles long and the British did not have the numbers to lay siege to such a large area. The original columns sent to attack Delhi were probably less than 2,000 strong and, although augmented by other units, were vastly outnumbered by the (estimated) 20,000 well-armed Sepoys whose numbers increased daily in the city. Another disadvantage that the Delhi Field Force suffered from was that no one remained permanently in command during the first month as each general in turn fell sick of cholera.

The British decided to capture and sit on the Delhi Ridge that ran north of the city, to invite attacks but to hold firm until reinforcements arrived. On 8 June, after two hours of sharp fighting, the Ridge was occupied and the mutineers chased to the city walls. As soon as Reid's men siezed this area the rebels mounted a fierce attack. Reid and his Battalion, supported by two companies of the 60th Rifles and guns from Scott's Battery, advanced to meet and defeat them. They fought for sixteen hours in terrific heat, and the victors were utterly exhausted. Their reward was to be cheered by the European troops on their return to the Ridge in the evening. The Gurkhas were now completely accepted as brothers in arms.

Fortunately for posterity, Major Charles Reid wrote and retained letters and notes throughout the seige of Delhi. In his own words, as he found leisure after march or battle, we learn how the struggle for Hindu Rao's House fared from the first clash on 8 June until the final victory in mid-September. He himself was appointed to command the main picquet and apart from his own Regiment, he had two companies of the 60th Rifles and two guns permanently under his orders. In addition, a further two companies of the 60th Rifles were held back in reserve and these were sent forward to Reid's support as and when the occasion demanded. In fact, such occasions were to number twenty-six major attacks by the rebels against Hindu Rao's House.

Hindu Rao's House was within 1,200 yards of the nearest rebel outpost and was soon to be sadly knocked about by their artillery. Although British guns gave heroic support throughout the seige, more often than not under direct fire, there was an initial grave shortage of twenty-four and eighteen pounder shot, so that the enemy shot had to be retrieved and fired back through the British guns – this did not help the accuracy or the effectiveness of their fire.

In the immediate pre-monsoon heat throughout June, Reid's small force was subjected to several attacks, often by as many as 8,000 rebels at a time. Charles Reid was no believer in static defence, nor did he believe that his Gurkhas' morale would remain at the highest level if they were to be continually attacked by shell and bullet without being a given chance to close with the mutineers and wield their kukris. As 'the rascals' or, another of Reid's terms, 'scoundrels' poured out of the city, so then, the alarm sounded and support troops in position, did Reid sally forth to close with them. Such actions were often costly but his offensive tactics were able to hide the weakness and numbers of his force and, as the days went by, gradually discouraged the mutineers from attempting anything ambitious without calling out a huge body of their soldiers. By the end of June the Sirmoor Rifles' casualties had reached 138 out of the original 490 men – almost identical to the losses sustained by the 60th Rifles during the same period.

An urgent call for reinforcements from Dehra Doon resulted in men being despatched, but they did not arrive until the end of July. The heavy strain on the defenders became so intolerable that four companies of the 60th Rifles, some 300 men from the Guides Corps and Coke's Rifles (later the 13th Frontier Force Rifles) were added to the number of defenders around the main picquet. Thus strengthened, Reid's force was able to silence new enemy batteries on the right of the British position by a very successful raid in which Tomb's Troop of guns distinguished themselves.

Many were the cases of extreme gallantry noted by Reid in his diary. A hero of the battle of Aliwal, Havildar Badalsing, again showed great powers of leadership, and not only was he decorated on the field of battle but also promoted to Jemadar. His men were happiest when allowed to attack. Reid mentioned one such request when, in his own words, 'One of my little fellows said "Sahib, here we are getting knocked over in cold blood; do let us jump over this breastwork and go at the enemy, they think we are afraid of them". "Have patience", was my reply, "and get under cover, I'll let you go presently", upon which he gave a broad grin and looked quite happy'. Charles Reid's admiration for his men, 'my little fellows', was no greater than the opinions he expressed about the 60th Rifles under his command. 'The feeling that existed between the 60th Rifles and my own men was admirable: they call one another brothers, shared their grog with each other. . . . My men used to speak of them as "our Rifles" and the men of the 60th as "them Gurkhees of ours".' This close fellowship and steel discipline was never to waver and in the end caused the defeat of the mutineers, after a total of three months and eight days' continuous struggle.

As July ended, the commanders of the Delhi Force were under severe pressure, not only from the politicians but also from the men under their command, to risk an all out assault on the city. The overall commander, General Archibald Wilson, procrastinated. One reverse would have been disastrous, with the whole of India watching events in Delhi. At last, when his force had been built up to about 8,000 men and included some heavy guns, Wilson was asked to reconsider the position. Unknown to him, one or two of his subordinates had already said that if he refused to attack, they were going to take steps to supplant him. Wilson agreed with reluctance, although he was careful to add a rider to the effect that if the attack failed he was not responsible.

The mutineers made their final attacks at the end of August. On the 30th, the date of the last attack, the King of Delhi, his ladies and retinue, took their places in specially erected seats to witness the downfall of Hindu Rao's House and the neighbouring Sammy's House to the south. As an incentive to his wavering army, which now totalled over 40,000 men, a written order from the King promised ten rupees for every Gurkha's head, the same price being offered for an English soldier's. In Reid's words: 'The rascals found me at home and took a sound thrashing'. It was to be their last major effort.

British plans were made to attack as soon as sixty heavy guns had arrived and been positioned. The lookout on Hindu Rao's House was an excellent place from which to observe the city walls and John Nicholson became a regular visitor there. After an initial meeting with Reid, who described him as 'having a haughty manner and peculiar sneer', they soon became the best of friends and Reid sought Nicholson's advice on several occasions thereafter. Reid last saw Nicholson on 13 September, the day before the attack in which he was killed.

The attack started at four a.m. on 14 September. Major Reid's column consisted of his own Battalion (now down to about 200 men), the Guides, detachments of the 60th Rifles, the 61st and 75th Foot, Coke's Rifles and the ever reliable Tomb's Troop of the Royal Horse Artillery – probably 2,500 men, a large force to be commanded by a major. Reid's plan was simple but effective. He intended making a feint attack from the front to mask the main assault, launched from the flank and from the rear. Unfortunately, just as he had completed his final arrangements, Reid was wounded in the head and his second-in-command, Capt Lawrence, took over.

This caused a delay and Reid's column did not progress as quickly as had originally been planned.

In the violent battle that followed, the Sepoys fought stubbornly and the struggle ebbed and flowed. But in all sectors the attackers had been given clear objectives and slowly fought their way forward to reach them. The siege as such was over, although some bitter fighting was to continue in certain parts of the city until 16 September and, regrettably, vengeance was taken against the innocent as well as the guilty by the attacking army.

Victory was not achieved without a heavy price. Charles Reid's column lost about a third of its strength while in the Sirmoor Battalion 370 out of the original 490 had been killed or wounded in or near Delhi. Only one British officer was to survive unscathed. A heavy price indeed, but with Delhi restored to British hands, the Mutiny lost any chance of gaining fresh support elsewhere in India.

The honours and messages of congratulations followed. For the survivors perhaps the greatest honour was when the 60th Rifles readily agreed to (the now) Colonel Reid's request that the men of the Sirmoor Battalion should be called Riflemen. Official agreement in 1858 also confirmed that the Sirmoor Battalion should be known as the Sirmoor Rifle Regiment and scarlet facings, as worn by the 60th Rifles, were adopted thereafter. Finally, the Governor-General granted the Regiment the exceptional honour of carrying a third special Colour 'on which the word Delhi was to be inscribed in Persian, Hindi and English'.

In 1863 Charles Reid handed over as Commandant. Although he later rose to be a general, his name is automatically associated with the seige of Delhi. Before he left the Regiment Reid received, at the command of Her Majesty Queen Victoria, a 'Truncheon' from the Commander-in-Chief at a ceremonial parade in Lahore in November, 1863. The Truncheon thus replaced the Colours which, as a Rifle regiment, the Sirmoor Rifles could no longer carry. It was indeed an appropriate end to Reid's command and the Truncheon to this day commemorates Delhi, Hindu Rao's House, and the successful outcome of the long siege which is observed as a Regimental Day on 14 September every year. On the evening of each Delhi Day, the

British officers dine, watched over by the Truncheon and parts of the table that was used for casualties in Hindu Rao's House during the Siege.

The Mutiny did not come to an end when Delhi fell. It had received its death blow but in various provinces disturbances still broke out and the Army's task continued for a further year or so.

Before leaving the Indian Mutiny the part played by the Nepalese Army itself must be recorded. In Kathmandu, the Prime Minister, Jangbahadur Rana, offered some 6,000 soldiers to the Governor-General, and his offer was readily accepted. The Nepalese Army Contingent was soon heavily engaged with the rebels in Northern India and suffered severe losses. Lord Canning asked Jangbahadur himself to take command and provide further reinforcements. Jangbahadur did not hesitate. Moving down to the besieged Lucknow where they joined General Sir Colin Campbell, the Nepalese Army played an important part in the attacks that led to the fall of the city.

The British did not forget such loyalty. The Terai was returned to Nepal for all time, and General Sir Colin Campbell arranged special escorts in honour of Jangbahadur's victorious contingent.

Loaded with plunder, the hillmen returned to Nepal after playing a notable part in the cause of their ally, Great Britain. Links forged by comrades in arms were thus extended to politicians and leaders in Kathmandu, New Delhi and, to a lesser extent, London.

Chapter 3

MANY military problems faced the British-Indian Government after the Mutiny, and these included both the North-West and Eastern frontiers of India. Over the years, the North-West Frontier has captured the imagination of soldiers and military historians alike; many units won battle-honours and the lessons learnt from the campaigns had an influence on tactics used in both World Wars. On the other hand, the Eastern Frontier has never found a prominent place in the story of India during the nineteenth century, although peace there was a rare commodity.

From 1860 until the outbreak of the First World War, one or other of the units which were later to form the British Brigade of Gurkhas was on active service in Assam or North-East Bengal. The hilly province of Assam was to remain the eastern boundary of the Indian Empire until 1885. During this period, Britain's interest in the area grew as the tea industry developed. Although encroachments were made into tribal areas in the wake and name of trade, it is easy to understand why the tribesmen viewed it all with grave suspicion. As time went by, they found it wise to make promises to obey the orders of the Government, even if they had no intention of keeping their word.

In 1858 the Abors broke the peace with a murderous attack on a village near Dibrugarh. The Abors were expert shots with bows from which they fired poisoned arrows. The 1st Assam Light Infantry made two sorties against the tribesmen; the first ended in failure, a result brought about by a complete lack of cooperation between the military commander and the civil officer who accompanied the expedition. The two men disagreed about everything from the route to be taken to the tactics to be adopted against the tribesmen. The result was an expedition that failed to achieve anything. Within sight of the final objective, the village of Kebni, the retreat was sounded before an assault had even been contemplated; so-called friendly villagers harassed the force during its withdrawal; and the recriminations between the military commander, Capt Lowther, and the civil officer were so furiously contended that a Court of Inquiry had to be convened by Col Hannay. The court's opinion was that Capt Lowther had led the expedition efficiently but that the civil officer had been particularly gullible in all respects and had placed far too much trust in the tribesmen.

Hannay's answer to this reverse was to lead the next expedition himself. Although on a small scale, it was an amphibious force with two Indian Navy gunboats and a naval contingent operating under his command. In 1859 this force attacked the three principal Abor villages. The Abors' spirited defence claimed forty-five casualties before their villages were captured. It was to be Col Hannay's last major action – he died in Dibrugarh two years later after commanding his Regiment for over twenty-two years.

It must be remembered that, until 1864 the Regiment contained two companies of Gurkhas only. Then the next official step was taken in an Army Order which stated that it would be 'chiefly Gurkhas and hillmen (Assamese) with a proportion not exceeding one fourth of strength of Hindustanis'. The title of the Regiment – which changed with monotonous regularity every few years – did not reflect the increased Gurkha contingent until 1886, when it then became the 42nd Rifle Regiment (Gurkha), The Bengal Infantry. As it transpired, this was the final step in the process of becoming a completely Gurkha unit, the final transition from its Indian origin to the modern 6th Gurkha Rifles. Nevertheless, it is of interest that the class composition of the Regiment was a matter of great controversy. Most officers urged that the Indians and Sikhs should be removed but Col Sheriff (who commanded for over eleven years) wanted to replace all the Gurkhas by Sikhs. The Regimental History commends two junior officers who 'appear to have been able to exert their influence, (and) saved the Regiment from this fate'.

The Government's intention was to use the 42nd and certain other units principally in the eastern provinces of India against the Nagas, Lushais, Abors and other tribesmen, all of whom continued to resist British authority. Of all the tribesmen who clashed with the British the Nagas probably caused the most trouble. The Angami Nagas were of medium height and resembled the New Zealand Maoris in build. Dressed in their full war paint and armed with their short spears, they were formidable looking warriors. From infancy they were brought up in an atmosphere of blood feuds, in which the exact number of losses had to be attained on both sides before a truce could be arranged. They wore a kilt, a *Toga Virilis* ornamented with cowrie shells which denoted each enemy slain. If they penetrated enemy country in anger, then it was considered fair game to kill women and children. They were a tough and robust people who only respected British power if it was permanently established in their territory. The British, however, did the worst thing possible by alternating between an aggressive 'forward policy' or vacillating and withdrawing.

Another warlike people were the Lushai. In the early 1870s the Lushais had carried out a series of raids against neighbouring tea gardens, particularly in the Cachar district, where they massacred many local coolies and some Europeans and also cut up one or two small frontier posts. The Government was stung into taking punitive action and columns were sent over difficult though beautiful country to seek out the Lushai tribes. The 42nd Regiment accompanied one column, of which Col F. S. Roberts (later Field-Marshal Lord Roberts) was Senior Staff Officer. Meanwhile, the Sirmoor Rifles, or 2nd Goorkhas as they were now called, entered the south Lushai hills with a column commanded by General Brownlowe. Both columns had many skirmishes but the main fight occurred when the 2nd Goorkhas attacked Lal Gnoora's village.

The Lushais, like the Nagas, built their villages on the tops of the hills for health reasons and to enjoy the cooler breezes, as well as for defence. The Government troops found each village a formidable task, particularly as they were surrounded by lines of bamboo spikes. At Lal Gnoora's village these spikes, *panjis*, were about eight or nine feet in height. The Lushais opened fire at the same time as some of their numbers began burning the village, prior to evacuation. Gurkha casualties in the centre company could well have been very heavy had it not been for the left flank commander, Major McIntyre, who scrambled over the stockade and disappeared into the smoke to harass the Lushais from an unexpected quarter. His men followed, the enemy broke and eventually dispersed without any more serious fighting. His gallant action saved many lives, and was recognized by the award of the Victoria Cross.

The Lushai campaign ended shortly afterwards; the capture of Lal Gnoora's village proved to be the turning point in the campaign. The 42nd Regiment and the 2nd Goorkhas, as part of the Lushai Expeditionary Force, had fully earned the campaign clasp issued with the Indian Medal – not because of the fighting but, in General Bouchier's words, because 'the history of the expedition has been sheer hard work'.

One small campaign was over but others continued throughout the eighteen-seventies and eighties. Regimental battle casualties were rarely measured in more than a dozen or so, but sickness, the tough nature of the country, and the necessity for vigilance by day and night, all placed a great strain on officers and men alike. Soon events on the North-West Frontier, added to the intransigency of the tribesmen on the North-East, influenced the Government of India into forming second battalions of the five original Gurkha regiments (1st to 5th Gurkha Rifles) in 1886. The 2nd Goorkhas raised its other battalion in a matter of three months; then, as now, recruiting of Gurkhas from the hills of Nepal did not pose any problems. At the same time, the 42nd Assam Light Infantry bade farewell to its Sikhs and Indians, and thereafter took the next step towards joining the modern Brigade of Gurkhas under another title, 42nd Gurkha Light Infantry.

Before the end of the nineteenth century there occurred an episode in the small state of Manipur that added little credit to the British reputation in India. The Maharaja was ousted by his younger brother in a *coup d'état* which was not recognized by the Government. Mr Quinton, Chief Commissioner of Assam, marched with a force to investigate and, if necessary, deal with the rebels. From the start there was complacency; for example, the mountain guns, then in possession of the 42nd Regiment, were not taken with the escort although a private warning was said to have been given Mr Quinton which stated that 'A big tiger was to be killed in Manipur'. The tiger was to be Mr Quinton himself. The story of the blunders made after the arrival of the force in Imphal makes sorry reading: bluster, vacillation and half-hearted measures only served to embolden the Manipuri rebels. The tragic outcome was that Mr Quinton and three other officers accepted a ceasefire, followed by an invitation to attend a durbar in the Palace grounds, where they went without escort. They were murdered in cold blood and many of the escorting force, leaderless and bewildered, scattered and ran in confusion from Imphal. Meanwhile, over 200 Gurkha soldiers were left behind, seemingly without any orders or leaders. Besieged in the Residency by several thousand Manipuris, they fought on until their ammunition gave out. By now the house was ablaze, and in the firelight they fought with kukri and bayonets until they were overpowered by sheer numbers. About fifty survived as prisoners in the hands of the Manipuri rebels.

News of the disaster quickly caused the Government to send forces to seek retribution, even if it was too late to retrieve reputations. Two officers in the original escort were court martialled and cashiered but their sentences were not made public for some time. Meanwhile, the three columns that set out for Manipur included the 42nd Regiment and the 1st Battalion of the 2nd Goorkhas, the original Sirmoor Rifles. Little fighting occurred, rebel leaders were seized, 'the pretender' brought to trial and hanged, and peace thereafter reigned. Always to remain in the men's memories were the marches across forest-clad hills in great heat; each man carried a greatcoat, waterproof sheet, 170 rounds of ammunition plus all his other kit. Cholera struck and the 2nd Goorkhas were to lose thirty-two men out of the fifty-eight cases; later the 42nd Regiment also suffered from the same disease, losing fifty-eight officers and men out of 105 victims. Throughout this period many more men died from cholera and malaria than in battle.

Thereafter service on the North-East Frontier was not to include anything quite as dramatic again. In 1899 the 42nd Regiment moved away from Assam to Abbotabad after a tour of duty in the east that had lasted seventy-seven years. It was indeed to be the final severing of their connections with the old Cuttack Legion of 1817. Four years later the modern title of 6th Gurkha Rifles was adopted.

Events which brought Burma into the British Empire also gave birth to the future 10th Gurkha Rifles. The Third Burma War lasted only nine days in November, 1885, but in its aftermath came anarchy and confusion; dacoits swarmed the countryside, spreading terror and destruction. The situation gradually improved until it became possible to withdraw most of the regular troops from upper Burma. In their place a semi-military force was raised to maintain law and order which became the Burma Military Police.

One of its original units was designated the Kubo Valley Military Police Battalion with the task of protecting the Kubo Valley, which lies between the Chindwin river and Manipur. Well-led and trained from the outset, the Kubo Valley Battalion, the majority of whose men had been recruited from the then little known Kiranti (Limbu and Rai) tribes of Eastern Nepal, soon made a name for itself on operations against dacoits. When, in 1890, the old 10th Madras Native Infantry was converted into a Gurkha regiment, the officers and men of the Kubo Valley Battalion formed the nucleus of the new unit, which established itself at the hill station of Maymyo in Burma. A close association, formed at this time with The Royal Scots, who trained and equipped its first pipers, continues to this day as a recognised affiliation and the pipers of this Gurkha regiment still wear the Hunting Stuart tartan. During the last few years of the nineteenth century the unit's title underwent several changes until, in 1901, it became the 10th Gurkha Rifles. Thereafter, like the other units of the Brigade of Gurkhas, most active soldiering between the two world wars was done on the North-West rather than the Eastern Frontier.

Chapter 4

THE NORTH-WEST FRONTIER BEFORE THE
FIRST WORLD WAR

'An enemy who made no stand in the open, but was unrivalled
as a skirmisher and marksman'.

SIR WILLIAM LOCKHART, 1898

ONE problem which the British never resolved was that posed
by the North-West Frontier. In Eastern India, especially
after the turn of the century, the peaceful interludes
increased as the years went by. It was not to be thus in the
north-west.

During this period British statesmen, both in New Delhi and
London, were highly sensitive to Russia's blatantly displayed
ambitions in Afghanistan. Now, with the benefit of hindsight, it is
easy to understand that the Russians had equal grounds for
suspecting the motives of the British. After the Mutiny, the British
moved north-west through the Punjab and reached the mountains
that separat India from Afghanistan. The mountains were a barrier
to the soft-hearted but a home for the proud and independent
Pathans. The Pathans greeted the British with suspicion and viewed
the encroachments into their territory with hatred. They did not
require any prompting by real or imaginary Russian agents in
Afghanistan to stir up their opposition to the British.

The Pathans, sub-divided into various tribes, often owned plots
of land on both sides of the frontier and moved their animals to the
best pastures without regard for the boundary line.

Such a situation posed many problems to successive Governors-
General and Viceroys during the nineteenth century. They were
tempted to leave the Pathans to their own devices. But British
suspicion of Russian intentions in Afghanistan deepened after the
Mutiny. Without a military presence in the tribal areas the
temptation for Russian agents to stir up trouble, particularly around

the vital passes from Afghanistan into India, was obviously far greater.

By the late eighteen-seventies relations with Afghanistan had become very delicate. The Afghans had been wooed by the British and Russians. Their ruler, Shere Ali, found difficulty in steering a course which satisfied the two big powers and, at the same time, resisted the extremists in his own country. All this was made more complicated by the differing views of successive Governors-General on the threat posed by the Russians in Afghanistan. Inconsistent British policies heightened the sense of insecurity and, in a sense, exacerbated an explosive situation.

In 1878 the Viceroy, Lord Lytton, took a more intransigent line and made certain demands which Shere Ali disregarded. The British forces were concentrated near the border during October and November of that year when the 2nd Goorkhas joined the Peshawar Valley Field Force, and for about five months operated on both sides of the Khyber Pass, without any major clash with the tribesmen. Shere Ali was to die in May of the following year and a treaty was signed with his eldest son, Yakub Khan, in the same month. Yakub Khan asked for a reassurance from the British that his country would remain immune from aggression and this was given. The war was officially over, but Yakub Khan was merely playing for time. In the late summer his intentions became clear.

On 5 September, 1879, came news of a massacre in Kabul. The British Envoy to His Highness the Amir of Kabul, Sir Louis Cavagnari, and his entire escort had been murdered by the Afghans. In India, shock soon turned to anger and a punitive force was concentrated with the greatest speed.

The Kabul Field Force under General Roberts was not a large army, but it compensated for its size by its speed and manœuvrability. Throughout September Yakub Khan continued to profess friendship for the British and to prevaricate, yet in secret he stirred up the tribesmen. Roberts finally decided to march on Kabul on 27 September. By the end of November, after suffering several reverses, including that at Charasiah, Yakub Khan elected to abdicate the Amirship. However, the insurrection was to continue.

The order for the Sirmoor Rifles, now known as the 2nd Goorkhas, their official Indian Army title, came too late for them to participate in the capture of Kabul on 24 December, 1879. Nevertheless, the Regiment was given exacting reconnaissance tasks during the severe winter, when they found themselves under command of an ex-commandant of the Regiment, Brigadier-General McPherson, VC, at Charasiah. Here two companies of the 2nd Goorkhas joined the Sikhs, the 72nd and the 92nd in a successful charge on a large body of Afghans who were in position on a hill. At first the steady fire of the Afghans held up the attackers, but, in the end, the tribesmen were in danger of being outflanked and they fled.

The campaign continued into 1880 with negotiations between the Afghan leaders and the Viceroy's representatives being carried out against a background of intrigue and violence. A further setback to the British was to occur when a brigade of the Kandahar Field Force at Naiwand was defeated by Ayub Khan, a contender for the throne of Afghanistan.

Kandahar was thus directly threatened and to its relief went General Roberts, with four brigades under his command, one of which was commanded by General McPherson in which the 92nd Highlanders and 2nd Goorkhas continued their happy association. A firm and lasting friendship between these units was established, the fruits of which were to be reaped in the battle for the Heights of Dargai, some twenty-seven years later.

General Roberts's march on Kandahar was commemorated by the award of a special ribbon and bronze star to all the units who took part in it. They fully earned the award. In twenty-three days they covered over 300 miles, an average of nearly fifteen miles a day over the most difficult country that can be imagined.

Battle was joined near the village of Sahibaad. The 2nd Goorkhas were commanded by Col. Battye, recently appointed Commandant of the Regiment. Battye's part in the attack on 31 August was brought to a premature end when he was wounded in the shoulder. By ten-thirty in the morning the village was taken, but the Highlanders and the 2nd Goorkhas found themselves confronted by some thousands of the enemy, occupying a position around two guns.

Volleys of fire poured into the massed tribesmen; Major White of the 92nd Highlanders ordered the charge to be sounded. Cheering hillmen from Scotland and Nepal sprang for the guns. A painting by Col Hobday, RA, shows a rifleman of the 2nd Goorkhas thrusting his cap down the muzzle of one of the Afghan guns in order to claim ownership. He is reputed to have shouted in Hindustani: 'This gun belongs to my Regiment – 2nd Goorkhas, Prince of Wales.' True or not, one of the guns was subsequently presented to the Regiment by the Government of India and now stands outside the Officers' Mess.

The Afghans were routed. The fighting had taken its toll of the British, with the 92nd Highlanders suffering heavy casualties. The 2nd Goorkhas lost some thirty killed and wounded while the Afghan figures were estimated to exceed a thousand. The sword of the British had conquered and the political situation was soon to be satisfactorily, if temporarily, established. Nevertheless, events in Afghanistan now influenced the Indian Government into making a further expansion of the Indian Army Gurkha Brigade, as it was then. This authorized, as already noted, the forming of a second battalion for the five Gurkha regiments, and these came into being during 1886.

Apart from the expansion of the Brigade, it is noticeable from the regimental records that the tempo and pace of training had changed. No longer could three or four British officers run a regiment, nor could they undertake duties outside their normal military ones. Field days were held and mountain warfare tactics suitable for the North-West Frontier were studied; officers of all ranks became much more professional in their outlook. Such a change in attitude had undoubtedly been brought about by their experience on the North-West Frontier. The test of their improved training was to come in 1897.

Discontent had been spreading from tribe to tribe until the main ones, the Waziris and Afridis in particular, resorted to open aggression. The Government's attitude to the tribesmen was normally rather like that of a benevolent school master. Pin pricks, even insults, were endured until patience was lost and the big stick, in the shape of troops, was wielded. Punishment invariably entailed burning the villages and destroying the crops. Such action was usually effective but in 1897 the initial raids by the Government forces were met with large-scale opposition. A campaign resulted which was to prove expensive both in money and in lives.

The 1st Battalion of the 2nd Goorkhas, under Col Travers, went on this campaign, but because of the short notice the equivalent of one company from their sister battalion was drafted in to make the unit up to full operational strength. Their early experiences were unpleasant; the August heat in the Kohat area was excessive, with several cases of heat stroke occurring. The tribesmen adopted hit-and-run tactics, firing a few shots, then disappearing to pop up again elsewhere to harass the marching columns and their baggage trains. The 2nd Goorkhas found themselves in the 1st Brigade where they renewed their friendship with the Gordon Highlanders. The association was to be fully tested on the ridge at Dargai.

On 18 October the Brigade was told to move to and secure the heights above Dargai which were known to be held by a large number of Afridis. Dargai was a village on a craggy spur and initially, on 18 October, the British were able to secure the ridge above the village. The tribesmen fought a skilful delaying action and as evening approached re-occupied the hills above Dargai, when the British withdrew and concentrated their force for the night. It was to be an expensive error because the Afridis fortified and prepared sangars throughout the 19th, whilst their opponents awaited the arrival of their guns. At 10 am on the 20 October the 2nd Goorkhas led the way up the ridge, with the Dorsets in support and the 92nd and 95th in reserve. An unearthly silence ensued as they worked their way up. Scarcely a shot was fired, although the enemy sangars were barely 300 yards away. The Afridis knew that these last 300 yards to their position led across an open saddle. This fact had not been discovered by Brigade Headquarters when the plan was made. The 2nd Goorkhas were to pay for this lack of reconnaissance; their attack was shot to ribbons. To quote from an eye witness:

> 'When all was ready, Col Eaton Travers, commanding the 2nd Goorkhas, stepped out in front, drew his sword and called on his

men to follow him. With a smothered shout the men scrambled up the few yards of shale and coarse grass which separated them from the glacis in front, and pouring over the top, came into view of the loopholes above. Instantly the whole line of sangars burst into smoke and flame and a torrent of bullets from front, right, and left, tore through the ranks; men literally fell in heaps and the stony slope was strewn with killed and wounded . . .'

Over sixty men fell, wounded men lay in the open, often receiving further wounds as some 500 breech-loading rifles pumped bullets into a strip of ground the size of two tennis courts.

On the Goorkhas' left the Dorsets suffered a similar reverse with their survivors joining Col Travers's small party hiding in dead ground under the final steep cliff before the objective. The attack had failed.

Although the British guns gave the maximum possible support, their fire was not very effective. A further assault was arranged with the Gordons in the centre and the van, supported by the 3rd Sikhs and, in the final rush, by Col Travers's Goorkhas. The assault went in and in the face of such numbers the Afridis melted away. The Dargai Heights were in British hands but if there was a victory it belonged to the Afridis, whose casualties throughout the battle were very few indeed. The Gordons held the heights but helped to carry down the wounded men from the Goorkhas and Dorsets; this touching display of comradeship has been commemorated in a painting. The 2nd Goorkhas had lost over sixty killed and wounded in this opening action of the Tirah Campaign.

Throughout October and November the British column reconnoitred valleys, seized and opened mountain passes, and destroyed villages which were known to have housed hostile tribesmen. No large-scale battles were fought but the utmost vigilance was required to counteract enemy action against isolated bodies and to deter them from constant harassment of rear guards and picquets. Casualties were never high but they occurred at regular intervals. However, by the beginning of 1898, resistance was virtually over, the Khyber had been reoccupied, and slowly, reluctantly, the tribesmen decided to accept the fines in rifles and money imposed on them by the Government. By April the campaign was over and it was with the deepest admiration and reluctance that the 2nd Goorkhas bade farewell to the Gordon Highlanders. To mark their association two ceremonial kukris were presented to the Gordon Highlanders by the 2nd Goorkhas and, in return, the latter presented a silver statuette and musketry challenge shield to commemorate their comradeship under the Heights of Dargai. To all those who had taken part in the campaign there was the satisfaction of adding another battle-honour to the Regiment's growing total.

By the year 1908 all the ten Gurkha regiments had raised second battalions. The Nepal Durbar had agreed to allow recruitment to maintain the minimum strength of twenty battalions in the Indian Army. This agreement was to continue until the partition and, as will be seen later, large expansions occurred during both world wars. From 1908 onwards, therefore, we follow the fortunes of four regiments, each with two battalions: the 2nd, 6th, 7th and 10th. The 7th Gurkha Rifles, not yet mentioned in this story, was formed at Quetta in 1907 from the 10th Gurkha Rifles, and the new unit, like its parent, was composed entirely of men from East Nepal. The 7th and 10th Gurkha Rifles have continued to recruit solely from East Nepal until the present day, while the 2nd and 6th have remained staunch supporters of the western Gurkhas. The respective merits of Eastern and Western Gurkhas have been argued over the years by their British officers – there is no such thing as an impartial observer because British officers of Gurkha regiments have never been expected to speak of their men in temperate terms!

Over the years the customs, habits and appearance of the men from East and West Nepal have become almost identical and old distinctions long forgotten. Nevertheless, each *jat,* or clan, still has its own language, although the *lingua franca,* Nepali, is now understood throughout the land. All recruitment from 1908 onwards has been from the hills as opposed to the plain of Kathmandu or the Terai, the strip of low-lying country alongside the Indian border. As the years have gone by the warrior clans have built up a tradition of service in the British-Indian Army Gurkha Brigade, and in more recent years, as part of the British Army itself. As hillmen, the Gurkhas were ideally suited for service in the North-

West Frontier and between the two World Wars their reputation was enhanced by several successful actions against the Pathans.

No more major actions occurred on the North-West Frontier until the First World War, although the 1st Battalion, 2nd Goorkhas was fortunate enough to be on an operation officially recognised by a service medal and clasp, Waziristan 1901–1902. This short campaign was memorable only for the introduction of the now traditional Gurkha hat. These hats were judged a success and together with the kukri are still part of the Gurkha soldier's dress.

In the years that preceded the First World War the battalions in the Brigade of Gurkhas were able to concentrate on peacetime activities – shooting competitions, manœuvres, attendance at Durbars and ceremonial parades. During this period the 2nd Goorkhas were the first of the four regiments to obtain a royal title, when they were designated 'King Edward's Own', with permission being given to wear the Prince of Wales's plume as a badge for headdress. Meanwhile, the battalions of the younger regiments, the 7th and 10th Gurkha Rifles, had become efficient and well-trained bodies of men who still awaited their first taste of active service. They had not long to wait.

Chapter 5

'1,200 yards gained, 12,000 men lost'
NEUVE CHAPELLE, MARCH, 1915

IN August, 1914 units of the Indian Army began mobilizing as quickly as possible when orders came for them to assist the King Emperor and his subjects in the war against Germany. In India, there was no pacifist movement, no Gandhi to cast doubts about the validity of the Allied cause. There was little heart-searching, though the fervent excitement that existed in England was not reflected to the same degree in the Indian Empire.

In 1914 only one battalion in the four regiments had any real experience of active soldiering—the 1st Battalion of the 2nd Goorkhas, the original Sirmoor Rifles, which had participated in several campaigns on the North-West Frontier, although those had been some years before the outbreak of the war. For the other battalions, their initiation into war was to come in the most testing manner possible. In particular, the 7th and 10th Gurkha Rifles had not only to prove themselves as regiments, but they had to show the rest of the Gurkha Brigade how well the men from East Nepal could acquit themselves as soldiers. The training of all battalions had been geared to the tactics required on the North-West Frontier. They had not trained to fight a long war of attrition in trenches, nor were they mentally prepared for the terrible artillery bombardments and the deadly machine-gun fire they were soon to experience.

In France, the efficient German army expected a repetition of the Franco-Prussian War of 1870 – a series of brilliantly executed encircling moves in accordance with carefully prepared plans. Their opponents were equally convinced that not only were such tactics inevitable but that they could, and would, be defeated by aggressive counter-moves on both of Germany's frontiers.

Unfortunately, only the first three weeks in late August, 1914 were to witness the type of fighting expected by the generals and, by the end of September, the power of the artillery and the accuracy of the machine-guns had caused soldiers on both sides to dig for protection. Trenches were prepared, dugouts constructed, and strong fortifications appeared along the whole of the Front. Trench warfare had begun.

On 15 October, 1914, two Indian divisions arrived at Marseilles – where they were designated the Indian Corps. The 2nd Battalion of the 2nd Goorkhas was in the Dehra Doon Brigade (Meerut Division). Prior to leaving India, the Battalion had mobilized in some speed and had received over 150 all ranks from the 1st Battalion, which was to remain in Dehra Doon for another two years. The decision to send the Indian Corps to France is one that has been queried by many military historians. Perhaps there were valid reasons for sending it, but what can be questioned is the timing of the move and the state of the troops, introduced, as they were, to trench warfare with so little preparation. Their equipment was poor, they had no machine-guns nor men trained to fire them, and their clothing was pitifully inadequate for soldiers unused to the damp cold of Northern Europe.

When the Division landed in France the struggle had already become one of endurance behind coils of barbed wire. Senior generals with inexperienced staffs to assist them found themselves in command of huge bodies of troops, without any real idea of how to handle them in the face of machine-guns and prepared enemy positions. Against this background, the Indian Corps was moved up to a sector north-east of Neuve Chapelle at the end of October, 1914; they proudly possessed two machine-guns in each battalion! The Indian Corps, more than their British or French allies, needed a relatively quiet sector in order to become acclimatized. They were not to get it.

The country around Neuve Chapelle was depressing. Heavy rain combined with the low-lying nature of the countryside had produced areas of flooding; incessant artillery fire had denuded the trees of foliage; artificial cover meant digging and invariably water was struck almost at once. And the Germans, in trenches often less than a hundred yards away, not only outgunned the Indian divisions but, at this time, outnumbered them. It was, for the Germans, an ideal time to strike at 'green troops', and strike they did, three days later.

The 2/2nd occupied a salient which had become more exposed since the Germans had occupied the village of Neuve Chapelle a few days before. Early on 2 November, the Battalion was subjected to a very heavy bombardment. Half-finished trenches and parapets were soon obliterated, so that the shaken survivors had to seek temporary cover elsewhere. The Germans moved forward and began occupying the front trenches, always supported by the heaviest of barrages. A very serious situation faced the Battalion. Only one thing saved them in this, their first real big action – the courage of their British officers.

The Corps historian was to write that: 'The heroism of the British officers has seldom been more brilliantly demonstrated than on this occasion. Not a single British officer of the 2nd Goorkhas in the front line got back alive, several being killed while leading attacks against vastly superior numbers'. The bravery of these officers encouraged their inexperienced and shaken men, until some cohesion was obtained and the Germans began to respect the stubborn resistance put up by these scattered groups of Gurkhas. Reserves filled the gaps in the rear and by nightfall the position had been stabilized. Thereafter individual acts of bravery by Gurkha VCOs and NCOs continued to rally the men until eventually the Battalion, shaken and bewildered, was withdrawn to refit and reorganise.

The casualty figures tell the sad story; out of a total of thirty-eight killed in the whole Battalion, seven were British officers.

By the middle of December, 1914, the Indian Corps, although now very short of men, was called on to make a series of diversionary attacks in order to assist a big offensive by General Smith-Dorrien at Messines. At La Quinque Rue, south of Neuve Chapelle, the 2/2nd were awaiting detailed instructions when, on 20 September, the Germans exploded a mine under a company position, following up with a heavy assault. Although that position had to be evacuated, the other companies held firm and for nearly forty-eight hours the Germans were unable to exploit their initial gains. The Battalion was able to hand over the sector intact on 22 September. The unit lost 152 officers and men in this battle.

Towards the end of December, the Indian Corps was withdrawn from the front line for a much-needed rest. At about this time, too, Major Boileau took over as Commandant, an appointment he was to hold until 1917 – a long period for a CO during the 1914–18 War. Meanwhile, during the rest period, reinforcements arrived and essential training exercises were carried out. The men returned to the trenches mentally and physically restored.

The first two months of 1915 were comparatively uneventful – days of cold discomfort and the never-ending process of repairing, extending and strengthening the trenches day and night. Casualties, fortunately, were few and the newly arrived drafts were given excellent opportunities to patrol and to learn the routine of life in the front line without too much pressure being put upon them. All this was to help the Battalion in March, 1915.

At this stage, with the winter behind them, the Allied commanders were optimistic about the overall situation. On the Russian front, the German General Hindenburg was under pressure and there were no signs of the terrible Russian reverses that were to follow. The French, too, had achieved successes in Champagne. In the hope that the Germans had depleted their numbers in the sector of Givenchy and Armentières, General Sir John French decided to launch a vigorous offensive, with the aim of recapturing Neuve Chapelle and seizing the Aubers Ridge near Lille. Once more, the 2nd Goorkhas were to find themselves near Neuve Chapelle, this time about a mile south of a large wood, the Bois du Biez.

In terms of relative strength within the Neuve Chapelle area, the British were much better off than the Germans. The administrative planning had been meticulously carried out and the logistic support for a big offensive had entailed weeks of preparation. Complicated staff tables for the move forward and breakthrough phases had been produced by the headquarters concerned. It must be remembered that Neuve Chapelle was the first of the real trench battles to be fought after the armies on the Western Front had settled down into conditions of stalemate. So much was experimental; the vast scale of the operations, the difficulty of observation over the low ground, the passage of information along archaic communication systems, had still to be satisfactorily resolved. The artillery relied on reasonable observation posts but these were hard to find in the low-lying plain. Although great efforts were made to maintain secrecy, the unusual movement forward in the British lines did not pass unnoticed by the Germans. Nevertheless, although the German High Command knew an attack was imminent, it was not until the last moment that they were certain as to where it would come from.

At 6 am on 10 March the first British batteries fired a few ranging shots. An hour and a half later the bombardment proper opened. The whole ground quivered as in an earthquake. Just after eight o'clock, the barrage lifted from the German forward trenches and the assaulting troops went over the top. The leading brigade (Garwal Brigade) cleared the now battered village of Neuve Chapelle within two hours and the first phase was over. The 2/2nd were told to advance on the Bois du Biez.

The move forward to the edge of the wood took until the late afternoon, due not to heavy opposition but to a series of obstacles, plus the fact that the unit on the right was held up by an obstinately defended position. Nevertheless, as darkness was falling, Nos 1 and 2 Companies not only reached and patrolled the north-west corner of the wood but found few signs of any enemy. A letter from Capt Mullaly mentions that he and another officer 'roamed the wood at will' while patrols forward failed to discover any trenches. A great opportunity appeared to exist, but orders from above told the companies to dig in and consolidate. A little while later fresh orders were received ordering a withdrawal of some 500 yards – the chance to inflict a heavy defeat on the Germans and break out of the trench war deadlock was lost forever. While it is difficult to understand why such a muddle occurred, it must be remembered that orders had to be passed up and down a very long chain of command and insufficient time was ever allowed for this process. After an order had been issued by a general, several hours elapsed before the troops and units actually moved; likewise accurate reports of progress made by units took an inordinately long time to reach the commanders in their headquarters.

Next day, the frustration of the leading troops was to be increased, by order, counter-order and further delays. Warned to attack in the early hours, the men of the 2nd Goorkhas occupied positions expectantly, only to be held back throughout a long and nerve-racking day. Finally at midday on 12 March the whole Brigade was withdrawn.

Neuve Chapelle village was to remain in British hands and an advance of about 1,000 yards on a two-mile front was held and consolidated. The Germans, on 12 March, mounted furious mass attacks in which they suffered terrible casualties. The British planned to make one last effort to take the now fortified Bois du Biez but fortunately a decision by Sir Douglas Haig prevented the attack from going in. Whose then was the victory? In terms of casualties both sides lost about the same numbers. In terms of ground, the gains have already been mentioned. At the time, both the British and German High Commands considered they had won a victory. Nevertheless, the British had failed in their aim of making a large-scale breakout towards Lille. Although the Germans had lost their forward positions, at no time did they lose control of the battle, even though their opponents had the advantage of surprise and weight of numbers at the outset.

At a lower level, as far as the 2nd Goorkhas was concerned, casualties were comparatively few and this was due to three reasons. Firstly, the very accurate and heavy bombardment on the morning of the 10th covered their initial approaches. Secondly, the enemy was not in any great strength in the Bois du Biez sector until later on in the battle. And, finally, the Gurkha riflemen were given a chance, albeit a fleeting one, to move away from the restrictions of trenches and to fight under conditions more suitable to their temperament and training. Although they make dogged defenders, it is in their nature to attack and, if possible, close with their enemy.

Neuve Chapelle was appropriately and deservedly the chief battle-honour of the First World War added by the 2nd Battalion to the 2nd

Goorkhas' roll. It was earned not only for the battle just
described but for the many weeks spent by the Battalion in the
Neuve Chapelle sector between November, 1914, and October of
the following year. Ten days later, on 24 March, the Battalion was
to return once more.

This renewal of life in the trenches was to bring back a flood of
tragic memories as the area was virtually the same as the
surviving members of the Battalion had occupied in November,
1914. Many bodies of their dead comrades were found and thus,
four months later, buried with due respect and honour. But on this
occasion the front line was quiet and it was to continue thus until
early May.

By this time the early spring optimism of the Allies had
evaporated, with the Russians now fighting desperately and the
French heavily engaged in the Verdun sector. The British planned
to launch a diversionary offensive between Neuve Chapelle and
Givenchy with the Indian Corps one of the three corps participating
in an assault against the now strongly held Ferme du Biez. The whole
operation, called the battle of Festubert, began on 9 May, 1915.

The aim of the offensive was to capture Aubers Ridge, a hill of
modest proportions – on the Western Front hillocks were of greater
military importance than mountains. The British had found it
virtually impossible to register their guns either by sight or from
the ground and the capture of the Ridge would provide observation
southwards and disturb the Germans on the French northern flank.
An impressive array of divisions was under command of the First
Army, but guns were few and the plan relied on a short sharp bombardment, followed by a large-scale infantry attack. Thus it was
hoped that the Germans would be surprised and would not have
time to react. The whole battle was based on an optimistic
misconception and the results were disastrous.

The official history sums it up:

'It was evident that for the most part the bombardment had
completely failed in its primary task, neutralization of the enemy's
fire power. Adequate lanes had not been cut in the wire and it
still formed a continuous obstacle; very few cracks had been made

in the German breastwork. For most of the batteries it was the first experience in wire cutting, and as only thirty minutes had been allowed, the results were not unnaturally incomplete.'

The Germans, after enduring a small bombardment, were able to creep forward and man the machine-guns they had set up in strategic positions. They then dealt with their opponents in merciless fashion.

The 2nd Goorkhas were one of the assaulting battalions. From two until five am all had been quiet, and then the guns began their opening bombardment which failed to silence the now chattering German machine guns. As the first two companies went over the top 'men were mown down and all their British officers were casualties within minutes'. The survivors crouched in a ditch, until three hours later a second bombardment by the Allied guns was arranged in order to help them forward. This, too, was disastrous, whilst along the whole sector other units were being checked in exactly the same manner.

No more attacks were made by the 2nd Goorkhas – who were relieved later that afternoon. The battle was a complete failure and the courage displayed and sacrifice of lives achieved absolutely nothing. The Battalion's casualties in the short and ill-fated appearance of a few hours numbered over one hundred. Although reinforcements were on their way, Col Boileau had under his command only about 400 effective soldiers for several weeks.

Behind the German front on 9 May there were two divisions in general reserve and, although they were alerted at the beginning of the British attack, neither of these were required during this phase of the battle. The Germans felt quite capable of handling the First Army merely by using local reserves.

To those who survived Festubert the battle was to be but a prologue rather than the finale. Although Haig's offensive cost over 17,000 dead and made but a dent in the German defences, the tragic lessons of the battle were not to be learnt by the senior commanders on the Western Front.

Fortunately, after the battle of Festubert, the role of the Battalion for the rest of the summer of 1915 saw it holding the line, nearly always in the Neuve Chapelle sector, and continuing with the now familiar make-and-mend of the parapets, dugouts and trenches. In August, the Battalion had to send a draft of picked men to join the 8th Gurkhas in Gallipoli. This gave rise to autumn rumours that the Indian Corps would not continue much longer in France.

Nevertheless, there remained one last big operation for the two Indian divisions. Once again, under command of Sir Douglas Haig's First Army, an offensive was to be launched to force a way into the Champagne district, east of Laon and Rheims. This battle, officially called the Battle of Loos, was mounted on the instigation of Joffre. If it had begun earlier, the Germans would have been unprepared. But, by the time the fighting commenced on 15 September, they had had ample time to strengthen their defences.

The role given to the Indian Corps was a subsidiary one. The decision was made to use gas in this battle but the wind was too light and the clouds of gas affected the British troops more than the Germans. The 2nd Goorkhas' role as first support involved hours of waiting, moves and counter-moves. For, although the assaulting echelons were at first successful, the Germans soon recaptured all their original trenches. A small party of British troops was cut off and No 2 Company of the 2nd Goorkhas attempted to contact them, without success and at the cost of several casualties. By the end of the day it was clear that the attack against an alert and prepared enemy in this particular sector had been a complete failure and no further offensive action was ordered. Elsewhere in the main sectors, the battle continued and was nothing short of a blood bath, so that by the time the offensive petered out in November, the Allies had lost nearly a quarter of a million men and gained no advantage whatever.

The Battalion's last casualties were received just before they withdrew for the last time from the front line on 2 November – exactly a year after their disastrous first action. 177 officers and men had been killed and buried in France, while the total of wounded and missing raised the casualty list to over 1,000. On 9 November the Battalion embarked at Marseilles and sailed for the Suez Canal. No active service was experienced during a three-month tour there, and in the following year Col Boileau landed at Karachi at the head of his men. Their war was over, although two uncomfortable years were to be spent in the inhospitable and barren country around Tank on the North-West Frontier. Hardship and danger were to be faced, but less than a dozen men's lives were lost, an enormous contrast to the cruel losses sustained in France during one year.

Chapter 6

IN the autumn of 1914, Great Britain was poorly equipped to fight a war in the Middle East and she had but a handful of forces available to meet the challenge posed by Turkey. Fortunately for Britain and her Empire, the Turks were in no better position and thus lost a wonderful opportunity to cut Britain's vital link with her possessions in the Far East.

The most important and vulnerable target was the Suez Canal. The threat was fully appreciated by the British Government but initially all that was available to defend the Canal were two brigades of Indian troops, hurriedly taken off troopships on their way to France. A few days later further reinforcements arrived in the shape of a partly trained British Territorial division.

No major incident occured during the last months of 1914, by which time the Sinai peninsula had been left to the Turkish Army under Djemal Pasha. Defensive works based on the Canal itself had been augmented by the guns of British and French warships. Only in numbers were the Turkish superior and Djemal Pasha completely underestimated the fighting potential of the troops that opposed his Army. He dismissed the newly-arrived Anzacs (Australians and New Zealand Army Corps) as complete amateurs. So they were, but they were keen, physically tough, and quick to learn.

The first major attack came in the vicinity of the Great Bitter Lake. To oppose it a mixed force of Indian troops, including the 2/10th Gurkha Rifles, was alerted. In the early morning of 3 February, the Turks attacked. Machine-guns mowed down the leading men and the attackers were beaten back to the east bank of the Canal. Subsequent assaults were hammered by accurate gunfire from Allied warships. Such gunfire played a big part in saving the

1. *A Gurkha Sepoy of the Bengal Light Infantry*

2. *A Native Commissioned Officer of the Cuttack Legion (now 6th Gurkha Rifles) in 1817* (p. 15)

3. *The remnant of the 2nd Goorkhas outside Hindu Rao's house, the key position in the seige of Delhi*

4. *Officers of the 42nd Gurkhas (now the 6th Queen Elizabeth's Own) at Kohima, 1893*

5. *Friendly Naga scouts employed with a Gurkha battalion in operations during the Abor Expedition, 1911–13*

day for the British as many Turkish guns were hit and put out of action. By the night of the 3rd the attackers had been defeated and the main Turkish force withdrawn. By this time another Gurkha Battalion, the 1/6th had come under fire for the first time since 1891. A successful brush with the Turks took place near Hill 70 at El Quantara and the Turks withdrew after suffering heavy casualties. Statements made by prisoners of war and intelligence reports, confirmed by aerial reconnaissance, indicated that Djemal Pasha's forces had moved back across the Sinai Desert. But General Maxwell, the commander in the Suez area, did not believe that the withdrawal was permanent and thus missed an excellent opportunity to harass the Turks as they withdrew.

In 30th Infantry Brigade the 2/7th Gurkha Rifles had their baptism of fire at El Kubri. The Turkish guns kept up harrassing fire but the bombardment did not herald an attack. A few days later, however, many of them were given the opportunity to see some real active service – the first since the Battalion's raising in 1908.

Under the Second-in-Command, Lt-Col Haldane, the detachments were sent on a mission shrouded in secrecy, for which they embarked in HMS *Minerva* on 10 February, 1915. A gang of Arab raiders, urged on by the Turks, was threatening the village of El Tur on the Gulf of Suez. A plan was made to land the troops south of the village in order to cut off the raiders, but this had to be abandoned because of rough seas. HMS *Minerva*, without lights, had to move in close to the coast in the darkness. The Gurkhas, indifferent sailors, had to climb down into open boats on a choppy sea. In silence and in darkness this was achieved although several men were desperately sea-sick. The landing was accomplished and the party set out on compass bearings towards the Arab village, some nine miles away. All went well and the final assault began at six in the morning. As the first troops moved into the village, firing broke out and the clearing of isolated groups of the enemy lasted until midday. By noon, the operation had been completed; the Arab raiders had lost some sixty dead and over a hundred prisoners of war were in the hands of the Gurkhas. One Gurkha was killed in this action, the first from the 7th Gurkha Rifles ever to fall in battle.

He was buried with full military honours, which included a firing party from the Royal Marines and with all HM ships in the vicinity flying their flags at half mast. The Regimental historian commented that 'It is improbable that any Gurkha Rifleman has ever been, or will ever be again, attended to his grave with so much honour'.

Meanwhile, the threat to the Suez Canal had lifted. Djemal Pasha had thrown away the best chance he was ever to have to disrupt traffic through the Canal, and the soldiers that remained in Egypt were able to continue their training for operations elsewhere. For two of the three Gurkha battalions, the 1/6th and 2/10th, it was but a prelude to the severe testing they were to undergo at Gallipoli. For the third, the 2/7th, the story was to continue in Mesopotamia.

MESOPOTAMIA, PERSIA AND PALESTINE

'I mean to defend Kut as I did Chitral'
GENERAL CHARLES TOWNSEND

In terms of troops deployed by both Turkey and Great Britain, Mesopotamia was a side-show when compared with the Western Front. Nevertheless, victory was vital for both sides; Muslims in Persia, in Afghanistan, and in India itself, watched events in Mesopotamia with the greatest interest. The defeat of the British would have had far-reaching consequences throughout the East, while a quick British victory would have ended all Turkish-German ambitions there.

The contestants were fighting in the most difficult country imaginable. A flat desert of barren earth, without trees and with the minimum of landmarks; nowhere was impassable but the scarcity of water tied armies to the main rivers. Rivers provided water and were the only means of transporting armies across a bleak and inhospitable land. Everything conspired to make a soldier's life one of discomfort; excessive heat in the summer, bitter cold in the winter, stifling sand which got into everything, and a plethora of flies by day and of mosquitoes by night.

To fight in such a country required good administration, quick and efficient medical support, and the basic necessities of life to make existence tolerable. Unfortunately, such a state of affairs did not pertain for a considerable time. There was a critical shortage of transport so that, on occasions, ammunition reserves had to be man-handled into action in the wake of the leading troops. Not only were operations curtailed but fresh food and a normal scale of rations were rarely obtainable. Everything was in short supply; tents to shelter the wounded, warm clothing for the nights and the winter, artillery ammunition, maps of the area – the list of major deficiencies was a long one. The wounded had to accept conditions reminiscent of those that prevailed during the Crimean War.

Britain's first intentions in Mesopotamia had been to secure Basra and to prevent any Turkish attempts to disrupt the oil-fields and the pipe line to Abadan. Thereafter the Government of India, who controlled the theatre with responsibility for all logistic supply, began taking an independent line from the one advised by Whitehall. A new commander, General Nixon, arrived with instructions from Delhi to obtain and retain complete control of lower Mesopotamia 'and such portions of neighbouring territories as may affect your operations'. Such a directive was to lure him on until the capture of Baghdad had become an obsession. Soon he had the complete support of the Viceroy of India, after early successes had seemed to promise an easy victory with far-reaching political rewards.

Six of the eight Gurkha battalions were to serve at one time or other in the Mesopotamia war. The first to arrive from the Gurkha Brigade were the 2/7th, fresh from their successful foray on HMS *Minerva*.

Although men of the 2/7th were near the battle zone of Shaiba, they did not take an active part in the fighting there which forced the Turks to retreat, a withdrawal which by its timing and speed took the British by surprise. It was impossible to follow up the retreating Turkish forces through the flooded countryside, so the newly-arrived commander of the 9th Indian Division, General Charles Townsend, was ordered to organize an amphibious opera-tion. But, once more, the Turks were quick to abandon positions and hastily retreated up the River Tigris. Townsend organized a flotilla of ships and, with himself in the van, chased the Turks up the river. In four days he and a handful of men captured over 2,000 Turkish prisoners.

The 7th Gurkhas formed part of a river flotilla which set out to capture Naseriya, considered by General Nixon to be the most likely base on the River Euphrates from which the Turks could launch a counter-offensive against Basra. It was no pleasure trip; boats had to be dragged across swamps by as many as 300 men and the steaming heat in the marshes claimed victims by the score from heat exhaustion and malaria. The Gurkha unit, by no means the worst hit, was reduced from 800 to some 350 men. In such a weakened condition, the force under General Gorringe met and pushed back the Turkish outposts until their last-ditch position was reached, some five miles down-river from Naseriya. After a long night approach, the decisive action was fought on 24 July. By this time the 7th Gurkhas 'looked forward to the approaching battle; we were confident'. Nevertheless, it was a tough struggle and for a few minutes, the Battalion's attack appeared to lose momentum. At this stage a young NCO made one of those unpredictable rushes that in battle can change the mood of those who falter and lose heart. The naik (corporal) charged the Turks with drawn kukri and, followed by his section, killed thirteen of the enemy. Other sub-units around them took up the charge and the battlefield belonged to the Gurkhas. After the battle was over, an eye-witness wrote that 'the appearance of the men was striking; they looked conquerors every inch, ready for anything'. The battle casualties were comparatively light – twenty killed and sixty wounded – and the Regiment's first major battle honour had been won. To this day, it is commemorated as a regimental holiday by the 7th Gurkha Rifles.

This latest success seemed to stimulate the Viceroy in India. Barely two days after the battle of Naseriya, he was urging the Secretary of State in Whitehall to accept the necessity of a further advance up the Tigris to Kut. Meanwhile, General Nixon had come to a similar conclusion and had decided that the best strategic centre was Kut because it was situated at the junction of the waterway that connects the Rivers Tigris and Euphrates. He maintained that it could be held by a small number of troops, but he did not add that it was a final stepping stone to Baghdad, and there is little doubt that the capture of the capital was his real objective. As the Regimental historian of the 7th Gurkhas commented: 'The opening chapter of the Mesopotamia campaign had shown how each objective gained made a further objective appear desirable – even necessary.' In the autumn of 1915 General Townsend was authorized to occupy Kut and began concentrating his force for the advance, due to start on 12 September.

Townsend had a total of about 11,000 soldiers under his command – three infantry brigades. The weather was very hot, 110–120°F, but the troops' morale was high and they were looking forward to another victory. At first, the Turkish outposts and reconnaissance parties watched but did not interfere with the advancing British forces. The battle for Kut-al-Amara, as it was later known, opened on the morning of 26 September, with Townsend relying on a plan which depended on deception and surprise. A feint attack was made on the right bank with the decisive attack being directed against the flank positions on the left bank of the river. Surprise was attained by making the approach marches to these positions at night and, in the end, General Townsend's stratagem paid off. The 7th Gurkhas played a minor part in this, the first battle of Kut, and entered the small town on 6 October. By this time General Townsend's vanguard had pursued the Turks up-stream where it was learnt that a large force was occupying a well-prepared position astride the river at Ctesiphon.

Once again, there was a major disagreement between those who wished to push on, led by General Nixon with the support of the Viceroy in India, and those who were opposed to any occupation of Baghdad, like Lord Kitchener in Whitehall. After a lot of vacillation, the British Government was swayed by the fact that a major victory seemed imminent and, as reinforcements from France were arriving in the shape of the 3rd Lahore and 7th Meerut Divisions, General Nixon was instructed to go on.

Unfortunately for his army, Nixon had a poor opinion of the Turkish generals and did not appreciate the fighting qualities of the men they led. He was right to doubt the leaders, but he was quite wrong to under-estimate the Turkish soldier. Moreover, his natural optimism did not take into account the fact that his own troops had campaigned throughout the very hot weather, and were badly in need of a rest. And, in view of the controversy about General Townsend that followed – and continues to this day – it must be recorded that Townsend considered that his force was inadequate for the task of capturing Baghdad. He was over-ruled by Nixon, and, in public, accepted his new directive. However, in his diary Townsend wrote: 'The British troops can be relied on as before but the Indians are now shaken and unreliable.' As far as the Gurkha conquerors of Naseriya were concerned, such a verdict was inaccurate and un-generous, as events were soon to prove at the battle of Ctesiphon.

General Townsend's leading troops were only twenty miles from Baghdad when they met a strong Turkish force led by General Nur-ud-Din. In fact, unknown to Townsend, the Turkish Army had a reserve division nearby and this extra strength meant that General Nur-ud-Din began the battle with superior numbers – and a card up his sleeve. Nevertheless, it was to be a hard-fought battle with neither side able to claim outright victory – although in the end, the tired and depleted British force had to retrace its steps in haste to Kut: strategically they had suffered a defeat of far-reaching consequences.

General Townsend's plan was simple but ambitious and depended on timings being adhered to by four separate columns which moved to attack the Turkish Army. These columns, he hoped, would deliver a rapid succession of blows which would keep the Turks fully stretched. In order to do this, the British commander did not keep any reserves under central control. He gambled on affairs going as he planned they would; this might well have happened if the terrain had been easy and accurate navigation possible. He gambled and lost.

The 7th Gurkhas formed part of a column commanded by General Delamain which had to cross some 5,000 yards of open desert before attacking their objective. All went well until the Turkish wire was met; a way was cut but by this time casualties were increasing. Nevertheless, the Gurkhas pressed on in company with the Dorsets and were soon well lodged within the Turkish position. However, the battle was not over; a strong counter-attack checked them, then forced the small body of Dorsets and Gurkhas to withdraw.

Townsend did not abandon hope and organized another attack on the Turkish second line of defences. This too failed, thus adding scores of wounded to the numbers who had already fallen in battle. Their evacuation by primitive hand carts down to the river was a slow and painful business, and many died from shock or loss of blood before they even reached the base hospitals.

An uneasy night followed, during which the opposing generals took stock of their positions. Neither had grounds for optimism and, more important, each lacked accurate information about the plight of his adversary. Dawn came, heralded by a severe sandstorm; then followed a strong Turkish attack on a low mound near the historic Arch of Ctesiphon. This mound, soon to be called Gurkha Mound, was defended by some 300 men from the 7th Gurkhas, and about a hundred soldiers from the 21st Punjab Regiment. A desperate struggle ensued; the small detachment was vulnerable and exposed and under attack by the 35th Turkish Division, who virtually surrounded the mound. Throughout the day the Turks tried to seize the post but by early evening they gave up the attempt.

A Turkish officer wrote: 'The 35th Division strove for hours in front of that brave, determined little force, alone on the little hill top and though it lost many men, did not gain its end. They did not succeed in even drawing near.' Later he added: 'I must confess to a deep hidden feeling of appreciation for that brave and self-sacrificing enemy detachment which, though only 400 strong, for hours opposed the thousands of riflemen of the 35th Division . . .' He classified the fight at Gurkha Mound as one of the outstanding feats of arms in the whole of the Mesopotamian campaign.

Although the Turks were driven from the field, General Townsend had to fall back. His division had been badly knocked about and was not capable of taking any offensive action. As soon as the British started withdrawing, the Turks turned about and pressed after them. Under pressure, the British withdrew for a week until, on 1 December, they were forced to turn and make a stand – then another retreat and finally on the morning of 3 December, they re-entered Kut. For the 7th Gurkhas the battle of Ctesiphon had been lost but honours had been won. Casualties had been heavy, sixty-two killed and nearly 200 wounded. This was one third of the Battalion's strength and yet, compared with other units, they had come off lightly. On 3 December, Townsend stood to watch the exhausted men trickling past him into Kut. In his diary he wrote: 'Courage and firmness in adversity were not wanting . . . in the Sixth Division'. The seven-and-a-half-day retreat was one of the most arduous ever experienced in the history of the British Army and the general's praise for his tired and depleted army was well deserved.

To his army and to the world, Townsend declared: 'I mean to defend Kut as I did Chitral', and his decision to do so was greeted with approval by General Nixon. The latter promised that reinforcements would soon be fighting their way through to relieve Kut but, as the Turks began to close in, it became apparent that with little food, insanitary conditions in the dirty town, and troops already exhausted, Townsend's defensive preparations could not match his brave and optimistic declaration. However, there was no alternative but to dig in, to tighten belts and to defy the Turks who were now in positions around the town.

The siege was to last from 3 December, 1915 to 29 April, 1916. Although the river that flowed in a loop around three sides of Kut was a protection, nevertheless it also prevented freedom of movement and left the garrison open to pressure from every direction. Meanwhile, throughout the winter, a force under General Aylmer, VC, began battering a way forward to try and relieve the garrison. In this force was the 1st Battalion the 2nd Goorkhas which had recently arrived from India and was experiencing its first action in the war. The unit's opening engagement was in many ways as costly and disastrous as the 2nd Battalion's in November, 1914, at Neuve Chapelle. On 8 March, 1916 the Battalion, as part of 37 Brigade, attacked the Dujailah Redoubt at the southern end of the Turkish main position. The Turks had recently been reinforced by battle-experienced veterans from Gallipoli, a fact that was not known by British Intelligence at that time, and the 2nd Goorkhas, initially in support, were sent in to assault in the early afternoon. Fierce hand-to-hand fighting took place between Turk and Gurkha, but the defenders, in superior numbers and aided by well-sited posts, eventually triumphed.

Such a heavy reverse, with nearly a hundred killed and over one hundred wounded, did not daunt the Battalion; but in a few hours they had learnt that the Turk was a foe to be respected.

This defeat was the final blow to chances of Kut-al-Amara being relieved. In the town itself, the news of Aylmer's setback was received in silence. There was no bitterness or dejection, as all realized that his force had failed in a task with the odds heavily against them. Rations had to be further reduced and the transport animals were slaughtered to provide horse-meat. Many Indian troops refused to eat the meat and grew weak and ill. But the Gurkhas, like their British comrades, ate it willingly. Attempts to drop food on the garrison by aeroplane had not proved successful, and one more bid to bring supplies and food past the blockade was made. The river steamer *Julna*, with some volunteer Royal Naval officers, came within a stone's throw of success. Almost before the eyes of the besieged garrison she ran against the cable across the river and drove on to a sand-bank, where the gallant venture died under the pounding of Turkish gunfire. There was now no alternative but to surrender.

The garrison consisted of about 8,500 men, while it is estimated that the relieving force lost about 20,000 from all causes, many of whom died of wounds and sickness because of inadequate medical arrangements and the scandalous deficiencies in transport. It was a sad ending to a brave adventure; the surrender of Kut set the whole world agog and 'shook the Empire'. Into captivity went the men of the 7th Gurkhas. The British officers were parted by their Turkish captors from the men they had led with such gallantry. Ahead of them all lay a long, uncomfortable period of captivity in primitive Turkish camps and prisons. The conduct of the 7th Gurkhas was steadfast and won the respect of the Turks and of the Germans. Although now without their officers, the NCOs continued to run the Battalion on normal regimental lines and thus discipline was maintained. The Turks were not deliberately cruel but a complete lack of interest in the fate of their captives was to cause hundreds of deaths.

The surrender was an inglorious end to a sad chapter of British military muddle. The main result was that the long overdue reorganization of the Army in Mesopotamia was carried out. The 1/2nd Goorkhas, after the setback at Dujaila in which one company was practically annihilated, faced a long and uncomfortable summer in which the average daily temperature reached 120° inside the tents, so that active operations came to a standstill. During this uncomfortable summer the third battalion whose story we are following, the 2/6th Gurkhas, arrived for its first experience of active service. Their initial brush with an enemy was not with the Turks but with Arab marauders, gangs of whom roamed the battlefield in search of victims, without regard to nationality. When isolated parties of Turks or British were found the Arabs attacked, showing no mercy to the wounded or sick. Two young NCOs and five riflemen of the 6th Gurkhas were set upon by over a hundred Arabs but fought with such determination and skill that some twenty-five Arabs were killed and wounded. A punitive expedition from the 6th Gurkhas exacted retribution and inflicted some eighty casualties as well as taking the local Sheik into custody. From then on until the fall of Baghdad the role of the 2/6th and the newly arrived 1/10th involved the unexciting but important work of guarding the long and complicated lines of communication back to Basra.

By September, 1916, each of the four regiments had a battalion serving in Mesopotamia. A decision was made to reform the 2/7th and, before the end of the year, starting from scratch, a new 2/7th Gurkhas came into being with the bulk of the reinforcements coming from their sister battalion, the 1/7th. It was fitting that the Battalion's first action was fought near Kut at the end of the year.

By September the War Office had taken over the responsibility for the Mesopotamian Campaign and a great improvement was soon felt. An energetic and able commander, General Sir Stanley Maude, quickly got things humming and by the end of December his army consisted of one cavalry and five infantry divisions, communications were secure, transport supplies reorganized, and his troops were ready to open the road to Baghdad – via Kut.

Still in 37 Brigade, the 1/2nd Gurkhas took part in the preliminary moves before Christmas of 1916. The battalion scouts (Reconnaissance Platoon) led the Brigade across a tributary of the Tigris as part of a series of probing moves and feints which were made to deceive the Turks and test their defences. After a few days, it became apparent that only hard fighting would drive the Turks from their positions south of and around the junction of the Rivers Tigris and Hai on the opposite bank to Kut-al-Amara.

The first big attack on the morning of 25 January was made by the two Sikh Battalions of 37 Brigade. Closely supported by the 2nd Goorkhas and 1/4th Devons, and preceded by 'bombers' from all four units, the Sikhs met with some initial successes. Hard-won gains were clung to with difficulty until 1 February when, once more, the Sikhs went into another assault. The attack was premature: the British guns had not registered on certain enemy machine-guns and the two Sikh battalions were mown down before they even reached the Turk defences, with casualties of over 500 in each battalion. The Turks had won the first round. That evening parties went out from both support battalions to help collect and bring in the wounded, all of which had to be done under continual sniping.

The next attack was ordered for the morning of 2 February with the 2nd Goorkhas and 1/4th Devons in the van. Both units had been six days in the trenches without rest or respite; they were now to attack over the same ground as the Sikhs had done, a ground still littered with the dead bodies of their Indian comrades. Tired but keyed-up troops twice climbed over the parapets prior to advancing, only to be recalled. Finally, the whole operation was delayed until the following day.

Such an inauspicious beginning deterred neither the men from the West Country of England nor the soldiers from Nepal. Supported by a well-executed barrage, the leading lines were soon amongst the Turks where the outcome was decided by bayonet and kukri. Bitterly contesting each yard, the Turks counter-attacked and withdrew only to come back again to hold up the British. By late afternoon 37 Brigade advanced about a mile, but the cost was high. The 2nd Goorkhas lost nearly a hundred killed and one company, No 3, was at half strength by the evening.

On the other side of the hill, the Turkish losses were disastrous and their High Command decided upon a complete withdrawal from the south bank of the Tigris. The battered 37 Brigade reorganized, with the Sikh battalions and the Devons being replaced, though the 2nd Goorkhas were to be asked to make one more supreme effort before some measure of rest was allowed. Between the British and Baghdad lay the Turks at Kut, and they also held three other likely crossing places along the Tigris. In addition the river, swollen by recent rain to a width of about 400 yards, made assault crossings doubly difficult. There were grave doubts, even in the highest headquarters, which were carelessly reflected in the operation order which stated that 'the crossing would be attempted'.

On 22 February, 37 Brigade was given the honour of leading what was considered by many to be a forlorn hope. The plan was to cross about six miles upriver from Kut with the prize being the possible capture of Khalil Bey's whole force. Three crossing points were selected about three or four hundred yards apart where the Norfolks, 2/9th Gurkha Rifles and the 2nd Goorkhas were to cross in boats, each of which carried about a dozen men plus the rowers. Although a careful artillery fire plan was prepared it was decided that this would only be used if the Turks discovered the crossing and opened fire.

During a long and bitterly cold night the units moved down and waited to embark. All was quiet, and at five-forty am the first boats moved across. The rowing was done by men from the Hampshire Regiment and the Royal Engineers. Theirs was a most unenviable task as fire was directed on them whichever way they were rowing. About eleven boats reached the far bank before the Turks opened fire, and then the carefully prepared plan went quickly awry.

The current of the river caused several boats to land right under the Turkish defences – boats sank and men died under a hail of bullets. Some boats were stranded on the enemy side of the river, while soldiers waiting to cross could only watch in anguish and dismay. Those who had already crossed, fifty-six men under two subalterns, Baker and Toogood, clung to a small bank and held the enemy at bay. But reinforcements could not reach them and by 9.30 am the decision was taken to abandon the 2nd Goorkhas' ferry point. This wise move proved to be the turning point in a day full of hazards.

The rest of the Battalion began crossing at the Norfolks' ferry point. By 5 pm a bridgehead had been seized and the group under the now wounded Toogood was substantially reinforced. As General Maude was later to say: 'Our troops have by unconquerable valour and determination forced a passage across a river 350 yards wide in face of heavy opposition'.

The 2nd Goorkhas lost eighty killed and forty-three wounded during the crossing of the Tigris on 23 February, 1916. Tigris Day has been observed as a Regimental Day ever since – a brave feat of arms across a dangerous river, against a determined enemy.

The fighting was not over. For two more days the Turks fought from prepared defences, from trenches and from barrack buildings. Casualties during those forty-eight hours were almost as heavy as those suffered during the crossing, but British successes elsewhere caused Khalil Bey's army to fall back during the night of 25 February; this time it was in full retreat – the way to Baghdad was open at last. The Turkish Army, harassed by the cavalry and relentlessly pursued by the tired but victorious British infantry, managed to avoid being cut off but their losses in men and materials were heavy indeed.

On 11 March, Baghdad was entered without any opposition and General Maude ceremoniously received the keys of the city.

After the fall of Baghdad, there was a pause as the cruelly hot summer approached and men found survival a problem and fighting almost impossible – feelings shared by both sides. In 1917 the health of the troops was much better, a direct result of the increased efficiency in all administrative matters since General Maude had taken command of the army.

But the campaign was not yet over. It is true that Baghdad had been the focus of the Turkish advance but they still had a force near Mosul. For three or four weeks, therefore, the British pushed north and north-west from Baghdad, meeting little opposition but always being taxed by the problems of movement, re-supply and the evacuation of the sick and wounded. During this phase of the operation 7 Brigade, in which the 2/7th were serving, tried to drive the Turks from a place called Ramadi. As this occurred before autumn, the intense heat and grave shortage of water nearly caused a complete disaster for the attackers. 'Officers and men succumbed to heat exhaustion, not in ones and twos but in scores. The want of water was acute' – so the Regimental History of the 7th Gurkhas describes this day of tribulation. By two-thirty pm the Battalion had lost 250 officers and men as victims of the heat which, added to the battle casualties (over sixty) meant that the Battalion was powerless to carry out its task. An hour later orders were received to withdraw.

A few days later, 15 Indian Division went into action at Ramadi to retrieve the gallant failure of 7 Brigade. The attack was carried out by 42 Brigade which consisted of three battalions of Gurkhas – the 1/5th, 2/5th and 2/6th, with the redoubtable support of the 1/4th Dorsets. The advance began before midnight over a distance of some 2,500 yards. Before dawn, the attack was launched and at about 6 am the 2/6th were told to recapture the Turkish trenches with the 1/4th Dorsets. In spite of heavy fire this was carried out with fewer casualties than had been anticipated. After daybreak, confused fighting continued until midday when the Battalion attacked Ramadi Ridge under heavy machine-gun fire. This was successful although the exposed position forced the battalion to seek cover until the other units of the Brigade had moved behind the right flank of the Turks. Early next morning huge parties of Turkish prisoners were seen moving towards the Battalion position and it became clear that the Turks were surrendering. The 2/6th had played a large part in this action, during which they lost three killed and eighty-two wounded. It was to be their last major action in the Mesopotamian Campaign.

A bitter blow to the army was the death, in November 1917, of

General Sir Stanley Maude from cholera. General Maude's great energy and determination had transformed the Army, instilling confidence, a sense of purpose and, most important of all, producing the success that had previously eluded the soldiers in Mesopotamia. The tide had now turned; never again were the Turks able to threaten the Persian Gulf or have the heart or resources to mount a dangerous offensive. Nevertheless, the task of the Gurkha battalions was not over. Guarding the long lines of communication against marauding Arabs was an unexciting and uncomfortable task, but a very necessary one if the Turks were to be evicted from Mesopotamia by an army fully equipped and efficiently administered.

The last major action in which the Gurkha battalions took part in Mesopotamia was in 1918 after the summer heat had died down. Careful preparations were carried out by Headquarters I Indian Corps assembled in the Tekrit area. By this time General Allenby had opened his final great offensive in Palestine and it was hoped that the *coup de grâce* could be administered in Mesopotamia at the same time. The Turkish main position was at Sharqat, with divisions held in positions to the rear. The British plan relied on speed for any delay would have enabled the Turks to concentrate a considerable force against the attackers. Two battalions of the British Brigade of Gurkhas took part in the ensuing battle for Sharqat – the 1/7th and the 1/10th, both composed of Rais and Limbus from Eastern Nepal.

The British line of advance was restricted to the Tigris, a course dictated by the lack of transport. An advance was made simultaneously on both banks of the river in an attempt to mislead the Turkish commander as to which would be the main attacking strike. The initial moves were successful. Out-manœuvred on the right bank and driven back on the left one, the Turks were compelled to evacuate the whole of their forward position and fall back on the right bank to their second line. By 24 October, the 1/7th Gurkhas had been under fire for the first time ever, losing one killed and twenty-one wounded. It was only a brush with the Turks, but all ranks were commended for their steadiness under fire. Thereafter, as part of 18 Division, the 1/7th shared with the cavalry the honours of the day – not least for a great march of thirty-six miles in twenty-six hours that brought the Battalion to the cavalry's aid in the rear of the Turks. General Marshal, the Commander-in-Chief, wrote:

'During the night 28/29 October the Turks made repeated efforts to break through to the north, but each time were repulsed. In this fighting, the Guides Cavalry and the 1st Battalion 7th Gurkha Rifles distinguished themselves by their staunchness.'

On the other bank, meanwhile, the 1/10th with 17 Division also had a lot of marching and fighting to do. Moving over ridges which were often under hostile machine-gun fire, the Battalion found the going very difficult. Staunch resistance by the Turks held them up, but events on the other bank drove the Turks out of their position and forced them to concentrate in strength on the right bank. Orders were received to move forward once again but enemy rearguards, plus the heavy marching on little food and severely rationed water, taxed the British, Indian and Gurkha troops to the limit. There was to be no respite, for the trap was closing on the Turks who now found their way to the north barred by 18 Division. Spurred on by the news that their comrades in the north were fighting desperately to prevent the Turks from escaping, the 1/10th did not hesitate when they came up against the enemy's advanced elements; increasingly heavy and accurate artillery fire fell upon them but although the broken nature of the ground slowed them up, it also prevented casualties from assuming serious proportions. By this time the Battalion was stretched over a large area and fresh troops were hurriedly sent up not only to maintain the momentum of the attack but also to hold the area against vigorous Turkish counter-attacks.

The night of 28 October was one of strain, and the first rays of light on the 29th saw a weary Battalion stand to for the next round of the battle. But the Turks had had enough. The gallant commander, Ismail Hakki Bey, knew that his army was now completely hemmed in with no possible chance of escape. White flags began to appear all along the Turkish defences and the long war in Mesopotamia, which had cost the British over 30,000 dead, was over at last. For the 1/10th Gurkhas, like the 1/7th, the battle-honour of Sharqat had been won by strenuous marches on limited rations and little water, by physical toughness and by courage more than equal to that shown by the Turkish soldiers themselves. Although the experiences of the prisoners of war who were unfortunate enough to be held in captivity by the Turks were harrowing, those who met the Turk in battle carried away kindly memories of him as a brave and honourable opponent.

The war in the Middle East was not over for all the Gurkha Battalions. The 1/2nd and 1/6th were ordered to leave Mesopotamia for Persia. Here, the Persians' sympathy undoubtedly still lay with the Germans. Both battalions had brushes with the Bolsheviks and took part in operations against a local guerrilla leader, one Kuchik Khan, whose force was called 'The Jangalis'. Fortunately, an early brush with these gentlemen in late July, 1918, found the Gurkhas getting well home into the enemy, which 'gave them a wholesome dread of the Gurkha kukri, the fame of which weapon spread through the countryside'. Both battalions had several spirited actions against the Jangalis before operations in Persia came to an end – nearly three years after the war in Europe had ended.

One more action has still to be recounted in which the 2/7th Gurkhas, the re-formed battalion, took part. As part of 3 Division they moved to Palestine to come under command of General Allenby. Although they arrived in the Lydda area in early May, 1918, no fighting was experienced until September. The first months of duty on the plains near the Auja river introduced the Gurkhas to a virulent type of mosquito and within six weeks 400 went down with a very bad type of malaria, of whom forty died.

By the middle of September, 1918, a new sense of excitement was in the air. Allenby had kept the Turks on tenterhooks. While threatening to move inland around their left flank, he had secretly massed overwhelming strength against their right on the narrow plain of Sharon, close to the sea. Five infantry divisions were to force a hole and swing back the Turks into the hills so that the coastal corridor would be open for the Desert Mounted Corps, three divisions of cavalry under General Chetwode, to ride through to the north. The attack, on 19 September, was the first decisive blow in the battle of Megiddo, which was to be an overwhelming victory for General Allenby and his army.

For the 2/7th Gurkhas as they moved up into position before light on 19 September, the part they had to play seemed small but, as events turned out, it was to have far-reaching effects. At 4.30 am pandemonium broke loose and the companies went off into the darkness, trying to accomplish a 'wheel'. In spite of the noise and confusion most of the Battalion, somehow or other, reached its objective and went through the wire to take the last of the trenches. At the same time Turkish machine-guns opened fire from a village some distance away so the Battalion, by now short of a few platoons but controlling men from other units, moved out to clear them away.

For some time the Gurkhas appeared to be on their own; their commanders received no orders nor did they know anything about the situation on either flank. Undeterred, they moved on until friendly units could be seen on their left. In a day of confusion, it was difficult for the infantry who fought in the battle to realise that their advance had pushed the Turks back to the hills – and the cavalry had thereafter swept rapidly north. It was hard going and particularly tough on the infantry. They outmarched supplies and went hungry – the pace was terrific and there was no relief. But on they went past Jezreel and Nazareth to the Sea of Galilee. Here, on 31 October, 1918, they learnt that the Turks had surrendered. The war in Palestine was over.

The spectacular part of the battle of Megiddo belonged to the horsemen who, in the space of some thirty-eight days, rode 350 miles, fighting brilliant actions on the way to Aleppo. There they met a small party of escaping Gurkha prisoners of war, amongst them men of the original 2/7th who had been captured in Kut. To the cavalry went the glory, but it must not be forgotten that the opportunities were made for them by the infantry on the opening day of the battle. The 2/7th Gurkhas lost nearly a hundred men, but took great pride in the part they had played in bringing the war in Palestine to a successful conclusion. The Battalion had helped to win eight battle-honours for its Regiment in four eventful years of war – and the Gurkhas had established a high reputation as courageous and efficient soldiers throughout the Middle East, a reputation that was to be maintained and even enhanced by the deeds of their sons in the Second World War.

Chapter 7

'Each little Gurkha might be worth his full weight in gold at Gallipoli.'

GENERAL SIR IAN HAMILTON, MARCH, 1915

GENERAL SIR IAN HAMILTON'S request, contained in a letter to Lord Kitchener, was granted in the shape of three Gurkha battalions; these were the 1/5th, 1/6th and 2/10th Gurkha Rifles. His confidence in the Gurkha soldier was justified in full measure and the achievements of the 1/5th, although not covered in this book, were in every respect equal to those of the other two battalions. So to Gallipoli – one of the most moving and tragic campaigns in all history, tragic not only in the severe loss of life but because from the British point of view, priceless opportunities were thrown away after the first landings on 25 April, 1915. Tragic too, because the morale of the Army that set out for Gallipoli was so high. Alas, from General Hamilton down to the private soldier, all lacked experience and knowledge about combined naval and military operations, so that British superiority at sea was not used to the best advantage.

It is not necessary to tell the story of the landings since the first Gurkha unit, as part of 29 Indian Brigade, did not arrive until five days later. General Sir Ian Hamilton's much-criticized plan of landing at six points on the southern peninsula of Gallipoli completely surprised his opponent, General Liman von Sanders, who wrote: 'The landing at so many points surprised many and filled them with apprehension because we could not discern at that moment where the enemy were actually seeking the decision'. As a consequence, Hamilton's force, although smaller than the defending Turkish one, had a superiority at the actual landing points. Things went awry thereafter when valuable time slipped by and the Turks were given the chance to recover their poise and mount strong counterattacks. After disembarking, the British and Dominion troops were bewildered by the rough terrain and, being raw and untrained, were apprehensive under Turkish gunfire. Even more tragic was the story at 'Y' beach where a landing force disembarked without meeting any opposition and thereafter sat for eleven hours, greatly out-numbering their opponents in the vicinity of the beach, whilst elsewhere stronger defences were being attacked by other men from the same (29th) division. To crown it all, 'Y' beach was later abandoned although by this time the Turks had pulled back their defenders. War is a series of 'ifs' but there is little doubt that inept leadership during the initial landings threw away an excellent opportunity and led to the long drawn out struggle that followed.

The 1/6th Gurkhas landed on 1 May. By this time the British and Dominion casualties had reached 9,000, of whom about 3,000 had been killed. The first hopes of a breakthrough had died, particularly when it was known that the Turks were rushing reinforcements with the greatest urgency, not only to check the landings but in an attempt to hurl back the invaders into the sea. Such was the situation when the 6th Gurkhas landed; within hours they were deployed in immediate reserve and had suffered their first casualties. For three days the battalion was moved hither and thither between points of the line threatened by the persistent attackers. Such was to be the role of the other units of 29 Brigade since there was no other reserve available to General Hamilton in the whole peninsula during the first half of May.

The 6th Gurkhas actually moved into the front line on 9 May and were immediately involved in a task of some magnitude. Two gallant attempts by the Royal Marines and the Royal Dublin Fusiliers had failed to capture a bluff of some 300 feet on the west of the beachhead. This bluff had been converted into a strong point by the Turks, and from prepared positions machine-guns were able to direct a raking fire against any attack from below.

Just before dusk three days later, the battalion moved out in an attempt to capture the bluff. The plan relied, to a great extent, on a quick dash by the leading company across a ravine and up to the

top of the bluff, while maximum fire support was given by the Royal
Navy and diversionary moves were made by other units in the line.
To the delight and astonishment of all, A Coy was on the top of the
bluff within two hours – the other companies moved up with speed
and determination so that the position was held by the battalion in
strength before the Turks could launch an organized counterattack.
That the attack was so successful was due to three main factors:
firstly, detailed and daring daylight reconnaissances by two senior
Gurkhas of A Coy, which enabled them to guide their Coy with
confidence and skill after dark; secondly, close and accurate support
for the rush across the ravine was given by HMS *Talbot* and *Dublin*
whose guns raked the upper wall of the gorge up to the very moment
that A Coy began their dash across the open space; and, thirdly, the
swift reinforcement of A Coy by the other companies so that before
the Turks attacked, the whole position had been well covered by the
6th Gurkhas. The cost in lives, by Gallipoli standards, was light; 18
killed and 42 wounded. The speed and daring of the attack was in
keeping with the character of the CO of the Battalion, the Hon
Charles Bruce, who, after the war, was to gain considerable fame as
leader of two expeditions to Mount Everest. For the battalion, it was
a great honour to hear that General Sir Ian Hamilton had decreed
in Army Orders that the bluff was to be known as 'Gurkha Bluff'
thereafter.

No other major engagement occurred in May but casualties steadily
mounted in trench warfare and raids. By the end of the month all
the original Company Commanders had been killed or wounded. By
this time too, the first two Battles of Krithia had been fought without
avail and the beach-heads remained pitifully small; gains were counted in yards and only under the protection of overhanging cliffs
could the troops seek rest and relaxation from Turkish gunfire and
the intense heat. As May changed to June so did the conditions
worsen; the pungent smell from the unburied dead in No Man's Land
tainted the food and flies swarmed everywhere. Dysentery spread
and claimed victims by the score while lice added to the discomforts
of the soldiers.

Into such a situation, the 2/10th Gurkha Rifles arrived on 3

June so that 29 Brigade now had three Gurkha battalions under command. The newly arrived battalions had not expected to take part in the Third Battle of Krithia which started in the early hours of the following morning but a severe reverse led to one of the battalions, the 1/5th, being used in an attack on the following day.

Meanwhile, the 1/6th Gurkhas took part in the opening stages of the Third Battle of Krithia, a battle that was preceded by the heaviest bombardment of the campaign so far, a bombardment intended to destroy the front line defences of the Turks. The Gurkhas fixed bayonets and cheered and then opened fire with rifles and machine guns. It was hoped that such a ruse would induce the Turks into manning their forward trenches which would then be subjected to a further bombardment by the guns. On some parts of the front the defenders were deceived but the 6th Gurkhas were not so fortunate. The bombardment had not destroyed the wire and as the Regimental Historian states: 'The Turks returned our fire in a most hearty manner'. C Company stormed and seized the end of the objective, Mushroom Redoubt, but nowhere else was 29 Brigade able to advance through a veritable curtain of fire. As a consequence, the men of C Company found themselves hemmed in on three sides; Colonel Bruce made the difficult but correct decision to withdraw the small force and, covered by Naval guns, the evacuation was successfully carried out.

Following this attempt, the 1/5th Gurkhas were ordered to follow the same route as C Company from their neighbouring battalion but the Turks were not to be surprised twice – the 1/5th were held up by the wire and the attack petered out, with heavy losses in officers and men. The Turkish lines held until the Allies had shot their bolt when, exhausted by their efforts, they faced the grisly task of burying the many dead and evacuating the wounded to the already crowded hospitals in the rear.

June passed with the 2/10th taking its share of duty in the front line until, at the end of the month, a major task was given to the battalion. On this occasion, three brigades including 29 Indian Brigade, were ordered to drive the Turks back about one thousand yards from their position north-west of Gurkha Bluff, on the left of the line. 28 June was the appointed day for the assault, an assault which led to a series of bloody actions in the Gully Ravine area.

The early morning of 28 June was fine and soon became hot as the British guns kept up a heavy bombardment for about two hours. The 2/10th moved under the cliff and, with the Gurkha soldiers using all available cover provided by the broken ground and scrub, the leading company climbed to the top of the cliff and routed the defenders. This was an encouraging start and the 1/6th Gurkhas moved over and extended the line. By this time, the Turks had been pushed back about half a mile but they were stung into a series of desperate and costly counterattacks which were to lose them over ten thousand men in a week. These counterattacks hit all the Gurkha battalions in turn and for eight days and nights the struggle continued, the outcome of local battles often being decided by hand-to-hand fighting in which the Gurkhas excelled and used their kukris with deadly effect. Nevertheless the 2/10th were to pay a high price in lives lost – seventy per cent of their British officers and nearly forty per cent of the Gurkha soldiers – all within five weeks of their arrival in Gallipoli.

Although General Hamilton was well pleased with the result of the Gully Ravine battle, 29 Brigade was badly in need of a break from the appalling conditions that now prevailed in the peninsula – the heat, flies and dysentery continued to plague the living soldiers while the dead lay unburied and rapidly decomposing in No Man's Land. It was therefore a most welcome relief for the three Gurkha battalions when they embarked for the Isle of Imbros where, for nearly a month, the men relaxed and reinforcements arrived to fill the sadly depleted rifle companies. In spite of security measures, rumours of another offensive reached the idyllic island although details were shrouded in secrecy. Belatedly, the British Government had promised Sir Ian Hamilton more divisions and the arrival of fresh troops gave the Army commander the chance, once more, to try and outflank the Turks north of Helles. The key to the peninsula appeared to be the main peaks of the Sari Bair Ridge with features which were soon to be household names in England: Battleship Hill, Chunuk Bair, Hill Q. The capture of these peaks would not only turn the Turkish positions that faced the Anzac beach-head but would have enabled the British to overlook and cut off the Turkish force on the tip of the peninsula. The night attack on the Sari Bair feature was intended to be the battle-winning blow, launched from the Anzac beach-head. The other two operations in support, the landing in Suvla Bay and a strong attack in the Cape Helles area, were ancillary to the major effort and were launched to help the Anzac force seize the peaks of Sari Bair.

About twenty thousand reinforcements landed at the Anzac beach to support the attack, amongst whom were the three Gurkha battalions. 29 Brigade was to be given the difficult task of leading an assault in the early hours of 7 August against Hill Q in the centre of the Sari Bair feature. The nature of the ground alone made it a forbidding task; rugged, steep spurs rose up from gullies which were covered with dense prickly clumps of scrub, the passage of which 'is difficult enough even in peace time for unencumbered tourists provided with a good map and setting out in daylight'. 29 Brigade set out in the dark, with inaccurate maps and without having had the chance to reconnoitre the ground beforehand. All told, it was a difficult enterprise, the successful outcome of which depended on the Chunuk Bair peak being captured before daylight on 7 August.

At about 10.30 pm the troops began to move along the beach from the Anzac position. Immediately north were the first two spurs of high ground that sloped toward the sea from Chunuk Bair in an almost east to west direction. In the early hours of the morning the lower peaks were reached and the road to Chunuk Bair appeared to be open. However, the lack of any prior reconnaissance by junior leaders then began to play an important part in the proceedings. Columns were delayed because the guides lost their way. For the Gurkha battalions the confusion was increased by an inexplicable decision from above which halted units about a thousand yards short of the summit of Chunuk Bair before daylight – a reversal of earlier instructions which had fatal consequences later. An attack in the early hours would have undoubtedly led to a brisk fight but an attack against a fully-manned position at 10.30 am even with Naval gun support, meant that the decisive battle on Chunuk Bair was doomed to failure, although fleeting opportunities to gain success were still to occur during the next two days.

The left assaulting column was truly international: Australian infantry, New Zealand engineers, British gunners, Sikhs from India and Gurkhas from Nepal. The battalions moved towards Hill Q after a night of confusion and the early hours of the morning were spent in trying to establish their correct position and in regaining control of scattered sub-units. The 2/10th found themselves on the right, next to a New Zealand Battalion, so that the CO, Lt-Col Sutton, offered to help the Kiwis in a daylight attack on Chunuk Bair. The plan was for three companies of the Battalion to attack on the left of the New Zealanders and, as the official history states with feeling, 'Seven and a half hours after scheduled time, the main attack by the right assaulting column whose strength on the spot amounted to four and a half battalions, was opened with five companies'. It was indeed several hours too late. The Turkish outposts were ready for them.

At 10.30 the attackers moved up the slopes and they were at once met by heavy rifle and machine-gun fire which bowled over the leading troops. The New Zealanders, subjected to a raking enfilade fire from Chunuk, were forced to retire, and the 2/10th companies were brought to a standstill. In particular No 3 Double Company was heavily hit and only about a dozen men rejoined the Battalion next day. The survivors of the other companies dug in and for the rest of the day, with some of the New Zealanders, clung to the position under incessant fire from the heights above. This was the end of an opportunity to achieve a victory on Chunuk Bair, an opportunity that might have been decisive if the attack had been launched before dawn as originally planned.

In the early hours of 8 August orders were received for a further attack and at 4.15 am the 1/6th advanced up the slopes of Hill Q. Five hours later they had reached a point two hundred yards below the crest of the ridge but there the attack petered out. The 6th Gurkhas did not accept defeat and throughout the day they tried to inch their way forward, gaining some fifty yards only and then being forced to fight desperately for the positions they had won. Reinforcements from the South Lancashire Regiment and the Warwickshire Regiment arrived; with the Warwickshire Regiment was Lt W.J. Slim, soon to transfer to the 6th Gurkhas, and many years later to be the famous commander of the Fourteenth Army in the Second World War.

August the 8th had been a hard day for the Turks as well. After the initial shock on the 7th, the Turks realised the importance of their positions on the crests and the high casualties thereafter testified to their determination to hold on at any cost. The conditions for both sides were cruel. There was little cover so that the men were blistered by the sun, parched with thirst, short of food and ammunition, and unable to evacuate their wounded by day. The long, hot day of 8 August changed to a night during which comparative peace reigned. The next Allied plan was to send up a Brigade of four British battalions under General Baldwin, moving past the point where the 6th Gurkhas were still clinging to hard won gains under their new Commanding Officer, Major Allanson, to renew the attack on Chunuk Bair. Unfortunately General Baldwin's guides lost the way and, after wandering here and there throughout the early hours of 9 August, they were still some distance from the start line when the attack was scheduled to start at dawn. As a result the assault was begun by the handful of troops already in position; on the left, the 1/6th with their supporting British companies; on the right, the 2/10th Gurkhas with the Royal Warwicks and a Maori Battalion from New Zealand. The right hand attack advanced to a position some sixty yards below the ridge but it was then stopped by heavy fire from Hill Q, as well as being bombarded by gunfire, thought at the time to be from the Royal Navy. All they could do was hold their own in the hope that Baldwin's troops would arrive, but this was not to happen. The Turks were quick to spot their lack of numbers and counterattacked in strength, forcing the 10th Gurkhas to give ground slowly. It was to be the end of any further aggression by the 10th Gurkhas for after an hour's struggle they could only muster two hundred soldiers who were still able to fight.

The 6th Gurkhas were to have better fortune. At dawn a fierce and accurate Naval bombardment continued until 5.30. Shells of all descriptions were hurled onto the Turkish position which was soon a mass of smoke, dust and flying clods of earth. Then there was silence and in the words of Major Allanson the drama that followed makes exciting reading: 'Then off we dashed, all hand in hand, most perfect advance and a wonderful sight. At the top we met the Turks; Le Marchand was down, a bayonet through the heart. I got one through the leg, and then for about what appeared to be ten minutes we fought hand to hand, we hit and fisted, and used rifles and pistols as clubs and then the Turks turned and fled, and I felt a very proud man: the key of the whole peninsula was ours, and our losses had not been so very great for such a result. Below I saw the straits, motors and wheeled transport on the road leading to Achi Baba. As I looked round I saw that we were not being supported and thought I could help best by going after those who had retreated in front of us. We dashed down towards Maidos but only got about two hundred feet down when suddenly our own Navy put six twelve-inch monitor shells into us and all was terrible confusion. It was a deplorable disaster; we were obviously mistaken for the Turks and we had to go back. . . . We all flew back to the summit and took our old positions just below. I remained on the crest with about fifteen men; it was a wonderful sight. . . .'

Major Allanson and his handful of men were the only Allied soldiers ever to see the view described above. Once again, the Turks commanded the heights, the way had been opened and for a few minutes there was an opportunity to strike a decisive blow but mistakes made by the guides with Baldwin's column during the darkness had far-reaching results. This was the last chance in the battle for the Sari Bair ridges. Thereafter during the rest of the 9th and the morning of the 10th, the remnants of the 6th and 10th Gurkhas, with their British comrades, clung to their precarious positions. By this time there was not a single British officer left with the 6th Gurkhas so that the senior Gurkha officer, Subedar Major Gambirsing Pun IOM, MN, commanded the Battalion. He did this with conspicuous success but had to rely on the Regimental doctor to translate communications and messages as he could speak no English. By now, both sides were utterly exhausted but no longer did the foothold on Hill Q have any military significance. A withdrawal was ordered and the attack on the whole Sari Bair feature was over. Twelve thousand Dominion and British troops had become casualties and the Turkish losses were correspondingly high. Sir Ian Hamilton commented in his diary that this effort, 'leaves us with a fine gain of ground though minus the vital crests. Next time we'll get them'. There was, however, to be no next time – the chance had been lost for ever.

For the soldiers it had been four days of hardship and suffering. Most of the wounded had to endure hours of pain before they were evacuated after darkness fell and the selfless devotion of the stretcher-bearers saved countless lives. General Godley was to write: 'I do not believe that any troops in the world could have accomplished more'. Gallantry was not enough, however.

Meanwhile the surprise landing at Suvla Bay had been achieved without any real opposition, but owing to inept leadership vital time was lost in the first few hours. Continued inaction by General Stopford, commanding IV Corps, eventually led to his dismissal but by that time the Turks were firmly on the heights above – and the battle was irretrievably lost on 9 August, when two Turkish divisions drove the invaders back to their starting positions.

General Hamilton decided to make one more major effort for which the now experienced 29 Division was brought round in trawlers by night from Cape Helles to Suvla Bay. His plan was to mount an offensive against the higher ground on the west of the Suvla plain; 29 Brigade was given the left hand sector, with the 10th Gurkhas leading and the 1/6th in reserve. The date selected was 21 August and the attack began in the afternoon. The sadly depleted 10th Gurkhas, led by a handful of British officers, soon ran into trouble which was accentuated by the inadequate bombardment which had preceded their advance. Thrown against intact, strong defences, Australians, New Zealanders and Gurkhas alike were all held up, short of their initial objectives. To support the 10th Gurkhas two companies from the 1/6th came forward. On the following morning, further attacks were mounted on Hill 60 which the Turks had turned into a maze of trenches and machine-gun nests; but in spite of valiant efforts, the attackers never penetrated the outer fringes. Slowly, inexorably, the offensive petered out until both sides were forced to consolidate and dig in – trench warfare had begun in yet another sector of the Gallipoli peninsula.

The hopeless struggle dragged on for another three months. Spells in the line brought misery, discomfort and casualties but the men accepted their misfortune with the usual cheerful stoicism of the Gurkha soldier. To add to their discomfort, at the end of November, a fierce gale swept across the Dardanelles and torrential rain, which lasted for twenty-four hours, flooded the trenches and turned streams into torrents and the dust into a quagmire of mud. The rain soon turned to snow and a blizzard then swept across the battle field; men died from frostbite and exposure while no fewer than ten thousand sick were evacuated. Both Gurkha Battalions were hit equally hard – the cases of severe frostbite were numerous and the men's feet suffered badly under these appalling conditions. When the blizzard died down the shaky and bedraggled Gurkha survivors found that their respective Battalions' strength had dropped to about a hundred.

The end of the Gallipoli adventure was approaching. After seeing the conditions himself during a personal visit to the Dardenelles, Lord Kitchener ordered a general evacuation. Prior to this, however, the 2/10th, who had suffered the heaviest casualties, were relieved and embarked for Mudros and eventually sailed to Alexandria. Of the original party that set out for Gallipoli from Egypt in May, 1915, only one British officer and seventy-nine Gurkha soldiers returned with the Battalion some six months later.

In October, 1915, General Sir Ian Hamilton was ordered back to London by Lord Kitchener with the words: 'The War Cabinet wish to make a change in the command which will give them an opportunity of seeing you'. In such a fashion was Ian Hamilton sacked. In a sense, he was the victim of his Government's prevarication and vacillation in the early stages of the campaign. In another respect he suffered from the bungling of his subordinates, one or two of whom were 'wished' upon him – General Stopford, for example. Nevertheless, Ian Hamilton's faith in his subordinates was implicit – and, at times, blind – and they often let him down. His original plan deserved to succeed; his attempts to snatch victory by launching the later assaults can be criticized as being without real hope or justification.

The final evacuation was decided upon and organized by the new Commander, Sir Charles Monro, and as an operation it was carried out with a degree of skill unequalled during the whole of the campaign. As far as the 6th Gurkhas were concerned, the moment for evacuation came after dusk on 9 December. The night, a perfect one, was peaceful and calm as the first men moved, leaving small groups to hold the Turks, whose positions were often less than a hundred yards away. Later, the last parties moved back without the Turks realising that the Gurkhas had disappeared into the night. Only one unfortunate Gurkha corporal was captured as a result of being separated from his comrades, otherwise the withdrawal of the Battalion went without noise or incident. Early the next day, the Turks attacked only to be pounded by naval guns until they were driven back from the Anzac position – only then did they realise that their foe had abandoned trenches and deserted their strongpoints during the previous night.

The survivors sailed away for Alexandria. Behind them on the battlefields remained the dead; one hundred and eighty officers and men of the 6th Gurkhas and two hundred and forty all ranks of the 10th Gurkha Rifles. 'They had poured out the full measure of their golden valour.' Their erstwhile Commander, General Sir Ian Hamilton, was not to forget their gallantry, courage and skill, his secretary later writing to the 6th Gurkhas: 'It is Sir Ian Hamilton's most cherished conviction that had he been given more Gurkhas in the Dardanelles then he would never have been held up by the Turks'.

There can be no better way of ending the story of the Gurkhas at Gallipoli.

NEPAL IN THE FIRST WORLD WAR

We have seen how the Gurkhas fared in France, in the Middle East, in the Dardanelles – but that is only a part of the story. Apart from the rapid expansion of the regular Gurkha Brigade Battalions, almost double the number of wartime units were raised; some two hundred thousand young men from the hills of Nepal volunteered to serve Britain's cause between 1914 and 1918. The Prime Minister (Maharaj) of Nepal's generous pledge to give help to his British friends encouraged and influenced the young men into joining the Indian Army.

Such a promise had been given readily and quickly by the Maharaj who, on the day before war was declared, wrote to the Viceroy of India in these terms: 'The whole military resources of Nepal are at His Majesty's disposal, we shall be proud to be of any service, however little it may be.' And the young men walked down to the plains of India to enlist and the old men and the women were left to till the fields and manage as best they could until war-weary survivors returned after the war was over, some with decorations for gallantry, others sick and disabled, and all with stories to tell in their mountain homes and hamlets.

The Maharaj did more than just allow his young hillmen to join the Indian Army. He sent units of Nepal's own army down into India where they took over duties in the large garrison towns and on the North-West Frontier Province – thus releasing troops that were urgently required in the operational theatres. Great Britain owed a great debt to the Maharaj of Nepal, Chandra Shamshere Jangabahadur Rana, as well as to the young regular and wartime soldiers of Nepal.

Twenty years later an even more serious crisis was to see the same spontaneous gesture and generous reaction to help and support Great Britain in her second War with Germany and, later, Japan.

6. *The Arch of Ctesiphon, near the Gurkha Mound* (p. 59).

7. *First line transport of a Gurkha Battalion in Flanders during the First World War*

8. *British and Gurkha officers at their H.Q. in France*

9. *Kukri inspection somewhere in France during the First World War*

10. *Honorary Captain Santabir Gurung, Sardar Bahadur, OBI, IOM holding the Truncheon (p. 26) after the Delhi Day parade of the 2/2 Goorkhas in Malakand, 1934*

11. *Rifleman (now Honorary Captain) Ganju Lama, VC, MM, late 1/7th Gurkha Rifles, is visited by his relatives while in hospital recovering from his wounds (p. 136)*

12. *Gurkhas advancing over rough ground, Tunisia; March, 1943*

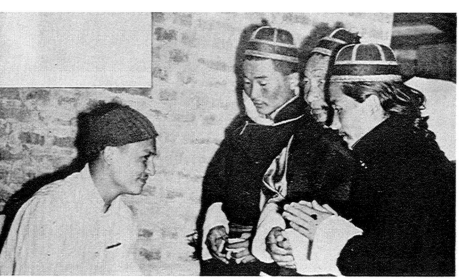

13. *Gurkhas moving through Faenza, Italy; December, 1944*

14. *Gurkhas advance past the grotesque* Chinthe *which guard the Temple at Prome, Burma, May, 1945*

The renown of the warriors from the small state of Nepal was enhanced during these wars by the deeds of her soldiers in many countries across the seas, strange lands that were miles away from the Himalayan peaks that overlook the humble homes of a proud but poor mountain people.

Chapter 8

Part I

THE YEARS BETWEEN THE WARS

IN April, 1921, three years after the rest of the world had been reaping the rewards and tackling the problems of peace, the last of our Gurkha Battalions, the 1/2nd, began a long journey home after nearly three years in Persia and, prior to that, two spent campaigning in Mesopotamia. The rest of the world did not include most units of the Gurkha Brigade who, on their return to India, were moved up to the North-West Frontier to meet and defeat the widespread Mahsud rising. Fortunately the war-time Gurkha Battalions had not been disbanded because Nepal's Maharaj, Chandra Shamshere Rana, had forecast the outbreak of violence – and because of his advice the expertise of experienced Gurkha soldiers was still available to the British Government to meet the new crisis.

Events in Afghanistan made the situation on the Indian side of the border very serious for the British. Amir Habibulla of Afghanistan had maintained a faithful neutrality during the war years but his assassination led to a reversal of policy by his third son, Amunulla, who took over as Amir and threw in his lot with the revolutionary movement in Waziristan. In such a way did the Third Afghan War start. It did not last long but imposed a great strain on the Indian Army which was then in the throes of demobilization; moreover it stirred up and fanned the hot air of revolution in the big cities throughout the continent of India.

All four regiments had one or more battalions participating in the short campaign; all were granted 'Afghanistan 1919' to add to the impressive list of First World War battle-honours. Units in the campaign found themselves marching long distances across bleak and inhospitable country rather than being actually involved in major actions. For example, the 7th Gurkhas force-marched some forty miles in twenty-four hours, as well as establishing a camp and picqueting several of the hills – only to miss the raiding tribesmen at the end.

September, 1919, saw the end of the Afghan War but the tribesmen in the Waziristan area were still up in arms. Against such a background, the regular battalions bade farewell to their wartime friends and thereafter spent many tours on active service on the Frontier before the outbreak of the Second World War. Such service under difficult conditions was to be an ideal way of keeping all ranks up to the mark in peacetime. Junior leaders were given the chance to command their men against a real enemy, although fortunately casualties were light. Moreover, a few officers and men were able to win decorations for gallantry under fire. Although taciturn by nature and modest in manner, the Gurkha soldier has always admired courage so that the holder of an award for bravery is respected by his fellow men, not only in the battalions but in the villages of Nepal.

Apart from service on the frontier, peace in India did not mean just routine soldiering or participation in military and sporting competitions or praising the exploits of British officers on the polo ground or as big game hunters. The Regimental diaries indeed do justice to all these aspects of life in the Gurkha Brigade but many other matters of interest are covered. The important topics of conversation in the messes in the 'twenties undoubtedly included the formal announcement of battle-honours to the four regiments; the sad but inevitable departure of old friends when each regiment contracted down to their two regular battalions: long overdue increases of pay for the Gurkha riflemen who, prior to 1921, received but 11 Rupees a month, although the new rate of 16 Rupees was still a meagre sum for men who were earning their living as mercenaries; and, the gradual, sad, but inevitable change from the pre-war pattern of paternal administration by a commanding officer who had governed the whole existence of his men, without any restrictive regulations encroaching on his independence. Nevertheless, in spite of the older officers' yearning for the pre-war days, these years before the world war of Adolf Hitler were undoubtedly happy ones and a welcome return to normal living for those who had survived the Great War.

With the 'thirties it is noticeable that the Regimental histories pay more attention to the serious aspects of soldiering. Large scale exercises and manœuvres are described in some detail; training became tougher and more realistic, although it would be wrong to imply that the regiments in the Gurkha Brigade had decided that war was inevitable and that the peacetime prizes at polo, football or shooting were of minor importance. Far from it – the imminence or probability of a war in Europe is never mentioned in Regimental histories until about 1938–9, although the more discerning of senior officers had stepped up the tempo of training because of their assessment of the political situation.

In 1934 Nepal experienced her most devastating earthquake of modern times. Several thousand dwellings were destroyed and severe damage done to many historic buildings in Kathmandu. A few weeks before Lady Houston's expedition had flown over the country and around the summit of Everest. The more superstitious people were convinced that the Gods who dwell among the mountain peaks of the Himalayas were so furious at this violation of their sacred homes that they had shaken the country of Nepal in anger. As a result, the Maharaj forbade the flying of aircraft over Nepal until the 1939 war began.

Less than a year later another earthquake was to strike Quetta, the capital of Baluchistan in North-West India. In the early hours of the morning of 31 May, 1935, the earth heaved in violent convulsions for thirty seconds – but in those thirty seconds the city fell into ruins and several thousand people were killed. Although the Quetta earthquake was the one that caught the headlines in the world press, the one in Nepal affected both the 7th and 10th Gurkhas to a greater degree as the havoc in the eastern districts, the homelands of the Rais and Limbus, destroyed the terraced fields; whole villages, men, women, children and cattle were swept down into the rivers whose banks had disappeared. News was scanty and rumours spread and although the distress was not as bad as had been anticipated, both Regiments had many men whose homes had suffered damage or whose relatives had perished in the earthquake. Meanwhile in Quetta, the 7th Gurkhas were fortunate as, although both battalions had been stationed there at various times, both were out of the cantonment when the violent tremors began. When the 2/7th returned to the city they found it an altogether strange and desolate place. By the time they left in 1938 a new city with reinforced buildings had arisen, phoenix-like, from the ashes.

As the last two or three years of peace were being enjoyed by the Gurkha Brigade, one or two officers who were soon to become famous were commanding Gurkha battalions. Lt-Col W. J. Slim transferred from the 6th Gurkhas to command the 2/7th Gurkha Rifles; Lt-Col 'Gertie' Tuker commanded the 1/2nd Gurkha Rifles; and in all four regimental histories other names of officers are mentioned who later reached high ranks before the end of the Second World War. Lt-Col Slim's tenure as Commanding Officer was a short one and not of the same significance as the contribution made by Gertie Tuker to his Regiment. Wars and skirmishes on the Frontier had always been fought on the premise that the tribesmen could only be defeated by a ponderous superiority of arms and men; no attempt was ever made to match the mobility of the tribesmen or outwit them, out-shoot them, or to establish a sense of individual superiority over them. Tuker had definite ideas on this and as soon as he was in command of the 1/2nd, he began training his unit on light scales and every officer and man, however junior, was encouraged to outwit his 'enemy' by using unconventional methods and tactics.

In May, 1937, he was given the chance to put his ideas into practice in the Razani area on the North-West Frontier. The tactics used by Col Tuker and his men were so successful that the tribesmen found themselves outwitted. Fortunately for the Indian Army, Tuker was a man not only eloquent in speech but also a writer of ability and distinction, so that within two years his ideas had gained the respect of a large audience. Tuker has been singled out but there were others like him, men with wide interests and talents not always expected in soldiers. To these men, the Indian Army owed a lot as their efforts in peacetime helped to prepare units for the war that lay ahead.

By 1939 it was clear, even to the most optimistic, that a second war with Germany was inevitable. In the Far East, too, Japan cast a hungry eye around the comparatively undefended but rich empires of France, Great Britain and Holland. In Delhi, like London, the mood of the times was radically different from the wild patriotic fervour that existed in August, 1914. As the last few days of August, 1939 passed, the declaration of war was greeted with relief but not with joy; no one talked about a quick victory or expected that the terrible struggle ahead would bring 'peace in our time'. India mobilized for war and within a few hours of Great Britain's declaration of war, her Government followed suit. By this time, Indian Army troops were already in the Middle East and Malaya, and it was to be in these theatres that the battalions whose fortunes we are following were to fight many of their most bitter battles of the Second World War.

Nepal's contribution to the Allied cause, notable in the Great War, was to be even more generous during the 1939/45 conflict. Not only did the ten Gurkha Regiments of the Brigade each raise a third battalion but during the black days of 1941, the Government of Nepal sanctioned the recruiting of men in order that each Regiment might form a fourth battalion. Scores of young Gurkha hillmen came down from the hills to enlist; never was Britain's need greater nor could she ever have expected such a contribution of precious manpower from so small an ally. By the end of the War the equivalent of fifty-five battalions of Gurkhas were serving in the Indian Army – a larger Corps of infantry than the present day British Army and one raised on a voluntary basis from a population of about eight million.

The Indian Army, and in particular the Gurkha Brigade, began the war as a well-trained body of men. The series of actions on the North-West Frontier had served to keep the edge on its training and although the Army as a whole was starved of modern equipment, the leaders and the men who followed them did not lack self-confidence as a result of their experience of being 'under fire'. The

Gurkhas, especially, reigned supreme in affairs of ambush and night patrolling and these qualities were to prove of the greatest value in the deserts of North Africa, on the mountains of Italy, as well as in the jungles of Malaya and Burma.

Part II

THE SECOND WORLD WAR – THE MIDDLE EAST AND EUROPE

'Why have I not been told of these Gurkhas before?'
[AMERICAN EDITOR in 1943]

Battalions from the 2nd, 6th, 7th and 10th Gurkha Rifles set out on the first of many journeys in the spring of 1941, journeys that were to take them, during four eventful years, to the Middle East, North Africa, Italy and Greece. They were never to be far from the centre of the stage, culminating in the bloody fighting in Northern Italy in which all four battalions helped to eject the Germans from the Italian mainland.

During May, 1941 the 2/7th Gurkha Rifles disembarked at Basra, only to find that the Iraqi Government had thrown in its lot with the Germans and, as a consequence, greeted the Gurkhas with bullets and not with cheers. For about two days the 2/7th had to deal with hostile forces and suffered a few fatal casualties. Here the newly-promoted Major-General W. J. Slim took command of the 10th Indian Division and, under his leadership, the tasks of relieving the RAF station at Habbaniya and defeating the government of Rashid Ali were soon accomplished. This was not to be the end of active service in the area because some Germans still held key posts in neighbouring Persia (Iran) where the Shah disregarded requests from the Allies that he should expel these technicians. Consequently, in July the British forces moved into Persia from the south and the Russians from the north. The campaign that followed, however, did not tax the invading armies to any extent. By this time the 1/2nd and 2/10th Gurkha Rifles had arrived, and together with the 2/7th, their soldiers revisited places that had been familiar to their fathers during the First World War. This time, however, there was no formidable enemy like the Turks to fight and active operations were soon over without a real scuffle. White flags appeared and the Persian Army, relieved that no bloodshed was necessary, welcomed their adversaries with dignity and, at one place, with a military band. Peace soon reigned around the Persian Gulf.

After such a beginning morale was high, although nearly six months were to elapse before the 1/2nd and 2/7th were called to join the already famous 4th Indian Division, under the command of General Gertie Tuker. Tuker's old battalion, the 1/2nd, was sent to Cyprus as part of 7 Indian Brigade. Cyprus at this time was, in the minds of both Germany and the Allies, a likely stepping-stone for an Axis invasion of Syria. From Crete and the mainland of Greece, German reconnaissance planes paid daily visits to check on the island defences which were scanty until 7 Brigade began constructing new ones. As the days passed so the danger of an Axis attack diminished; however, time was not wasted because hard and realistic training was carried out during the last four months. But the situation in Africa had changed during this period – for the worse as far as the British were concerned.

The German Afrika Korps had won a series of brilliant victories which had forced the British Eighth Army to retreat in haste and disorder into Egypt. Once more, the small port of Tobruk lay exposed to German assault – but during the first days of June, 1941, Tobruk was not like the tough little garrison that had withstood bombs, bullets and a series of Axis attacks during the eight-month siege which had ended in December, 1940. This time, the defences were not ready and the troops, hurriedly moved into the town, had to attempt to hold a thirty-five mile perimeter; a task that would have been beyond the capabilities of 2nd South African Division and 11 Indian Brigade, even if they had been given more time and warning to prepare the defences against the ordeal that lay ahead of them.

In 11 Indian Brigade was the 2/7th Gurkha Rifles. Throughout the early days of June, the battalion waited while disaster after disaster hit General Richie's Eighth Army; on 12 and 13 June came the blackest days of all which ended in Tobruk becoming the Eighth Army's foremost defended locality – and left to stand alone.

In General Headquarters, Cairo, there had been no intention to defend Tobruk yet again, chiefly because the strain on the Royal Navy had been such a severe one during the 1940 seige. Suddenly the decision was changed. Winston Churchill expected Tobruk once more to become a thorn in Rommel's flesh and his exhortations overcame doubts in GHQ Cairo, although the deficiencies of the defences were not revealed to the British Government. These were well known by the South Africans, British, Indians and men of the 7th Gurkhas, who faced a hopeless task. 'The destiny of Tobruk was once more in the hands of the Almighty and the conviction that all ranks would fight to the last rank and last round'.

For the men of the 2/7th, the majority of them pre-war regulars, the prologue before the first and only act was to be tragically short. All the long months of training were going to be tested in a drastic manner and all ranks in the battalion were to prove to themselves, as well as to friend and foe, that they belonged to a first-class fighting unit. But the odds against them were far too great. Around the perimeter mines and wire had been removed for use elsewhere. The 2nd South African Division, although full of enthusiasm, had never seen active service before. To make matters more difficult, the Division had a new commander, General Klopper, who had been badly briefed about the Tobruk defences; and, finally, the tank and artillery support left behind to help the infantry hold the long perimeter was too pitifully inadequate to cope with Rommel's Panzers, or the dive-bombing Stukas which ruled the sky over Tobruk without any opposition. This time, Field-Marshal Rommel was determined that Tobruk would be captured before his march on Cairo began.

The opening shots of the battle were fired on 21 June when the Germans displayed their intentions before dawn broke by launching a powerful attack against the Indian Battalion in 11 Brigade, the

2/5th Maharattas. The Indian soldiers were bombed by Stukas and pounded by the German 88-mm guns before being attacked by a whole brigade. One by one, the Maharatta companies were overrun and forced to surrender without the rest of 11 Brigade being able to move to their support, the long perimeter having forced the defenders into putting everything forward 'in the shop window'.

This breach in the defences was exploited with such speed and determination that Headquarters 11 Brigade was overrun as were the guns of the supporting Field Regiment. In effect, Rommel had split the British defences in half and by nightfall he was already claiming that his troops had captured the town of Tobruk. The fighting, however, was not over as on both sides of the corridor the Cameron Highlanders and the 2/7th Gurkhas stood firm, fully resolved to fight it out to the end. General Klopper's original plan was to try and break out through the Germans during the night, but he was dissuaded from this by his own South African brigades. After much indecision, it was decided to fight on, but when the artillery reported that their ammunition supply was almost exhausted, Klopper reluctantly ordered a surrender. Such an order did not reach either the Camerons or the Gurkhas, nor did they realize that at six-thirty on the morning of the 21st white flags had been raised by the South Africans who were fighting alongside them. It must be remembered that communications had broken down and, to keep matters in perspective, that the distance between the two battalions of 11 Brigade was nearly six miles.

During the night of the 20th/21st the 7th Gurkhas Battalion Headquarters was attacked and forced to seek protection with C Company. The next move was a German attack against D Company which began at dawn on 21 June. Like the Maharatta companies on the previous day, D Company fought it out until their ammunition was finished and there was no alternative but to surrender. Then it was B Company's turn. They beat off the first attack by two Italian battalions – but the Italians returned, this time reinforced by a German battalion, and by midday this company too was forced to surrender. Although the fight was hopeless, one officer who took part in the battle eventually wrote:

'The men were fairly bursting with confidence. Things were a bit chaotic but this really was war . . . They had knocked everything for six that had come against them and had received almost perfect battle inoculation. Their sense of superiority did not leave them until the end. After they had fought it out against overwhelming odds, and had lost, the stunned expression on their faces was a sight that few who saw it will ever forget.'

It was the turn of C Company and Battalion Headquarters. Here again, the men fought until they could do no more. At 1 pm Lt-Col Orgill, the Commanding Officer, realized that the situation was hopeless and, having ordered a small party to try and break out, decided to surrender. The Regimental History records that the Germans, after it was all over, held a ceremonial parade in the old C Company position and presented Iron Crosses to six of their men who had distinguished themselves during the battle that day.

For the second time in its history, the 7th Gurkhas lost their Second Battalion into prisoner-of-war camps. An even more remarkable coincidence was that official permission was again given for a new 2/7th Gurkhas to be raised; from the survivors, the few of them who managed to rejoin the Eighth Army after crossing miles of desert with adventures galore, from the officers and men who had been left out of the battle in reinforcement camps or on courses, with drafts of men posted in from other battalions of the Brigade, in such a way the new 2/7th became, once more, a fighting unit and part of 4th Indian Division that was to fight in the Italian campaign during 1944.

Before we leave Tobruk, due honour must be paid to the 2nd Queen's Own Cameron Highlanders, who like the Gurkhas, continued fighting after the official surrender. Then, on the morning of 22 June, led by their pipers, the Scots moved into captivity. Appropriately too, this battalion was also reformed and later fought alongside the 2/7th Gurkhas against the Germans in Italy.

Back to the 1/2nd Goorkhas, who moved from Cyprus after the fall of Tobruk. Cairo in August, 1942, was seething with rumours, shaken in spirit, lacking in confidence. The Afrika Korps appeared to be on the very doorstep of the city. Another offensive was feared at any moment when 7 Brigade landed and joined General Tuker's

4th Indian Division. However, on 28 August, even before the Battalion had moved forward from Cairo, the blackest day in the history of the Regiment occurred. Almost the whole of Headquarter Company was wiped out in one second when a sapper instructor inadvertently inserted a detonator into a live mine and pressed the plunger. Sixty-eight officers and men, who were watching the demonstration, were killed outright and another eighty-five were severely injured. Nearly all the victims were specialist signallers, mortarmen and drivers. In no battle had the 2nd Goorkhas ever lost so many killed and wounded in a whole day's fighting, let alone in one disastrous second. A few days later the Battalion had to move forward into the desert minus most of their specialists; fortunately a month's grace was granted before the El Alamein battle was launched, so that replacements arrived from other Gurkha battalions and from the Regiment's centre at Dehra Doon.

Initially, front line duty involved patrolling and probing the German defences but, as the days passed, tension built up when it became clear that the British were preparing for a new offensive; an optimistic spirit permeated down to the youngest and most junior of soldiers. A new commander, General Montgomery, had taken over the experienced but jaded Eighth Army, while precious reserves of tanks, planes and ammunition also arrived at this critical stage. Rommel was to be hit and hit hard; the place was to be El Alamein and the date, 23 October, 1942.

El Alamein was the turning point of the long see-saw struggle in the desert war. Meticulously planned, deliberately fought, the battle was a classic example of careful but controlled generalship by the then unknown General Montgomery. Many historians have described the battle from the opening salvoes of 1,200 guns, on 23 October, until the final rout of the Axis armies, twelve days later. The part played by 4th Indian Division was, to their chagrin, not a spectacular one, even if vital in the overall army plan. Their task was to contain the Axis troops on the inland flank by a series of raids and deception schemes so that when the British armoured break-through occurred on the coast, Rommel could not call on support from his divisions inland.

The 1/2nd was asked to carry out a small raid as part of the divisional plan and a tough fight occurred, when C Company, supported by the carrier platoon, came to grips with an enemy stronghold. Not without losses, the raiding force withdrew, but its part had been played to fit in with the overall plan. Then, as the Afrika Korps began to disengage, so did the battalion's role become more interesting when raiding columns were formed and despatched against a confused enemy. Many of the Italians saw and took the chance to surrender; the battalion took over 2,000, including one or two high-ranking generals.

Exhilaration in the victory soon turned to disappointment as far as 4th Indian Division was concerned when they were ordered to stay behind and 'clear the battlefield'. In fact, the pursuit of the Africa Korps produced such a strain on the available transport that the temporary grounding of some formations was inevitable. Nevertheless, four months were to elapse before 4th Indian rejoined the frontline troops; needless to say, General Tuker used every day during this period to perfect the training of his division and his untiring efforts helped to produce a division which became one of the most efficient formations in the whole of the Middle East. More important, he helped to erase suspicions about the Indian Army that undoubtedly existed in the minds of some senior British Army generals.

When 4th Indian Division rejoined in March, 1943, the Eighth Army had reached Tunisia with its barriers of mountains and salt marshes. Rommel was preparing to fight on the Mareth Line, a series of fortifications which led inland to the Matmata mountains.

4th Indian Division's part in the Mareth Line battle was to be a subsidiary one, but it provided them with an opportunity to show their prowess as mountain troops by seizing two of the passes in the Matmata mountain massif. Such an action involved movement through villainous terrain which the Germans had made more deadly by the liberal and skilful use of mines. The crest above had just been reached by the forward troops when it was learnt that the British armour had burst through on the coastal flank of the enemy positions. For the troops of 4th Indian Division it had been a hard slog for nothing, but by then General Tuker was certain that a similar role for his mountain troops would soon come again. It did barely twenty miles away, at the battle of Wadi Akarit.

Field-Marshal Rommel was showing as great a skill in adversity as he had displayed in success. Hampered by unreliable Italian allies, and subject to irrational decrees from Hitler, Rommel faced the two Allied armies, closing in on his Afrika Korps, with courage and decision. A sudden savage attack on 2nd US Corps in the First Army sent them reeling back some fifty miles. Then he made a quick switch to hold up the Eighth Army before a salt marsh which stretched from the Mediterranean for over 120 miles inland. The wide Wadi Akarit ran through this while rolling hills to the west overlooked the natural obstacles. These hills culminated in a high pinnacled feature of extravagant contours which was known as the Fatnassa. Rommel had indeed selected a strong position and he believed that his enemy would be forced to strike near the coast or against the gentler features in the centre of his line. To the defence of the Fatnassa he had sent two Italian divisions, although there were German elements in support close by.

The Eighth Army planners originally advocated an attack near the coast, just as Rommel had anticipated they would, but General Tuker, with the courage of his convictions and the utmost confidence in his men, persuaded General Montgomery into letting 4th Indian Division undertake a task of vital importance in the battle. His troops were to seize the key feature of the Fatnassa heights by a silent night assault and thus open a corridor for a thrust behind the Axis defences.

In this attack two Gurkha units, the 1/2nd Goorkhas and the 1/9th Gurkhas, were given the leading roles, with the former being selected to scale and seize the first pinnacle in order to open up the way for the next brigade to pass through. Such a task was to require expert navigation, the silent ascent of rocky precipices and slopes, and the utmost speed before the enemy could react to the unforeseen threat. Careful planning and reconnaissance were vital but even these were of minor importance compared with the quality of the troops available for the undertaking. Tuker knew it had to be victory or destruction and to a friend said: 'Perhaps I have asked too much of them and have set them a task beyond human accomplishment'.

His doubts were set at rest during the night of 5 April, 1943. The 1/2nd had an approach march of over six miles before the companies began to climb towards their objectives. All was silent until an Italian sentry, before death, raised the alarm. From then on, surprise lost, the Gurkhas moved like mountain goats, hurling themselves against the defenders before planned counter-measures could be effected. Two hours before dawn all the important features were in the hands of the 2nd Goorkhas, so that on 6 April the next brigade passed through.

To recount the story of each Rifle company or describe the many acts of gallantry would take too long. One outstanding display of leadership was shown by Subedar Lalbahadur Thapa, the second-in-command of D Company. With a handful of men he rushed to seize the vital passage leading up to the top of the most important feature. The path led up a steep cliff where several enemy posts were dealt with by Lalbahadur at the head of his men. On they went until just below the final crest, Subedar Lalbahadur, now with only two riflemen in support, killed several enemy before the remainder fled. The gallantry of the Gurkha officer led to the capture of the feature and his bravery was recognized with the immediate award of the Victoria Cross.

As dawn broke on the next day, the Germans, now aware of the threat to their rear, brought heavy fire down on the Indian Division positions. Communications broke down, but the commanders were able to move from hill to hill to keep in touch with each other. Counter-attacks by German troops were pressed home with great courage but the Gurkhas, splendidly supported by the magnificent divisional artillery, stood firm. In the early hours of 7 April there was silence. The battle was over and, considering the task given to the 1/2nd, the loss of some fifty all ranks was gratifyingly small. A victory had been won, a victory that led to increased public interest in the Gurkhas from Nepal.

Although Rommel saw that the end of the campaign was drawing near, he was, as always, subject to orders from Hitler who rarely agreed to territory being given up for tactical reasons. Resistance to the Eighth Army stiffened around Enfidaville where the Germans clung to the mountain peaks and their observers directed artillery and mortar fire against the British to great effect. Fierce fighting influenced General Alexander, the Allied ground Force Commander, into making the momentous decision to reinforce the First Army in the west with elements from the veteran Eighth Army. 4th Indian Division was one of the formations so selected.

The dramatic switch began on 20 April and after a move of over 200 miles, the troops went straight into battle on 5 May. Surprise was complete, and within a week the war in North Africa was over.

While other formations began special training for the invasion of Sicily and subsequently Italy, 4th Indian Division quietly slipped out of the limelight and away from the Eighth Army. Away they went to the east, first to Egypt, thence to Palestine, Syria and to the Lebanon. Here the Division went onto a special establishment to become a mountain (light) division. Training in rock climbing and mountain warfare began apace, spurred on by General Tuker's desire to increase the mobility of his troops to fit them for special tasks in Italy. By November a strong sense of imminence was felt by all ranks. Although the Italian Government had surrendered, the Germans were fighting with determination and efficiency south of Naples. A tough campaign was unfolding. Once again Eighth Army sent for 4th Indian Division and on 8 December the first Indian and Gurkha soldiers landed at Taranto in southern Italy.

Conditions in the Italian campaign were more like those of the Western Front in the Great War than any other theatre of operations during the Second World War. The strength of the forces deployed by both sides on a comparatively narrow front made manœuvre difficult, while the weather and terrain curtailed the seasons and areas available for effective operations. The sudden collapse of the Italians had presented opportunities to the Allies and problems for the Germans, but the highly professional techniques of the divisions under Field-Marshal Kesselring kept the Allied armies at full stretch until 1945. It is wise to remember, however, that the aim of the campaign, as given to General Alexander by the Chiefs of Staff, was to force Germany into using her strategic reserves to fill the vacuum created by the defeat of Italy. As to whether the cost of achieving this aim, in manpower and lives, was worth it, is still being discussed to this day by military writers. One thing they all agree on is that it was primarily an infantryman's war, tough, uncomfortable, costly in lives, with some of the most experienced soldiers in the world locked in a grim struggle.

Although initially 4th Indian Division saw some action on the Adriatic coast of Italy as part of the British Eighth Army, the situation in central Italy, on Fifth Army's front, soon became so pressing that reinforcements were urgently required and the two most experienced divisions of the Eighth Army, 4th Indian and 2nd New Zealand, were ordered to move over to become part of the hurriedly formed New Zealand Corps under General Sir Bernard Freyberg, VC.

When the New Zealand Corps arrived in the rear areas of the Fifth Army, the German defence system was firmly hinged on the mountains north-east of Cassino and linked to the key strong-points around Monte Cassino. The road to Rome, Route 6, curled into and around the town of Cassino which nestled below the beautiful monastery on the mountain above. From their observation posts on Monte Cassino and to the north-east on the high peaks of Monte Cairo, the Germans had a complete view of the battlefield which lay below them. With these advantages afforded them by nature, the Germans were quick to construct and devise defences which included machine-guns, mines and a series of well-sited guns and mortars. Cassino was as nearly impregnable as any defence could be; it needed only crack fanatical troops like the German Para Division to ensure that its capture would be a terrific problem – and the Para Division took over its defence at the same time as New Zealand Corps prepared to launch their first attacks.

Ironically, air superiority was the one thing that influenced the Allied generals into carrying out three direct assaults against the famous monastery, although fully appreciating the strength of the defences around that building. Assured that the Air Forces 'could whip out Cassino like an old tooth', General Alexander agreed, despite early doubts, to the New Zealand Corps carrying out two frontal attacks, after the gallant US 34th Division had clawed a foothold at great cost on the high ground to the north-east of the monastery. Unfortunately, 4th Indian Division entered the battle without General Tuker, who was struck down by a chronic tropical illness. This was a sad blow. Tuker had already proposed a plan for an encircling movement against the weaker links in the German defences, rather than a direct attack which substituted heavy supporting fire for surprise. Without Tuker's voice in dissent, the alternative plan was adopted by General Freyberg.

In early February the 1/2nd climbed up the narrow path to the forward areas in the hills near the monastery, on their way to relieve the exhausted Americans who had displayed courage beyond praise in holding on to their hard-won gains. The Battalion was not to wait long before orders were received for the first assault against the monastery. By this time, 11 Brigade had also arrived in the battle-zone. Two companies of the 2/7th Gurkhas were attached to the 1/2nd to act as porters, carrying ammunition and stores behind their fellow Gurkhas to the positions which were to be wrested from the defenders.

On 15 February, the aerial bombardment of the monastery began. It is not the place here to argue the ethics of the decision to bomb the building. What can be said is that the bombing was not correlated to any ground assault or timed to assist forward movement of troops so that, militarily, the bombing was a failure. Thereafter the 2nd Goorkhas in 7 Brigade, were given the supreme prize of the battle, the capture of the monastery, while on their right the Royal Sussex, old comrades in many a battle, were to capture a vital strongpoint, Point 593. The attack was scheduled to begin at 4 am on 18 February, three days after the first bombs had landed on the monastery.

At the appointed time, the Gurkha companies topped the ridge in front of them and advanced towards the monastery, less than 800 yards away. Pandemonium broke loose as devastating fire was opened by Spandau groups on the right, from machine-guns on the crest of the spur, and from posts sited under the walls of the monastery. The leading Gurkhas made a dash for the nearest scrub, only to leap into a deathtrap. The scrub was thorn thicket, sewn with mines and booby traps. Within minutes B and C Companies were struck down with more than half their number out of action. The other companies were to fare no better. The CO, Col Showers, fell shot through the body, other officers were hit and under this short, deadly hail of fire, nearly 150 all ranks were killed, eventually declared missing or seriously wounded.

By nine o'clock next morning those remnants of the Battalion who had found cover of a sort along the rough slopes took up positions near their original jumping-off position. On their right the Royal Sussex had also failed to take Point 593. Heroism and courage were not enough to overcome well-planned defences, manned by first-class fighting men. The porters provided by the 7th Gurkhas suffered many casualties trying to perform the thankless task of carrying heavy loads up the rough tracks under incessant mortaring and shelling. They had to take punishment without being given the chance to fight back.

For some time defenders and assailants in the 7 Brigade area were so close that supporting fire was not called for by either side. Below them, the New Zealanders fought with the utmost gallantry but had been unable to enter the now battered town of Cassino; the first attack by the New Zealand Corps had failed.

The story of the second attack by these two divisions begins with a period of frustration that lasted nearly three weeks, three weeks of delays and postponements. By this time the 2/7th Gurkhas had taken over a sector of the 7 Brigade front and were soon tested by probing German attacks. The second assault was scheduled to begin on 24 February but the weather broke into fierce rain, snow and sleet, so that air operations became impossible. For the tired, wet troops these days were miserable indeed. Relief was impossible and the forward areas were subject to continual 'stonks' by German guns and mortars. No day passed without casualties, no night without patrol activity or minor alarms. At last, the skies cleared, and on 15 March, 500 heavy bombers opened the second attempt by the New Zealand Corps to capture Monte Cassino and the town below.

In this, 7 Brigade had a holding role while the New Zealanders and

5 Brigade from 4th Indian Division attempted to strike side by side through the town and then up the slopes towards the monastery. Another Gurkha Battalion, 1/9th Gurkhas was to win the unstinted admiration of friend and foe alike by clinging to a rocky feature, Hangman's Hill, for several days right under the monastery itself. The Germans tried desperately to cut all communications with the 1/9th and, in particular, sought to capture a key point, Castle Hill, through which all reinforcements and supplies had to pass. A Company of the 2/7th moved down to help the defenders of Castle Hill, 1/4th Essex, and held out in bitter fighting against determined attacks by the German parachutists. All this was to be of no avail, however, as the defenders in Cassino town, shaken by the bombing but benefitting from the rubble that resulted, stood firm against the New Zealand Division. The bombing had created such destruction that Allied tanks could not move forward to support the infantry. Eventually, to prevent further heavy losses, the attack was called off; the 1/9th Gurkha Rifles infiltrated their way back to the Allied positions and two very exhausted veteran divisions waited patiently for their relief after nearly six weeks of non-stop fighting, the memories of which are brought alive to this day by the rows of graves that stand above the newly built town and in the shadow of the magnificent, new monastery on the mountain top.

The relief of both the 1/2nd and 2/7th Gurkhas was completed by the end of March; in two days they had recovered their normal high spirits, though losses had been heavy in both battalions. 4th Indian Division moved over to the Adriatic front near Orsogno. The German 334 Infantry Division greeted them with pamphlets which read: 'It wasn't much of a rest you had, was it? You need not think you will be allowed to complete the rest on this sector, although you may have been told that it was quiet'. And the very efficient enemy kept their promise. However, Eighth Army's final battle for Cassino opened on 11 May and this time the Germans were unable to with-stand an assault delivered in such unexpectedly overwhelming strength. They gave way and both Monastery Hill and the road to Rome were captured at last. The Polish flag flew over the ruins of the monastery and the Anzio divisions were soon biting into the enemy as they withdrew. Soon, too, the Adriatic defences were abandoned by the Germans and the long retreat to the north of Rome was under way. For a few days, the Gurkhas, Indians, British and other soldiers from the many nations who served the Allies in Italy, tasted the fruits of victory, enjoyed the heady wine of liberators as they entered towns and villages to the cheers of their erstwhile, albeit reluctant, enemies.

The grim business of war began again as both the Fifth US and Eighth Armies left Rome and moved into Central Italy. Field-Marshal Kesselring had no other intention but to buy time until the Gothic Line defences in the north were ready. The wooded country-side, with high isolated hilltops around Florence and Arezzo, was ideal for such delaying tactics; small groups of Germans supported by mortar fire or self-propelled guns were able to hold up advancing troops for hours before slipping silently away; demolitions and the generous use of mines caused even the bravest soldiers to pause and to tread warily.

Both the 1/2nd and 2/7th fought spirited actions during the months of July and early August. The 1/2nd had to employ all four rifle companies before they were able to seize and hold a crescent-shaped ridge near Arezzo by the name of Pian di Maggio. The timely arrival of the reserve company, after the three forward companies had been out of radio contact with their CO, saved the situation, although the Battalion lost some fifty casualties in the hour of victory. Likewise, the 2/7th had to mount a battalion attack on a feature called Poggio del Grillo. Monte Grillo was a place of some importance which the Germans had already defended against attacks made by the Cameron Highlanders – during one of which a complete Cameron company was surrounded and forced to surrender. The attack by the Gurkhas was preceded by an approach march of close on three miles over broken country which had to be carried out after dark. There was no hitch and surprise was complete. The Germans did not stay to fight, although they mounted counter-attacks during the next three days before finally deciding that they had had enough. It was at this stage that 4th Indian Division was once more withdrawn from active operations and, while resting near Lake Trasimeno, the officers were briefed about the imminent Gothic Line battles in which their units were to play a prominent part.

To achieve surprise against these well-prepared defences, Field-Marshal Alexander (as he had now become) reinforced 5 Corps on the Adriatic sector until it contained seven divisions. The greatest care was taken to deceive Axis agents, with complicated moves being made at night and all insignia and formation signs removed; the staff work was brilliant and, once again, Alexander caught Kesselring off balance, only for the latter to react so quickly that the outcome of the offensive was only decided after weeks of intensive fighting. But now there were to be more than these Gurkha battalions of 4th Indian Division in the battle. The 43rd Gurkha Lorried Infantry Brigade joined the Eighth Army for their initiation into war as fought in Italy. The Brigade consisted of the 2nd Battalions of the 6th, 8th and 10th Gurkha Rifles, all of whom had served on active service for about three years in the Middle East without taking part in any major operations. In spite of the long delay, the Brigade had trained hard, its discipline was excellent, and its arrival in northern Italy helped to meet a requirement for more infantry in the 1st Armoured Division. Nevertheless, the 4th Indian Division was in the thick of the battle for the Gothic Line before 43rd Lorried Brigade was tested in war for the first time.

At the end of August, 4th Indian was given the left hand sector up in the foothills of the Apennines, on the western flank of Alexander's offensive. 5 and 11 Brigades led off with the drive towards Tavoleto, a village on a hilltop that held out until just after midnight on 3 September. Then the 2/7th Gurkhas, spearheaded by their C Company, cleared the village after hours of confused fighting by small groups of men. It was a great achievement for which, after the war was over, the Battalion was given 'Tavoleto' as a battle-honour. This was a rare tribute as no other unit gained the same battle-honour.

Seven Brigade's watching role was soon over and the 2nd Goorkhas were told to take the village of Auditore and the steep hill behind it, Poggio San Giovanni. Initially Auditore fell to a night attack without much trouble. The next move, in the small hours of 3 September, was an attack on Poggio San Giovanni. Heavy opposition greeted them, although the first attacks were successful. As dawn broke the 1/2nd looked in vain for the tanks which were due to join them. For several reasons the armour was two hours late and during this time the infantry were in serious trouble. German self-propelled guns with machine-gunners riding on the front rolled down the road and desperate fighting ensued until the situation was eventually saved by the belated arrival of the British tanks.

This tough fight was summed up by the Corps Intelligence appreciation in the words: 'Auditore and Monte San Giovanni were occupied against slight opposition'. In fact, both sides had lost a lot of men and, not for the first time in Italy, the Intelligence report reflected a wishful forecast rather than the experiences of the men who did the fighting.

The Gurkha Lorried Brigade made its début by leading an assault timed for midnight, 12/13 September. They fought as infantry and such was to be their role until the last few days of the war in Italy. Final orders for the big attack were issued on 12 September; in this the 2/8th and 2/10th led the advance with the 2/6th held back in reserve.

After dark on 12 September the Rifle companies of the 2/10th moved up towards the Passano Ridge. All hell broke out as the leading groups reached the German positions. Owing to the broken nature of the country, co-ordinated attacks were not possible so that small bodies of men, nothing daunted during this, their first taste of battle, closed with the Germans in fierce hand-to-hand fighting and threw them off the Ridge. Then it was their turn to be buffeted by the Germans with heavy mortar and artillery fire. For a time it was touch and go but the men of the 10th Gurkhas stayed where they were to win the day. Fortunately the Battalion's casualties were not as heavy as had been expected. Winston Churchill subsequently referred to the Passano Ridge battle as 'a brilliant feat of arms'; truly a remarkable beginning by 43rd Lorried Brigade.

The 2/6th Gurkhas were not in reserve for long; they took over as leading battalion during the next phase, which entailed the seizing of certain peaks on the Mulazzno Ridge, on the north banks of the

River Marano. The actual crossing of the river was facilitated by an intense and accurate Allied artillery shoot onto known German positions on the Ridge which was captured without much trouble. Here for a day there was a lull, during which time it was announced that, owing to heavy tank losses in the 1st Armoured Division, 43rd Brigade was to transfer its allegiance to 56 London Division, its next task being to establish a bridgehead across the River Marecchia, the crossing of which had already been disputed for three days. A period of confusion, order and counter-order preceded the advance which was suddenly brought forward by twenty-four hours. On this occasion, the 2/10th attacked on the left, the 2/8th on the right, with the 2/6th in reserve. Unfortunately, higher HQ Intelligence staffs were sceptical about recent unit patrol reports which clearly indicated that the Germans were ready to resist any crossing with determination; for possibly the same reason, it was decided to send the leading Gurkha battalions across the river without tank support or guns to help out the forward troops until the following day. Such a gamble was to be a costly one and the Gurkhas in 43rd Brigade paid for it.

The German Spandau teams shot at the leading troops as they crossed the river bed. Fortunately, many of the machine-guns fired high so that the 10th Gurkhas were able to reach their objectives before daylight on 23 September. This proved to be but the beginning of a long, fierce battle. D Company, in dire trouble from a German counter-attack supported by tanks, held on grimly while C Company's platoons struggled forward to their aid. But they, too, ran into heavy opposition and could not advance any further. Without any tank support or anti-tank guns, D Company fought on until their posts were overrun and the Company ceased to exist as a fighting unit.

The long daylight hours of 23 September proved full of anguish for the whole Brigade. Confusion reigned and casualties mounted so that by midday the 6th Gurkhas had to be moved forward to relieve the 2/8th. Later, as darkness fell, the 6th drove towards the crest of the Ridge and held on to their gains after overcoming the resistance. Prior to this a few British tanks had managed to get across the river and their presence had a big psychological effect on friend and foe alike.

By midday on 24 September the battle was over – the most vicious battle the 2/10th were to experience in the Italian campaign and the one that caused them the heaviest casualties. By this time the whole Brigade had been in continuous action for eleven days and had behaved like veterans throughout.

Meanwhile, inland, the 1/2nd and 2/7th Gurkhas, still in the van of 4th Indian Division's advance, were fast approaching the end of their days in Italy. Near the River Rubicon, the Division learnt that their part in the Italian campaign was over and that others would be given the chance to defeat Field-Marshal Kesselring's army – they were to move to Greece forthwith.

For 43rd Brigade the pattern during the winter became a question of 'one more river to cross' and frequent switches from one division to another. Under 10th Indian Division, the 6th Gurkhas crossed the River Fiumicino and seized the Monte Codruzzo feature before first light on 11 October. The German defenders, lulled into a false sense of security by the steep slopes below their post, did not allow for the mountaineering skills of the Gurkha soldiers; surprise was complete and the 10th Gurkhas passed through on the following day. For the next few days the Gurkha Battalions, in turn, struggled forward along the ridge towards Monte Chicco, which fell to the 6th after desperate fighting for a German strongpoint, the White House. The struggle for the White House was fierce and it changed hands several times before the Gurkhas finally triumphed. Much of the fighting had to be done at close quarters where the Gurkhas used their kukris to deadly effect. Among the casualties was the CO of the 2/6th Gurkhas, Lt-Col Bulfield, whose wounded knee prevented him from returning to command the Battalion again.

One more major action occurred before the winter – the crossing of the River Ronco, which, being in spate, was some twelve foot deep. Once across the Ronco, Eighth Army could advance on Forli. The initial crossing caused more problems than the actual establishment of a bridgehead thereafter. In the 2/10th sector, in particular, the depth of the water and the swiftness of the current were such that not a single patrol was able to cross during the night. In the end, an aqueduct, which had been crossed by a company of the 2/8th Gurkha Rifles, was used to build up and expand the brigdehead and, on 29 October, the 6th and 10th Gurkhas crossed. The bridgehead was then enlarged to a depth of over 3,000 yards, which was enough to turn the enemy defences. The reward for the Gurkha battalions in 43rd Brigade was a well-earned break from operations, the first real rest they had enjoyed since early September.

During December, they saw action on the Montone and Lamone river lines, thence under command of 2nd New Zealand Division for an attack on Faenza. The association with the New Zealanders was a happy one and the Brigade was to work with efficiency under their command on several occasions before the end of the war.

As spring approached, plans for the offensive to attack and destroy the German army south of the River Po were made; at unit level special attention was paid to practising river crossings, including the use of assault boats and cooperation with other arms, while the tempo of fitness training was stepped up. During this period Lt-Col A. G. Stewart, who had commanded the 2/10th Gurkha Rifles for four years, left them on posting. It was ironic that, having led the Battalion in many countries and under many climates, he should miss, by a few weeks, the climax of the Italian campaign. Much of the Battalion's high reputation was due to his outstanding leadership.

The Eighth Army plan was to attack across the Rivers Senio and Santerno. 43rd Brigade was given the role of pursuit group under the Polish Corps, with its general mission, once the rivers had been crossed, of striking deep into enemy-held territory and disrupting communications in the rear. The attack began on 9 April and for the first two or three days went well without 43rd Brigade being asked to take any active part in the operation. The 10th Gurkhas were the first into action with a brilliant attack across the Sillaro River in the early morning of 16 April. At the outset they had had heavy casualties but the assault across the Sillaro River was a complete success; all the objectives on the far bank were taken and large numbers of prisoners captured. Through them passed the pursuit group, led by A Squadron, 14th/20th Hussars and the 2/6th Gurkha Rifles. The friendship between the 6th Gurkha Rifles and 14th/20th Hussars was one that was forged in battle and continues to this day. Both Regiments proudly possess the same battle honour, Medicina; the 14th/20th wear the crossed kukri badge and the 6th Gurkhas the hawk on the right sleeve of their uniform. Two companies of the 2/6th in Kangaroos – armoured troop-carriers – supported by tanks from the 14th/20th, roared into the town of Medicina, sweeping aside all resistance on the outskirts before meeting opposition in the centre of the town. German self-propelled guns were knocked out, another self-propelled gun was captured intact with its complete crew, and many prisoners were taken. Such was the speed of the assault that the Germans were completely overrun. Medicina was firmly in British hands after 'a glorious mix-up of confused fighting'. German prisoners admitted that they had been ordered to hold Medicina and fight it out to the end, but had been surprised by the speed and dash shown by the 6th Gurkhas and 14th/20th Hussars.

One more action remained, the crossing of the Gaiana River by 43rd Brigade. A and D Companies of the 6th were ordered to cross but it soon became apparent that the Germans were going to stand and fight. Both companies took heavy punishment when crossing and were so weak that there was little hope of withstanding another counterattack. The survivors were ordered to retire so that a fresh and stronger attack could be launched in which the 2/8th and 2/10th both took part. For the 6th Gurkhas' attack against heavy odds, the Battalion won twelve decorations.

The war was virtually over for the 43rd Gurkha Lorried Brigade and, on 2 May 1945, the great news was received that the German armies in Italy had capitulated.

Finally, before we leave Europe, a quick look at the situation that faced 4th Indian Division when they arrived in Greece. Many of the units had been on very active service since the early days of the war and the peaceful liberation of Greece sounded an attractive proposition. The expected welcome when the three Brigades landed in

Salonica, Athens and Patras was genuine and warm but it didn't last long. The Communist party, ELAS, was well organized and determined not only to eliminate the pseudo-traitors in Greece but take over the government of the whole country. Well-armed, and with many able leaders ELAS soon turned their welcome of the British into direct enmity. Open warfare began in Athens where 5 Brigade of 4th Indian Division, with other British formations by their side, soon found themselves deeply involved. Fortunately, the other big cities, in particular Salonica and Patras, although dominated by the ELAS forces, remained quiet while awaiting the outcome of the struggle in Athens.

The atmosphere was extremely tense. In the neighbourhood of Salonica, 8,000 Communist troops were on call with field guns at their disposal. In Patras, ELAS had at least one division opposing 11 Indian Brigade. Precautionary steps in both cities were taken in as unostentatious a manner as possible, while the ELAS soldiers arrogantly strutted the streets, confident that victory would be theirs in Athens, a victory that would signal their attack on 7 Brigade in Salonica and against 11 Brigade in Patras. Fortunately for the future of Greece, the British prevailed in Athens and the dispirited local ELAS leaders saw the writing on the wall. On 14 January, 1945, the 2/7th Gurkhas set out from Patras to cross the hills and to clear the rebels away from the city. One small but spirited action took place when C Company killed thirty-two rebels, wounded thirty-eight and took several prisoners – for the loss of two Gurkha soldiers. It was enough to break local resistance and was the only action fought by either the 1/2nd or 2/7th during their tour in Greece. Arms were handed in to the Indian Division as they gradually occupied more and more of the rural areas and slowly the suspicion of Greek villagers was changed to smiles of genuine welcome.

At the end of December, 1945 the time had come for 4th Indian Division to return to India. The 1/2 Gurkhas after four and a half years' service in ten countries, returned to their regimental home in Dehra Doon. Likewise, back in India, the 2/7th Gurkhas' veterans of Italy met many old comrades of the original Battalion who had been taken prisoner in Tobruk. However, the India they returned to was not the same India they had left in the first years of the war. Now, it was a country in turmoil, and the exhilaration of peace and the joy of reunion with old friends quickly gave place to doubts and fears about the future of the whole Gurkha Brigade if and when the British left India.

Chapter 9

'The Almighty created in the Gurkha an ideal infantryman . . . brave, tough, patient, adaptable, skilled in fieldcraft'

FIELD-MARSHAL VISCOUNT SLIM

IN the Far East, Japan made no secret of her ambitions but, until her German ally had crushed Western Europe and driven deep into Russia, she stood aside to bide her time. With Great Britain alone of the European powers still controlling her Far Eastern Empire, and the United States clinging to an isolationist policy, the Japanese Military Command struck without warning. Pearl Harbour was their first blow; other disasters to the Allies were to follow in quick succession.

Plans for the defence of the Federated States of Malaya were implemented as soon as troops were available. The 2/2nd Goorkhas moved to Malaya in early September, 1941, and for three months life in the north-west, near Ipoh, was reasonably pleasant, although relations between Japan and the USA gave rise to several alerts and stand-tos. On the morning of 7 December all doubts were ended by the attack on Pearl Harbour, by Japanese landings on the beaches of north-east Malaya and by the first bombs falling on Singapore. No one on the Allied side expected an easy campaign; all were shocked by the speed and ease with which Japan conquered Malaya.

Within twenty-four hours, the 2/2nd had moved up to north of Alor Star. Within the same time the Japanese had thrust their way through inadequate defences near the Siamese border while the British High Command wavered between two pre-planned operations – one of forward aggressive defence and the other, the occupation of a half-prepared line south of the Malaya-Siam border. The hesitation was fatal and neither course proved possible. Off balance from the start, the British, Indian and Australian troops began the long, ill-starred retreat down the mainland to the so called 'fortress' of Singapore. At various places improvised plans were drawn up and hurried defences prepared, only for the speed of the Japanese advance to cause them to be discarded or abandoned. The Japs were to retain the initiative throughout.

The 2nd Goorkhas' first brush with the enemy came during the night of 11 December. By this time the Japanese infantry had infiltrated into the heart of the defensive positions; they scorned supporting fire except that required to distract their opponents; their audacity and mobility had already spread confusion and no one knew where their leading units would appear next. The Gurkhas went to the aid of 15 Brigade but within hours an immediate disengagement became necessary. Although it was planned to use troop-carrying vehicles, these never appeared; for four days and three sleepless nights the 2nd Goorkhas marched south. A measure of defiance was shown at Gurun, but it took a few days for 11th Indian Division to recover from the early reverses. Only the Battalion of the 2nd Goorkhas remained intact, although desperately tired.

Their first real clash with the Japanese was to occur on 28th December when two companies dealt severely with the enemy advance guard. On even terms, the Japanese had been repulsed, but there was to be no respite. Taking advantage of complete air superiority they were landing troops with impunity behind the British lines; the Royal Navy had little left, even in Singapore. Another move back to the Slim River, fifty miles away, was ordered. Defences were being prepared there when suddenly the enemy began an all-out assault.

Here, at Slim River on 7 January, 11th Indian Division fought with spirit but within a few hours its units were completely disorganized. The Japanese spearheaded their attack with a 'death ride' of some fifty tanks jammed tight, head to tail. Although the first few were destroyed, the Allies had no aircraft with which to attack those waiting behind, so on they went to overrun two Brigade headquarters and to burn the British transport which lay defenceless before them. Complete chaos and confusion reigned.

During this time, the 2/2nd Goorkhas and the other Gurkha unit of 11th Division, the 2/9th Gurkhas, found themselves cut off on the northern bank of the River Slim behind the Japanese advance. The decision was made to split the 2/2nd and separate routes were selected for each half to cross the river and rejoin the retreating British forces. One party, in single file, was able to cross over the partially destroyed railway bridge. The other two companies, joined by some men of the 2/9th Gurkhas, were not so fortunate. Many crossed the river by improvised means, only to find the Japanese waiting for them. In desperation, a handful of officers decided to lead the remainder on a wide outflanking march through dense jungle and over 2,000-foot high hills. Tired, ill-clad, the men moved on for a day, but it became apparent that the size of the force would soon lead to their detection. Small groups, each of three or four men, were organized and sent off in an attempt to follow the line of the main road, moving in the undergrowth whenever possible. Few managed to escape, although many subsisted for several weeks before finally being taken prisoner. It was the finish of A and C Companies of the 2/2nd Goorkhas until the war ended.

On the same day, General Wavell, Allied Commander-in-Chief, made the decision to abandon the Malayan mainland and to concentrate all available resources to defend the island of Singapore. The decision, difficult to make, was no easier to implement as the exhausted British, Indian, Gurkha and Australian soldiers made their withdrawal.

A week later, the Gurkhas were in their last position on the mainland, twenty-five miles from the Straits of Johore. They were astounded to see social life going on, with gay dresses and dinner jackets being donned at sundown in the local club. They were equally surprised to see one or two friendly aircraft for the first time in the campaign. During this short respite, a few officers of 11th Division found time to record their thoughts about the five long weeks of fighting and retreating, retreating and fighting again – unrelieved, short of men, bewildered and with no confidence in themselves or their senior commanders. To those who were present, it was quite clear that the jungle training of the Japanese was far

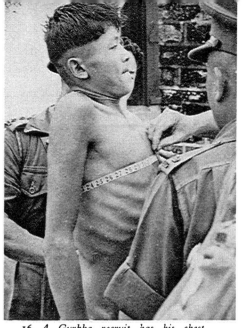

15. *Lance Naik Dambarbahadur Sunwar inspects a Japanese bunker on 'Scraggy'* (p. 135)

16. *A Gurkha recruit has his chest measured*

17. *Men of the 1/10th Gurkha rifles capture an Indonesian parachutist in Malaya, during the confrontation*

18. *Swamp and jungle became a second home to the Gurkha soldiers in Malaya during the Emergency, 1948–60*

19. *Corporal Rambahadur Limbu, VC, 10th Princess Mary's Own Gurkha Rifles with members of Queen Alexandra's Royal Army Nursing Corps, also from Nepal*

20. *Gurkha paratroopers swim a river in Brunei while their equipment, in ponchos, remains dry*

21. *A young Gurkha NCO with his wife and daughter*

22. *Major Harkasing Rai, MC, IDSM, MM, 6th Queen Elizabeth's Own Gurkha Rifles* (p. 160)

23. *A Gurkha soldier in a Belvedere in Borneo during the Confrontation*

superior to that of the British, Indian or Australian armies. To the Japanese the Malayan jungle might have been neutral, but to the British and Indian it was a deadly enemy – no one had bothered o train them in elementary movement and tactics or to teach them ᵗto fend for themselves in the jungle.

On 31 January, at dawn, the Causeway to the mainland was blown up with the last organized bodies of the British forces safely across on the island of Singapore. The siege of Singapore had begun.

A lot of publicity had been given to the strength of the fortress of Singapore. Some of it was inspired by the hope that the Japanese might be deterred from attempting to capture the island base. The Japanese High Command had a more accurate picture of the true state of Singapore than did the British Government back in Whitehall. For months before the outbreak of hostilities, Japanese agents had been busily ferreting out likely British plans for the defence. The reports that reached Japan confirmed that there were concrete fortifications, that heavy guns had been installed and air fields existed for mounting offensive and defensive operations: all these assets were in the defender's favour if the Japanese had attacked the island from the sea. Unfortunately, an invasion from across the Straits of Johore had never been seriously considered by the British and the defences were sited accordingly. But there were other equally valid reasons why Singapore had the flimsiest of pretexts to claim the title of 'fortress'. There were eighty miles of coast line, about a quarter of which faced the mainland at distances as close as 1,200 yards. The Naval Base was empty because the Japanese air force had dealt crippling blows to the Royal Navy when they sank the *Prince of Wales* and *Repulse* off the east coast of Malaya before the invasion had even begun. The Navy had been withdrawn and now, as the Japanese lobbed shells across the Straits of Johore, the RAF airfields had to be abandoned also. Lastly, the huge civilian population, mainly Chinese but with strong elements of Malays and Tamils, were mostly indifferent to the dire predicament of their British masters, for the latter had made little effort to prepare them for the war. The water consumption of such a population in a hot climate is high but the precious water had to come across the

Causeway from Johore. When this was destroyed, Singapore began living on its none-too-plentiful reserves.

After the 500-mile retreat, morale in the 2/2nd Goorkhas was still reasonably high. The Battalion was given a sector near the Naval Base and they did not have to wait long before the Japanese struck. During the night of 8/9th February the enemy crossed in various types of craft and hurled themselves against the sector held by the Australians. By sunrise, 5,000 Japanese had landed and infiltrated inland to seize valuable ground on the Island. 11th Division on the right was untouched, and indeed heard only the scantiest reports about the progress of the struggle. A day later, this was to prove disastrous: the Australians, forced to withdraw, did not, or were not able to inform the Indian Division. The latter made great efforts to protect the open four-mile flank, but the strain on the depleted units was too great. In danger of being completely isolated, they had no alternative but to pull back.

Even then, the Japanese were one step ahead of them, for the 2nd Goorkhas found themselves fired on from the rear as well as from the north. At this stage confusion reigned throughout the Island as groups of soldiers from both sides moved about, fought and moved away, without knowing where their Headquarters was or what the next task should be. In the middle of the destruction the dazed and bewildered Chinese population either sat as passive spectators or began looting. Singapore's days were numbered, although plans were made to pull back the perimeter and defend the city itself.

At four pm on 15 February the ceasefire began. Prior to this, the 2/2nd Goorkhas, with their friends from the 2/9th, had fought grimly, dead tired and dressed in a varied assortment of uniform and rags. After a nightmare move back to the perimeter selected for the final stand, both Gurkha battalions had prepared positions and benefitted from a day's rest. The men were ready to sell the position and their lives dearly when, to their disbelief and shocked amazement, the news of the surrender reached them on the 15th.

Many excellent accounts of life as prisoners of war have been written by the survivors of the 85,000 British, Indians and Australians who marched into captivity after 15 February. The

Gurkhas, like all other Indian Army units, found that their British officers were segregated by the Japanese in an attempt not only to degrade the officers but to coerce the Indians and Gurkhas into joining the motley gang who called themselves the Indian National Army. Few, very few, Gurkhas were to join and several of these did so only to attempt an escape from Japanese forward positions in Burma at a later stage in the war.

The 2/2nd Goorkhas then began the three long and terrible years of captivity. In the men's camp, Subedar Major Harising Bohra, blind and suffering internal hæmorrhages, died after severe ill treatment. This Gurkha officer refused to submit to Japanese exhortations to join and bring his men into the ranks of the Indian National Army. In this same camp the senior officer was Capt Hari Chand Badhwar of the Third Cavalry. At the end of the war his citation read: 'The enemy regarded him as an arch ringleader in resisting attempts to undermine the loyalty of the Indian soldiers.' He was subjected to extraordinary punishments; suspended for eighty-five days in a cage, unable to sit or lie down, exposed to the sun by day and under the cruel beam of a spotlight by night; yet this tough, loyal, magnificent man survived. Appropriately enough it was Capt Hari Badhwar who handed back the Gurkhas to their British officers on 8 September, 1945. The Regiment elected him as an honorary life member of their Mess, but his welcome in India was to be insignificant compared to the public lionizing of the members of the INA by the Government of India under Pandit Nehru.

While Malaya was falling and the British forces withdrew to Singapore, the Japanese began their invasion of Burma. The 1/7th Gurkhas took up positions near the Siamese frontier, the companies being positioned at likely crossing places. The first fighting occurred when the officer commanding D Company, speaking on the civil telephone line, reported that he was being attacked by Japanese using mortars and machine-guns; an hour later he again called and told his CO that he was surrounded; then the line went dead. Intense firing was heard from the direction of the Company position and then there was silence. But the Battalion could not move to D

Company's assistance because Japanese aircraft began a series of dive-bombing attacks against the other companies, unchallenged by any British aircraft. Then a pattern of events began that was to be repeated many times throughout the first Burma campaign: the Japanese infiltrated round behind the Gurkhas who, on Brigade's orders, had to retire in haste and in some confusion. This went on for nearly a week before they were able to rest and re-equip at Kywegan. Even more important, they were joined there by the missing D Company. The intense firing that had been heard had heralded their break through the Japanese surrounding the Company position. The Company Commander then led his men by compass march through the jungle to the River Salween where, having obtained a barge, he and his soldiers had floated down the river to rejoin the Battalion. While out of touch with the Battalion, they had listened on a portable radio to the BBC and had learnt that things had not been going well for the defenders of Burma.

By now the Headquarters of 17th Indian Division under Major-General Jackie Smythe, VC, had taken command of the three brigades in Burma. With 48 Brigade came the 3/7th Gurkhas, one of the war-time units who, within a few weeks of completing their recruit training, found themselves in the front line against the superbly trained and successful Japanese enemy. A third battalion of our British Brigade of Gurkhas, the 1/10th Gurkhas arrived during March as part of 63 Brigade to fight in this first phase of the Burma campaign.

There were no roads between India and Burma so that the British Army depended on Rangoon for supplies and reinforcements. Small as the invading force was, it far outnumbered the British and only by holding the port of Rangoon could the defending army be built up and maintained. The Japanese made for Rangoon and, in particular, sought to seize the Sittang Bridge, a vital link if their advance was not to be held up. In mid-February, the already over-stretched 17th Division found that a fresh force of Japanese was streaming to the west, obviously making for the Sittang Bridge. A grim race now took place; the Japanese hoped to capture the bridge intact while the retreating British hoped to destroy it after their troops had crossed to the other side. The Japanese drove a number of wedges between the bridgehead guard and the British and Indian units desperately trying to reach the bridge. Units and sub-units became separated and there was little overall control – each had to do the best it could against whatever opposition was encountered. Both the battalions of the 7th Gurkhas, 1st and 3rd, were continually attacked by the Japanese and were unable to join up with the bridgehead force. Then, at five-thirty am on the 23rd two tremendous flashes lit the sky, followed by explosions. For a short time there was complete silence and those still on the east bank of the Sittang did not know whether the Japanese had seized the bridge and blown it up or whether it had been destroyed by the British. In fact, the commander of the bridgehead guard had reported to General Smythe that the bridge could not be held any more and, although it meant sacrificing many of his division, General Smythe had had to make the terrible decision to give the order to blow it up. General Smythe, in his book *The Valiant,* subsequently wrote:

'But hard as the decision was, neither Punch Cowan (Chief of Staff) nor I had any doubt that I must give this permission. Nor indeed, despite the controversy which subsequently surrounded this operation, have we ever doubted its necessity.'

On the east bank of the Sittang it was left to junior officers and their men to find some way to cross the river. Below the Sittang Bridge the river was 1,200 yards wide with a tide that flowed strongly; there were no boats but there was bamboo in the jungle, and in the local villages there was a lot of wood. Anything that could float was carried to the river's edge. A few rafts were made, for the wounded, but most men had to wade into the river and, clinging to whatever support they found, try to cross the 1,200-yard gap. Many were drowned, others were carried out to sea by the current and even the strongest swimmers had to abandon boots and equipment before reaching the other bank. The exact losses in the two battalions of the 7th Gurkhas have never been accurately ascertained. The Regimental History gives an estimate of 350.

Even in 1946, when prisoners of war had been recovered, about 300 all ranks of the two battalions remained unaccounted for and could not be traced. Some of these undoubtedly died later in Japanese hands, but the majority perished in their attempt to cross the Sittang River.

The immediate effect of this disaster was to reduce the 17th Indian Division to a brigade group only and it was at this stage that the 63rd Gurkha Brigade, which included the 1/10th Gurkhas, joined the depleted division. For much of the war thereafter, 17th Indian Division was to consist of the two brigades – 48th and 63rd.

The 1/10th Gurkha Rifles were introduced to the Burma war in a dramatic fashion. A Japanese force had by-passed Pegu and the Brigade R Group, in wheeled carriers, ran into an enemy road block on 6 March where it was very severely handled. Lt-Col R. G. Leonard, the CO of the 10th Gurkhas, was in the second carrier with his Brigade Commander and all in it were killed or wounded. The wounded driver managed to turn the carrier round and drive it back to Brigade Headquarters. Col Leonard's troubles were not over, however. The ambulance taking him to hospital was ambushed and Japanese bullets ripped up the slats below his stretcher. Gurkha soldiers tried to come to the rescue and for over an hour a battle raged around the ambulance. Eventually the Japanese were driven off and the badly wounded Leonard was saved.

By now the decision had been made to evacuate Rangoon. On 7 March, Army Headquarters and rear-guards from the city managed to pull out. Meanwhile, the survivors of the two 7th Gurkha Battalions were joined together to form one unit with a combined strength of about 500 under command of the new 48 Brigade. At Pegu the men were reclothed and, as far as possible, re-equipped. Then, a day or two later, 48 Brigade was ordered to fall back from Pegu to conform with the withdrawal from Rangoon. Road blocks set up by the Japanese had to be cleared, which inevitably meant tough fighting even when the Japanese were met in small groups. Unless the assaults made against the road blocks were properly organized, the Japanese would cling like limpets to their positions, causing the maximum casualties and inconvenience to the retreating forces. The strain on the men was considerable. Days of strenuous marching with irregular and infrequent meals were interspersed with desperate confused fighting against Japanese ambush groups, sent ahead in an attempt to seal the escape routes back to India.

In these encounters the Japanese displayed superior techniques in jungle fighting as well as being stronger numerically, and with air support on call. In contrast, the 10th Gurkhas had over 450 recruits with less than six months training. Additionally, all units lacked efficient and serviceable radio equipment and men trained to operate the new sets were few. Nevertheless, there were one or two occasions when the Gurkhas stood firm and dealt severe blows to their Japanese opponents – learning from their experiences and giving the enemy a foretaste of what was going to happen when they were to meet on even terms during the later phases of the Burma campaign.

One example of fighting spirit in adversity can be given before the curtain is drawn on the first act of the struggle for Burma. On 28 April at Kyaukse, 48 Brigade fought a sharp action and severely handled the newly arrived 18th Japanese Division in its first big battle. 48 Brigade consisted of three Gurkha units, one whose fortunes we are following, the 1/7th, together with the 1/4th and 2/5th. The Gurkha battalions took up a position forward of the already gutted town and through their positions the withdrawing Chinese 5th Army passed on 27 April, followed by the other brigade of 17 Division, 63rd Brigade.

Next evening, under bright moonlight, the unsuspecting Japanese were allowed to approach to within a hundred yards of the Gurkhas' position before heavy and accurate fire was opened up. The enemy, with a lot of shouting, fled in confusion, harrassed by the British artillery. An hour or two later, they advanced again but once more heavy firing drove them away. Later, after daybreak, D Company, 7th Gurkhas was ordered to counter-attack and burst through to capture the village, routing the enemy and adding to the already high Japanese casualty list – over a hundred were killed.

During the morning the Japanese renewed their efforts to thrust a way through and the bitter fighting continued. In the late afternoon,

Headquarters 48 Brigade heard that the Chinese Army had completed its withdrawal over the Ava Bridge and so, one by one, the Gurkha battalions were ordered to withdraw. Kyaukse was indeed a model rearguard action as it had caused the Japanese to deploy in strength and thereafter many casualties were inflicted on them. The 7th Gurkha Regimental Historian summed it up: 'At Kyaukse we were masters of the situation from the start'.

However, any hopes that General Alexander had of holding North Burma disappeared when the Japanese seized Monywa on the Chindwin. Without vital supplies from the oil fields and deprived of the rich and abundant Shwebo rice fields, it was no longer possible or advantageous to seek to retain a foothold on Burmese soil. The history of 17th Indian Division states:

'It was a race against the weather because, if the rains broke, the road would become an impassable quagmire. It was a race against starvation because, if the withdrawal took too long, the reported meagre stocks along the road would become exhausted. It was a race against the enemy, because he could make the journey to Kalewa by river in 24 hours ... and finally cut off the Army of Burma.'

At Shwegyin, the Japanese made a last attempt to destroy the British rearguard. Once more they came up against 48 Brigade and on 10 May attacked the Indian Battalion, the Jats. Three companies of the combined 7th Gurkhas Battalion moved to their assistance. It was in the middle of this battle that General Bill Slim noticed that an old friend, Subedar-Major Saharman Rai of the regiment he had once commanded, was laughing at him: 'I asked him coldly what he was laughing at and he replied that it was funny to see the General Sahib wandering along there by himself, not knowing what to do.'

After some tough fighting, the Japanese were cleared away so that the river steamers could continue to ferry men, guns and equipment from Shwegyin to Kalewa. Many of the vehicles and most of the very heavy equipment had to be destroyed or abandoned during this withdrawal.

And so both the 7th and 1/10th Gurkhas came out of Burma by 21 May, just as the monsoon broke. A war-weary and ragged 17th

Division moved into Imphal, tired and defeated, but certain that it was not the end and that they would return to win the final round. The soldiers had earned a period of rest and recuperation, but Imphal was in a shambles after some recent Japanese bombing. Accommodation had to be improvised and the conditions and lack of reception arrangements raised bitter comments from the commanding officers of the Division. However, both sides were faced with similar problems; disease was rife, in particular malaria, communications were badly over-stretched and the rain poured down for days on end. These factors brought major operations to an end until early in 1943.

Although General Wavell, by now Commander-in-Chief in India, appreciated that it would not be possible to take any offensive action for some considerable time, he was attracted by the idea of British and Indian forces operating behind the Japanese foward positions with all supplies being air-dropped whenever the situation so permitted. The exponent of this theory, the Commander of 77 Brigade, was soon to be a famous figure in the Burma war: a man who slouched but possessed a restless temperament, who was eccentric in dress, speech and habit but yet had the complete confidence of the taciturn General Wavell, a leader whose personality has been described by many writers and whose exploits are still championed, disputed and denigrated by modern military historians. His name was Orde Wingate. Wingate had many convictions and theories about jungle fighting, all of which he imparted in crisp, sizzling language and these were soon to be practised by his troops in a series of tough imaginative exercises in Central India.

Under his command were the 3/2nd Goorkhas. They were selected because Wingate maintained that a newly raised unit could be easily moulded to his ideas: he accepted their inexperience and he assumed the responsibility for the training that would outweigh their immaturity. With some of the older men in the King's Liverpool Regiment, the experiment probably succeeded. With the young men from Nepal, many of them aged only sixteen or seventeen, the results were not so fortunate. If the unit had fought under its own officers, then the story might have been different. As it was, units and sub-units were deliberately mixed. The junior commanders were as inexperienced as the men they led, while few of the officers could speak Gurkhali well enough to explain the reasons behind the very intricate jungle tactics practised by the early Chindits.

Wingate was to criticize the Gurkhas as being mentally unsuited for the role given them in the first Chindit Expedition. Events since 1948 have, in fact, shown the Gurkhas to be ideal troops for guerrilla and anti-guerrilla warfare in the jungle. Their fitness, ability to carry great weights and cheerful patience in discomfort and adversity have always existed. But, by splitting the men up, by mixing units and, quite simply, not understanding that Gurkha soldiers need a different type of leadership to the British, Wingate failed to exploit their best qualities.

Originally the strategic concept behind the first Chindit Expedition was to divert the Japanese while the Chinese recaptured the key to Northern Burma, the town of Myitkyina. This promised offensive never materialized, but by this time Wingate's columns were poised to cross into Burma from Manipur. Wingate was adamant that although the Japanese were now free to concentrate against his men, 'The chances of getting the Brigade through and of extricating them again were good and that the experience to be gained would be invaluable and well worth the risk.' Wavell gave his consent and reviewed the men before they marched off into enemy-held Burma on 6 February, 1943. They were part of a calculated experiment; human guinea-pigs from whose experiences in life and death many lessons were to be learnt.

The whole Chindit Brigade was divided into decoy and striking forces, the 3/2nd Goorkhas being split up between four columns. The CO of the Battalion, Lt-Col L. A. Alexander, was given two columns in the decoy group. Their story was to be one of limited success. Initially, all went reasonably well but once the Japanese learnt about the foe in their midst, things started going wrong. One of the parties was expertly ambushed, about half joining up with their CO while the other group, having lost their radio, were unable to ask for orders or, even more important, call for replenishment of food and ammunition. Leaderless, dispirited, they found their way back to India where they were to incur the unreasonable displeasure of Wingate. They survived, albeit without credit – others died from drowning, sickness, starvation, by the bullet and at the ruthless hands of their Japanese captors. To tell the story of each column would require a book in itself – and the records of the battalion columns are conflicting in many details, chiefly because Col Alexander died of wounds and did not survive to give his report. Only the exploits of C Company have been accurately recorded – their column commander was a Sapper officer who was soon to be famous in Burma, Major Mike Calvert.

Mike Calvert had all the attributes of a guerrilla commander and without being foolhardy, took calculated risks that brought success. His column achieved a lot and although often in contact with the Japs, Calvert invariably kept them out of serious trouble by well-timed dispersal and the ingenious and liberal use of booby traps and mines. Eventually, the Japanese were like a lot of angry hornets roused to anger by the demolitions and destruction caused by Calvert: as a result, the column commander reluctantly decided to split his 360 men into nine groups of forty who were then sent off by various routes to attempt the return to India. Over 200 arrived back safely. Calvert's columns could claim that their journey and tribulations had produced definite results. In India, the 3/2nd Goorkhas gradually re-formed as parties returned, a few men ready to fight immediately but the majority suffering from under-nourishment, sickness and exhaustion, both mental and physical. The emaciated and fever-riddenmen had suffered a reverse in which they had lost 446 from their battalion (150 of whom subsequently returned.)

While the Allied press praised the gallant Chindits and lionized the eccentric figure of Orde Wingate, the survivors inevitably asked the question: 'What was the point, was it worth it?'. In 1943, Lord Wavell reported that 'the enterprise had no strategic value and about one third of the force which entered Burma was lost, but the experience gained . . . was invaluable. The enemy was obviously surprised and at a loss . . . In general, Brigadier Wingate's theories of leadership were fully vindicated.' Nevertheless, the very selection of a young, untried Gurkha battalion was an error and arbitrary carving-up into segments, which were mostly under the command of officers who were complete strangers to Gurkhas, was too big a psychological burden for the young men from Nepal to overcome in such a hazardous operation.

The lessons were evaluated and Wingate, with the full support of Mr Winston Churchill and other Allied senior commanders, asked for troops of the highest quality for his next venture. This time, the Special Force was on a much bigger scale and three Gurkha battalions were selected – again, none of these were regular units and included the 3/6th Gurkha Rifles. Like the 3/2nd Goorkhas before them, the 6th Gurkhas came under the command of Mike Calvert in 77 Infantry Brigade. The training carried out was even more strenuous than before the first Chindit operation; this time it was not to be a tip-and-run affair but part of an overall plan designed to retake Burma.

Although slightly out of chronological order, the fortunes of the 3/6th will be followed before returning to see how the other British Gurkha battalions fared during 1943 and 1944. Wingate planned to establish 'strongholds' which were to be bases for rest and resupply, sited in 'country so inaccessible that only lightly equipped enemy infantry can penetrate to it . . . We can transport our defensive stores there by air; the enemy cannot'. These strongholds were guarded by artillery and had in some cases light aircraft and even fighters based on them.

'D Day' was fixed for 5 March, 1944 and a galaxy of senior commanders gathered on Hailakandi airfield to witness the start. At the last moment it was reported that one of the strongholds, called 'Piccadilly', had been blocked with felled trees and Wingate considered that the operation should be cancelled as he feared that his plans had been compromised. Calvert was keen to go on with the operation and General Slim overruled Wingate. The 6th Gurkhas went in during the follow-up phase; their fly-in was carried out in full moonlight and passed without incident or hitch.

The Battalion's first big skirmish occurred when, with Brigadier Calvert present, Pagoda Hill near Henu was captured. In this action a mixed force of South Staffords and 6th Gurkhas killed forty-two Japanese. Thereafter the supplies poured in from the Allied aircraft and because of the hundreds of white parachutes hanging out of reach in the tall trees, the position became known as White City. The Japanese reacted with fury and for several weeks made strenuous efforts to re-take White City. After a period of desperate defence, Calvert decided to clear the town of Mawou about a mile away, a base that was being used by the Japanese for their attacks against the Chindit position. Two companies of the 6th Gurkhas took part in this attack which was led with great dash and determination but C Company commander and one of his Gurkha officers were killed. For a few days, this successful attack brought respite but once more from the first week in April the Japanese renewed their attempts to destroy the White City position. From records, it is clear that they expected to meet light opposition similar to that encountered when dealing with the first Chindits – they were very surprised to be engaged by all types of guns and to see heavy equipment brought in by the Dakotas which had landed on the newly-constructed airstrip. For twelve nights the battle for White City went on with each night heralding a more intense struggle than the previous one. The most bitter fighting raged around O P Hill, the highest point, where a platoon of the 6th Gurkhas supported by medium machine-guns held on for fifteen days until their many casualties forced the small party to be withdrawn.

Meanwhile, events in other parts of Burma had been moving fast and the long-term role of the Chindits was still uncertain. The Chindits had another commander when Major-General Joe Lentaigne was promoted to succeed General Wingate, who had been killed in an aircraft crash in the jungles of Burma. Unfortunately, too, the Chinese forces under General Stilwell had made little progress and had not yet captured Kanaung or Mogaung. Although by this time the men of 77 Brigade were tired and fully expected to be flown out, they were given orders to move over 150 miles north and capture the town of Mogaung. The march was very strenuous, especially as the monsoon had broken in all its fury. Before the end of May came, the men had not changed their clothes for weeks, everyone was lousy and most of the column walked in torn and soggy rags. General Stilwell's agents reported that Mogaung was occupied by only 100 Japanese; the battalion was therefore ordered to 'strafe, assault, capture and hold Mogaung'. To the 6th Gurkhas this order came as a shock because it was well known that the town was strongly held and fortified. Fortunately, the orders were changed and the whole of 77 Brigade was detailed for the attack. Some valuable information was brought in by a little Gurkha, a prisoner of war from the 7th Gurkha Rifles who had escaped from a gaol in Mandalay. He and his fellows had been selling milk to the Japanese and he was able to pass on information of value to 77 Brigade.

Operations began on the night of 6/7 June and for three days the Lancashire Fusiliers, the South Staffordshire Regiment and C Company of the 3/6th saw some hard fighting before capturing objectives outside Mogaung itself. A vital bridge on the western approaches was strongly held by the enemy and defied firstly, the Lancashire Fusiliers, then a company of the 6th Gurkhas who lost thirty men and were pinned down. Only after outstanding bravery by Capt Michael Almand were the Japanese defenders overcome and the bridge captured. Although the way was open to attack the town itself, the Japanese resisted with their usual fanatical bravery and progress was painfully slow. It was not until the night of 21 June that the centre of the town was reached, and at no time had the Japanese ceased to fight for every yard, preferring death in battle to the dishonourable state of captivity in British hands.

In the early hours of 23 June, the greatest day in the history of the 3/6th Gurkhas occurred. On the right, C Company drove onto the railway bridge. B Company had a tough struggle against a Japanese stronghold called the Red House, and only after a terrific fight was the position captured. Two members of B Company were to receive the Victoria Cross. Capt Michael Almand, who had already distinguished himself with two acts of outstanding bravery, although suffering so badly from trench foot that he could hardly walk, struggled alone through deep mud and charged a Japanese machine-gun position single-handed before he fell mortally wounded. He was carried back to the hospital on the east of Mogaung but died during the night of 23 June. Fortunately the winner of the other Victoria Cross, Rfn Tulbahadur Pun, was to survive the attack on Red House. His section was reduced to three men. With two men, he charged the House, going on alone when his companions fell badly wounded. Firing a Bren gun from the hip, Tulbahadur covered some thirty yards of open ground before reaching the building. There he killed three Japs, captured two machine-guns and put the other defenders to flight. The courage of these men played a big part in the capture of Mogaung by the 6th Gurkha Rifles.

After the attack was over, the Battalion took stock and found that casualties had been extremely heavy. Since flying into Burma in March, three months before, they had lost 126 killed and over 350 wounded – a heavy price to pay even if it is remembered that the Japanese had suffered heavier casualties in their encounters with the Gurkhas. The weary and depleted 77 Brigade could not continue in action any longer and after a march of a further fifty miles, the tired troops emplaned and returned to India. For a few weeks the praise and plaudits received helped the weary soldiers to recover their spirits; however, it was to be the last action by the Chindits, who were disbanded, the units being sent to other formations. Although the 3/6th Gurkhas were to return to Burma just before the war ended, the climax of their short history was the battle of Mogaung.

It is now time to turn the clock back and look at the decisive battles in the Arakan, at Imphal, and around Kohima.

During most of 1943 17th Division's two Brigades in turn watched the Tiddim road along which the Japanese had to come if they were to capture Imphal. By October both sides had brought up fresh divisions and minor operations were launched to seize the best vantage points. In these, both the 1/7th and 1/10th Gurkhas played their full part. Likewise, one of the war-time Battalions from the 10th Gurkhas, the 3/10th, carried out operations in 23rd Division, covering some of the 150 mile sector at the southern end of the Imphal Plain. The newly raised battalion showed all the skills that made the Japs dread and detest the name 'Gurkha'. Their patrols harried and killed the enemy, quickly learnt to move with stealth and skill in the jungle, and showed a natural instinct for hunting their quarry. One story of a patrol serves as an example of similar stories that other Gurkha battalions could produce:

'First patrol (L/Nk and riflemen) came across approximately 100 Japanese – laid ambush, killed ten Japs including two officers. Rifleman was wounded with five bullet wounds but escaped. L/Nk was about to throw a grenade when Japs took him prisoner. They tied him to a tree and bayonetted him in the face, then took him towards Intha. Near Intha Japs were ambushed by another 3/10th GR patrol of a Havildar and one soldier. Nine Japs escorting the Rifleman killed and remainder ran away. Rifleman escaped into the jungle and returned to unit. Later the other three Gurkhas returned although two were wounded – total enemy killed 25.'

Of the battalions whose fortunes we are following, only the 3/2nd Goorkhas took part in the Arakan Battle at the end of 1943. Elsewhere three battalions from the 10th Gurkha Rifles and one from the 7th Gurkhas (1/7th GR) were to be severely tested when the Japanese launched their Imphal offensive in the second week of March, 1944. Although General Slim was aware of the Japanese intentions, he was surprised by the speed of their initial advances towards Imphal. However, Slim reacted with speed and determination so that reinforcements came by air, by rail and by road to defend Assam and East Bengal. Nevertheless, 17th Division, east of Imphal, had to fight many battles, clear many road blocks, and cover many miles in non-stop fighting for four months before the Japanese threat was defeated.

One of the first indications that the Japanese columns were moving west came from the report of a young rifleman of the 1/10th Gurkhas who became separated from the patrol he was with. Soon other reports followed and 17th Division was ordered to fall back on Tiddim This order came as a shock to both the 1/7th and 1/10th Gurkha Rifles who, in local clashes and by aggressive patrolling, had gained a moral superiority over the Japanese. However, Slim now knew that three Japanese divisions were moving west and 17th Division was soon under pressure, as well as being in danger of being cut off when the Japanese positioned themselves across the Tiddim Road near Tuitam Ridge.

The 1/10th played a notable part in the fierce struggle for possession of the Tuitam Ridge. It was imperative to dislodge the Japanese so that the main road could be opened once more. A Company of the 1/10th was sent into the attack but could not take the whole position – later, the 1/3rd Gurkhas followed and took the position without any real resistance. The withdrawal of the Division could then continue, but the 1/10th were told to remain in positions on the Ridge, acting as rear-guard for the other units as they withdrew along the road. Thereafter a battle raged for several days and nights as the Japanese hurled themselves again and again against the defenders. The 10th Gurkhas took the brunt of these onslaughts but held firm until relieved by another Gurkha battalion.

For the 1/10th the battle for Tuitam Ridge was probably their most successful action during the Burma campaign and a delighted Divisional Commander singled the unit out for high praise, as well as granting them the unique privilege of flying his divisional Black Cat banner, with the Regimental Crest superimposed upon it, outside the Quarter Guard – a custom that continues to this day. A well remembered event for the 1/10th occurred shortly after when, continuing the withdrawal, they passed through their own 3rd Battalion who had been sent up the Tiddim road to take over as rearguard.

Imphal was the forward base for IV Corps. The Tiddim road was not the only approach to it; there were two other major routes for the Japanese Army to move along, one from Tamu in the south-east over the Shenam Pass and the other from the north-east down the track from Ukhrul. In defence of these three main routes many battles were fought, all of which contributed to the defence of Imphal. The three battalions of the 10th Gurkhas between them were to suffer over 1,000 casualties before the last of the Japanese road blocks was cleared on the Imphal-Kohima road by 21 June, 1944. The battle-honour 'Imphal' was awarded to all three battalions, a fitting reward for the Regiment's contribution to the victory gained near Imphal in 1944.

So far no mention has been made of the other wartime 10th Gurkha battalion, the 4th, which under 20th Indian Division operated in the Khabaw (Kubo) Valley south-east of Imphal. The 4/10th had had a quiet and successful battle inoculation during the first few weeks of 1944 before the Japanese Shenam Pass Force advanced up the Khabaw Valley. On 13 March, the Japanese sprung a surprise, not only on the Battalion but on the British High Command, when they used their tanks for the first time in the war in Burma. In addition, medium guns also appeared in the valley. After the initial shock, the 10th Gurkhas hurriedly revised their Piat drills and positions were improved in the expectation of full scale tank attacks. Thereafter the fighting became confused and although A and C Companies beat off local Japanese attacks, a message was received which indicated that the Japanese had crossed the Chindwin and that the whole British force would have to evacuate the Khabaw Valley and withdraw in haste to Shenam.

This pre-planned withdrawal went wrong from the start. The British artillery was ordered to move first and thus left the infantry without any anti-tank or artillery support – this in turn forced the battalions to move away from the main track. Left without protection on the track, the administrative columns were ambushed by the Japanese and thereafter panic and confusion reigned, with mules stampeding and communications between companies and units breaking down. For a time, the Japanese had it nearly all their own way and renewed their efforts in an attempt to break through into India. The 4/10th Gurkhas concentrated on the Shenam Ridge by the evening of 1 April and from here its C Company was sent on a gallant but abortive attack against a Japanese strongpoint, a position that was only captured by the Devons after a full scale battalion attack combined with generous fire support. C Company, without support and on its own, lost the equivalent of one platoon killed and wounded. In spite of this setback the 4/10th continued to fight well; B Company successfully ambushed a battalion of the so-called Indian National Army. The INA received a bloody nose about which the Japanese 15th Army had this to say: 'The Gandhi Brigade (INA) advanced south of Pallal . . . and met a strong counter-offensive by the Indian Army together with attacks from the air; they retreated thereafter and were very cautious in their actions.' The Regimental

History commented: 'Never were so many so utterly routed and put to disorderly flight by so few.'

Meanwhile the 3/10th Gurkhas made a great name for themselves during late May and early June, when battles were fought on the high Shenam Pass features which dominated the Tamu road. One of the peaks, nicknamed 'Scraggy' because of its appearance, was the foremost defended locality on the Pass. With the enemy only forty yards away, the Battalion took up positions on this feature. For four days and nights the Japanese poured fire on the Gurkhas and repeatedly launched attacks during the night. The Japanese made repeated attempts to rush the position. Gurkhas rarely need an excuse to join in hand-to-hand fighting and this they did, driving the Japanese back wherever they met in open conflict. In one morning attack, on a knife-edged pinnacle known as 'Gibraltar', the Japanese dead numbered no fewer than ninety-three. Nevertheless, the Japanese did not give up, and although the Battalion was withdrawn for a short rest in the middle of June they were back fighting over the same ground. The whole of the 'Scraggy' feature was not to be completely cleared of the enemy until B Company spearheaded the 10th Gurkhas' pre-dawn attack on 24 June. Shouting 'Ayo Gurkhali',* the Gurkhas surged forward until eventually the Japanese had had enough. Another great battle had been won by the 10th Gurkha Rifles. In all this fighting the 3/3rd and 3/5th Gurkhas bore an equal part with the 3/10th and the three battalions, as 37th Gurkha Infantry Brigade, made a great name for themselves.

Near Imphal each of the four battalions, three from the 10th and one from the 7th, had many stories to tell about the fighting in May and June of 1944. The 1/10th, in one of the hardest fought actions of their war, captured the village of Potsangban, about twenty miles south of Imphal. At first, things did not go well when the British guns brought down a concentration on C Company, causing thirty-five casualties. This and other reasons led to a new plan, the object of which was to capture the village by a *coup de main*. With the neighbouring 1/3rd carrying out a diversionary attack, 1/10th went across open flat paddy fields, with the riflemen crawling from the

* 'The Gurkhas are upon you'

'Start Line' to keep their movements secret. Luckily the night was very dark. The diversion caused by the neighbouring Gurkha battalion was a complete success. The 10th Gurkhas burst into the village without much trouble, although they lost many casualties through booby traps and, because the Battalion was thereafter concentrated in such a small space, losses from enemy shelling and mortaring were high.

Although casualties during these engagements were heavy, the Japanese had been losing far more men, their situation being aggravated by the fact that reinforcements had been prevented from reaching the forward troops. Moreover, the British had begun an advance from Kohima towards Imphal. 48 Brigade in 17th Division had a hard fight for the village of Ningthoughong. During this fighting, the 1/7th lost some 200 casualties. Half of the village of Ningthoughong was held by the Japanese and it took six weeks of incessant attacks by the three battalions of 48 Brigade before they were evicted. On 12 June, when the 2/5th Gurkhas were under great pressure, the 7th Gurkhas sent two companies to their assistance. The leading platoons were pinned down by three Japanese tanks. Rfn Ganju Lama, who had already won the MM for destroying two enemy tanks in a previous operation, crawled forward on his own to attack these three tanks. Three times he was wounded in the arms and legs, his left wrist being broken, but he struggled forward and destroyed first one and then a second tank, killing the crews. An anti-tank shell hit the third: Ganju moved nearer and flung his grenades at the escaping tank crew. For his single-handed battle against the tanks, Rifleman Ganju Lama, MM was awarded the Victoria Cross. It is a measure of the severity of the fighting there that four Victoria Crosses were won in the month of June, 1944. However, Ganju Lama's great day did not bring immediate victory – the fight went on and the village that earned the 7th Gurkhas their only VC cost the 1st Battalion 130 casualties.

As June ended it was clear to Slim and his staff that the Japanese offensive had failed. The breaking of the monsoon made the enemy's situation hopeless and by mid-July, the Japanese had started a reluctant withdrawal which was to end in Rangoon. For the soldiers of 17th Indian Division, after fighting non-stop for months, there was a welcome interlude in India for rest and re-training before they returned as a spearhead to strike one of the decisive blows of the war in Burma. Of 100,000 Japanese who marched on Manipur it is estimated that 75,000 were killed or died of wounds, disease or starvation. What may not be appreciated now is that their enterprise so very nearly succeeded: it is to General Slim's credit that in the darkest days and during the most anxious hours he retained a steadfast belief in his overall strategy and the utmost confidence in the troops that he led. Many of them were Gurkhas, and they did not let him down. Now it was Slim's turn to put into effect his plans for the re-conquest of Burma.

In the autumn of 1943 the rejuvenated 3/2nd Gurkhas joined 25th Indian Division and a few months later, in March, 1944, moved into the Arakan. A more unpleasant country could not be imagined. The coast consisted of tidal waterways of swamp and marsh with mangrove swamps stretching inland to join the spine of the main Arakan peninsula.

After a series of skirmishes, the 3/2nd was given the task of capturing a strongly defended position on a peak, Point 1433. The attack began on 8 September, 1944 and it took two days of hard fighting, assisted by the continuous pounding of the Japanese bunkers by British artillery, before the enemy silently withdrew, leaving the peak in British hands. The Battalion lost a total of ninety-one men during this operation.

Later that year, the Japanese withdrew completely from Northern Arakan and on the first day of January, 1945, the leading platoon from the 3/2nd Gurkhas found that Akyab had been abandoned by the enemy. Not a civilian walked in the streets and only the jackals roamed the deserted gardens at night. Two years of RAF bombing had completely destroyed the once proud port of Akyab. Thence, using British sea and air superiority, a series of combined landings were launched in the rear of the Japanese, thus forcing them to withdraw from previously prepared positions. In all these the 3/2nd played its full part.

Although resistance was stubborn, by the end of February, 1945 the Allies were within sight of closing the final escape route of the enemy force in the Arakan. It was here that 3/2nd was to have its biggest, toughest and, as it was to transpire, final battle of the war. The feature the Gurkhas were to fight for was a ridge nicknamed 'Snowdon'. This was occupied with barely a shot being fired on 4 March. That very evening the Japanese decided to fight for its recovery and by next morning at least half the hill was in their hands, although the defending Gurkha platoon fought with the greatest gallantry until over half their number lay dead or severely wounded.

Next morning D Company was ordered to re-capture Snowdon East. The company's exploits were both overshadowed and enhanced by the supreme gallantry shown by one young rifleman, Bhanbhagta Gurung. Bhanbhagta was in the leading section when he decided to take the objective alone if necessary. Five times his platoon was pinned down and five times Bhanbhagta rushed forward and engaged the enemy single-handed. Near the top he killed the last Japs in a bunker with his kukri and then, with two other riflemen, faced the final, despairing enemy counter-attack. This was stopped at close range by the accurate fire of Bhanbhagta and his friends. Rfn Bhanbhagta Gurung was awarded the Victoria Cross.

The fighting died away and the grim count of casualties revealed that B Company, 3/2nd Gurkhas had lost a third of their number. On the battle-scarred ridge over sixty Japanese bodies were recovered Other units passed through and the enemy escape routes were closed. The Arakan campaign was over – apart from one or two suicide parties who clung to their warrens in the jungle until the bitter end.

Meanwhile, in Central Burma, the Japanese had withdrawn across the Irrawaddy during early January 1945, whereupon General Slim had sent the 19th Indian 'Dagger' Division after them. In this Division were two battalions of the 6th Gurkha Rifles; the regular battalion, 1/6th, and the wartime 4/6th, both of whom were meeting the Japanese for the first time. The target for 19th Division was Mandalay. At the same time, 17th Division was to strike for Meiktila, some seventy miles south of Mandalay. The Japanese had decided that they would fight for both places.

In order to draw off large forces of defenders from Mandalay, 20th Indian Division went across the River Irrawaddy opposite Myinmu. In this Division was the 4/10th Gurkhas who, by their exploits when on an independent battalion mission at the end of 1944, the crossing of the Wainggyo Gorge, earned the nickname of 'the non-stop Gurkhas' – a title given them by the military correspondent of *The Times*. Now, for some fourteen days and nights in the middle of February, the Battalion was to face its toughest struggle and win its finest victory. Having captured the village of Talingon, the 4/10th found themselves attacked repeatedly by the Japanese. At times it looked as if the Japanese would overwhelm the companies by superior numbers, but the CO did not hesitate to bring down defensive fire, even on top of one of his own company positions. D Company was singled out by the Japanese for attack after attack. The intimation of the final and most dangerous assault came from two Gurkhas up a tree in an observation post when, having reported to their Company Commander by telephone, the men found that they could not escape from their tree because the Japanese then held an 'orders group' under it. Without any regard to their own safety, they dropped grenades on them, killing five Japanese officers but suffering wounds in their own nether regions by the upper blast from their own grenades. Extraordinary to relate, the Japanese did not realize where the grenades came from and the two brave men remained up their tree throughout the night and were able to witness the successful outcome of the battle which raged below them. After the battle was over, the 4/10th actually counted 504 Japanese bodies and two armoured bulldozers had to be called in to dispose of the corpses.

Although Mandalay itself did not fall until 20 March, the climax of the battle took place nearly fifty miles north at the little village of Kyaukmyaung where, in the middle of January, 19 Division established a bridgehead on the east bank of the Irrawaddy. The actual assault crossing went according to plan but the Japanese reaction thereafter was violent and for five weeks everything was flung into the battle in an attempt to destroy the British bridgehead. A feature, 'Pear Hill', changed hands several times as the Japanese deployed ever-increasing forces against both battalions of the 6th Gurkhas. But behind the hand-to-hand fighting, the build-up of the bridge-head continued and on 22 February the 'Dagger Division' broke out towards the south. During this phase, mixed columns of tanks, armoured cars, infantry and guns streamed across the plain towards Mandalay. Although occasionally the Japanese stood firm, the momentum of the breakthrough was maintained and on 7 March the British were at the gates of Mandalay.

While the Japanese defended the town stubbornly, the 6th Gurkhas, having learnt their trade in the jungle, had their first experience of street fighting. The key to Mandalay was the Monastery on Mandalay Hill, overlooking the town. Two thirds of the hill was captured by the 4/4th Gurkhas and the Royal Berkshire Regiment, after a bitterly contested struggle. Both battalions of 6th Gurkhas thereafter took part in the final stages before the Japanese evacuated the position. Neither battalion escaped lightly; a total of over 200 killed in both battalions and approximately 500 wounded bear witness to the way the Japanese fought for Mandalay.

Meanwhile, the motorized and armoured troops of 17th Indian Division, two days before the fall of Mandalay, passed through the bridgehead and set out for Meiktila, the nodal point for communications between the Japanese 15th and 33rd Armies. In the vanguard of 63 Brigade, the 1/10th Gurkhas had one setback when its D Company, through a misunderstanding of orders, turned north instead of south and drove straight into an enemy roadblock. The Company Commander was killed and only inspired leadership by another young British officer, assisted by the senior Gurkha officer, reorganized the men until tanks came up and supported a successful counter-attack against the Japanese. Apart from this incident, the sweep across the plain to Meiktila was an exhilarating experience after countless weeks of cautious, silent movement in the jungle.

The town of Meiktila was divided into two halves by a lake so that both brigades in 17 Division were given clearly defined sectors of responsibility. 1/10th Gurkhas and the other units in 63 Brigade were to advance from the west while 48 Brigade, which included the 1/7th Gurkhas, was ordered to move round and attack from the north.

Neither brigade was to have an easy time. The 1/7th Gurkhas tried to advance across open ground over a causeway but the Japanese exploded bombs which, aided by accurate heavy machine gun fire from the area of the pagoda, brought the advance to a standstill. All the battalion could do was to dig in and hold firm until the following day when, supported by tanks from the Deccan Horse, an assault was launched against the north-east corner of the town. This time, the soldiers of the 7th Gurkhas advanced slowly with the help of the tanks and enemy pockets of resistance were gradually overcome. General Slim was subsequently to write about A Company's exploits: 'It was one of the neatest and most workmanlike bits of infantry and armoured minor tactics I had ever seen'. It was by such tactics, in conjunction with tanks, that the companies eventually triumphed, killing 105 of the Japanese defenders.

In the western half of the sector the 1/10th Gurkhas, using the same tactics as the 7th, at first advanced with little difficulty although the Japanese, with callous brutality, deliberately and needlessly defended the area of a hospital which included some 300 of their own sick and wounded. Every effort was made by the British not to bombard this area but eventually a direct attack had to be launched on the hospital and most of the unfortunate Japanese invalids were killed. On this day B Company of the 1/10th probably had the toughest fighting, counting twenty-seven Japanese as a result of their own efforts. Meiktila fell the next day but this was only the first phase of the battle. The Japanese Commander lost no time in calling in other troops to recapture the town and 17 Division found itself besieged. The divisional supply line was in enemy hands and the British hold on the airfields was contested with such violence that more than once these changed hands. Major-General Cowan, the Divisional Commander, decided to organize a constant, energetic series of sorties in which strong columns of infantry and tanks, heavily supported from the air, sought out enemy concentrations wherever they had been reported. These sweeps usually lasted for 48 hours and both battalions took part in them. By the end of March enemy resistance had been broken: General Kimura, Commander-in-Chief Japanese Burma Army Area, described the Meiktila operations as the 'master stroke of the whole campaign in Burma' – the stroke which sealed the fate of the Japanese armies in that theatre.

The race for Rangoon began, a race not only between British and Indian divisions to get there first but a race against the weather because it was essential to open the supply port before the monsoon broke and left the 14th Army floundering in the plains with its vehicles and its armour bogged down in a quagmire of mud. General Slim was determined that Rangoon would be occupied before the middle of May. At the end of April the leading troops heard guns of the Fleet bombarding Elephant Point below Rangoon, prior to the landing of 15 Corps. The OC 1/10th Gurkhas wrote: 'It was a thrilling, and at the same time a depressing sound reverberating in the distance. Depressing because we now knew that 15 Corps would be in Rangoon before us, a race we had set our hearts on winning.' For the 7th Gurkhas there was a slight consolation because in 50 Parachute Brigade were many men of the original 3rd Battalion who had fought the battle of the Sittang Bridge in 1942, with their comrades of the 1/7th Gurkhas.

The fight for Burma was over although hundreds more Japanese were to die as they tried, in vain, to batter an escape route through the British and Indian troops in Central Burma. One major attempt was made in mid-July and the waiting 17 and 19 Indian Divisions inflicted terrible punishment on the Japanese. Eight days later, the Japanese in Burma capitulated.

In the autumn of 1945 the British landed in Malaya just after the Japanese had surrendered. Here as elsewhere in the Far East, the problem caused by the sudden surrender called for the presence of British and Indian troops to police the areas and to guard the large bodies of bewildered and dejected prisoners of war. The 4/2nd Gurkhas, after a brief but successful war in Burma moved with 20 Division to French Indo-China, as did the 4/10th Gurkhas. The Nationalist groups were already clashing with the advanced elements of the French Colonial régime who were returning to a much changed country. The Gurkha battalions landed in Saigon to find a menacing situation. Open conflict between the French and their former subjects had already resulted in bloodshed. Shortage of

British troops forced the GOC of 20 Division, General Gracey, into using the Japanese prisoners of war in a variety of tasks, often as assistants and collaborators and even as comrades in arms.

For about a month the Gurkhas in Saigon were virtually at war again. The rebel forces showed that they had already studied the art of guerrilla warfare as the 2nd Goorkhas' diarist complained: 'In such a country the Ammanites always had the first shot. It was annoying that they never stayed to bear the brunt of the attack but always faded into the countryside where it was almost impossible to follow them without sustaining casualties.' Shades of Vietnam! Soon the French were outwardly in control and they bade farewell to 'les jolis Gurkhas' with gratitude and smiles.

An area where matters were even more delicate was Java; the 3/10th Gurkha Rifles, in 23 Indian Division, prior to carrying out an assault landing at Semarang, were informed by the Force Commander that in some cases the Japanese had handed over arms and overall control to the Indonesian nationalists who had quickly seized Dutch internees and prisoners of war as hostages. Fortunately for the battalion, the local Japanese commander in Semarang, a Major Kido, had appreciated the danger and despite the fact that many of his men had been disarmed, was taking energetic steps to clear the town and to protect the Dutch internee camps. This was the position on the morning of 19 October, 1945 when the leading companies of the 3/10th were put ashore from landing craft. A confused situation ensued involving Gurkhas, Japanese and Indonesians, and inevitably there were casualties, but by evening the internee camps were occupied and the Battalion was in full control.

Open fighting broke out again and again, however, and at Magelang, in the centre of the island, the 3/10th Gurkhas, ably supported by a company of Japanese under the direction of a British officer of the battalion, fought off repeated attacks until negotiations became possible and Dr Sukarno himself arrived to arrange a truce. Faced with arrogance and provocation the Gurkhas maintained their normal discipline and possible bloodshed on a major scale was avoided.

Negotiated truces did not last long. In a rapid move, in November, from Magelang to Ambarava, where large internee camps, containing many thousands of women and children, were being mortared and set on fire, the Gurkhas dealt swiftly with obstacles and ambushes and one platoon of D Company killed twenty-five out of twenty-six Indonesians manning the main roadblock, which caused them to view the Gurkhas with far greater respect thereafter. Only just in time the Gurkhas entered Ambarava at nightfall and a well-nigh desperate situation was soon under firm control.

For nearly a year, the 3/10th continued to serve in various parts of Indonesia, never free from tension and always meeting insults. The Regimental Historian described it aptly as 'the Java Nightmare'. It showed, not for the first time, that the Gurkha with his happy disposition and tolerance is in every respect as good a keeper of the peace as his British counterpart.

By 1946 South-East Asia had been restored to some degree of stability, even if in many countries this was to be short-lived. Gurkha battalions raised in wartime were disbanded back in India, an India on the verge of complete independence from the British Raj. Waves of unrest and hatred between Hindu and Muslim swept across the Continent. Day by day deeds of violence became more common. Major questions were now asked about the Gurkha Brigade; what was its future to be? Was it to be part of the new army of India under Indian officers or an integral part of the British Army elsewhere in the Far East? The war was over, but its aftermath did not bring peace.

Chapter 10

THE end of the war in the Far East found some fifty battalions of Gurkha soldiers serving in the Indian Army. Nepal had sent nearly a quarter of a million of her sons to fight against Germany and Japan and, by September, 1945, the Gurkha soldiers' numerical strength, reputation and renown were at the highest point ever.

In India splits were quick to appear and the stability achieved under 'Pax Britannica' was changed almost overnight into a religious war between Hindus and Muslims. The Indian Army remained one element which gave some promise of eventual sanity – in spite of the fact that old and established regiments had to be split between Pakistan and India. In the middle of the turmoil of a civil war, the Indian Army Brigade of Gurkhas waited for decisions to be made about its future. All kinds of rumours only served to increase the feelings of doubt and uncertainty in the minds of British officers and their Gurkha soldiers. Rumours abounded, but to those who waited other details were immaterial: the answer sought was the one to the question: 'Does my Paltan [Regiment] stay with the British or remain to serve in the new India?'

To those who expected an elaborate conference or a degree of formality, the telegram which casually announced decisions on the Brigade was indeed a disappointment. This telegram stated that the 2nd, 6th, 7th and 10th Gurkha Rifles had been selected to serve HM Government, while the other six regiments were to remain as part of the re-fashioned Indian Army. Thereafter a period of confusion followed, because the Terms of Service for the new British Army Brigade had still to be finalized – in contrast to the Indians who had already made several promises about life in their Army. Eventually, it was announced that all men serving in the four

British regiments were to be given the chance to opt for one of three courses: to remain with their regiment as part of the British Army; to transfer to another Gurkha regiment remaining in the Indian Army; or to go on discharge with some sort of compensation. Each man was required to give his answer to a tribunal of three officers from Nepal, India and Great Britain. It was made clear to all ranks that the choice was to be an individual one without any coercion or propaganda but there is no doubt that many of the men were subjected to a lot of pressure from senior Viceroy's Commissioned Officers (VCOs) and NCOs, particularly when the former had decided to 'opt' for India. They tried to justify a personal decision by taking many of the men with them. Battalions were inevitably subjected to a lot of strain, and bad feeling crept in to darken the last few months of service in the Indian Army.

When a Gurkha soldier said 'I will serve HMG' it meant that his association with the Indian Army had ended. It also meant that he would be serving permanently overseas, something that had never happened before in peacetime. In one or two battalions the number of men who opted for service with HMG was surprisingly low. Nevertheless, these few carried the hopes and traditions of their regiments across the seas to begin a new chapter in a long history. It was sad to see so many old friends select service with India yet, in many respects, it was to prove easier to mould comparatively new battalions to a different life as part of the British Army in Malaya.

In January, 1948 the four infantry regiments, each with two battalions, left India for Malaya. One or two were at very low strength. For the older officers and men it had been a nostalgic and sad occasion when they said farewell to their regimental depots, now handed over to new guardians in the shape of Indian officers. Memories of the years gone by could not be lightly dismissed even when the future seemed to hold promise of an exciting life in the British Army.

Scores of new recruits were enlisted in the first few weeks of 1948 so that, on paper, the fledgling British Brigade of Gurkhas was soon brought up to strength. There were many shortages; a dearth of senior Gurkha VCOs (re-titled Queen's Gurkha Officer in the

British Army) and specialists such as drivers, signallers and clerks were sadly lacking in every unit. Nevertheless, the youthful air of the whole Brigade meant that there was a sense of urgency and keenness in rebuilding the battalions to reach a high standard of efficiency, but the precious commodity of time was not given because, with dramatic speed, the future of the country was threatened by the Communist Insurrection. For a long time, the outlook in Malaya was grim and the chances of democracy surviving against the continued successes won by the Chinese Communists were slim indeed. In a situation where infantry were at a premium, the Gurkha battalions had to be deployed from the first days of the Emergency; young soldiers were sent into the jungle both to learn and to fight. As our American friends put it, 'They were training for real'.

One of the first successes achieved against the Communist bandits by the Gurkhas happened during July, 1948 in the Ipoh district. Just after midnight on 12 July, Major Neill, B Company Commander in the 2/2nd Goorkhas, was aroused from his sleep by a telephone call from his Commanding Officer. A few minutes later the CO and the Chief Police Officer of Perak brought a Chinese informer, a rubber tapper, along to the Company Commander's room. The rubber tapper, through an interpreter, said that he had seen about fifty armed Chinese bandits in uniform, living in a large house in the jungle nearby, and could lead the soldiers to the very spot.

Early next morning, well before first light, the men of B Company 2/2nd Goorkhas moved in single file through a rubber estate in pitch darkness. An hour of frustration followed which Major Neill described:

'Judging from the direction indicated by my compass needle and from certain recognizable landmarks which kept on reappearing, I felt sure that my guide was closely related to the Duke of York. Accordingly, I halted the column and, through the interpreter, told the guide that I thought he was trying to play a double game and I would take him aside and shoot him without further ado if he failed to put me on the right track to the bandit camp. I think the informer took my words to heart.'

The rubber tapper asked for a small escort and went off to try and find his bearings. After an hour he returned, saying he now knew where he was. The column trudged on, each man holding onto the belt of the man in front. Once more the guide lost his way and again he searched around before claiming, with his face wreathed in a broad smile, that he had at last found the track to the jungle hut.

Every second counted as it was now getting light. Major Neill put the informer in front of the patrol and they moved off at a jogging trot through the rubber to the edge of the jungle where with pride the Chinese tapper pointed out new tracks. In the soft mud there were definite imprints of hockey boots so on the Gurkhas went, this time rather more slowly. Suddenly, with a low shout in Malay of 'Rumah' [House] the guide spun round and darted off into the jungle. Barely ten yards away from the Company Commander was a lean-to atap shelter – it was a small shelter, nowhere near what the informer had said it was.

A second or two later, with shouts of alarm, ten figures in khaki uniform burst out of the shelter, moving away from where Major Neill stood. He had no time to give any orders, so raising his Sten gun to his shoulder, he fired three bursts and brought down seven of the men.

After searching the area no sign of the other three was found. The informer returned, pleased with his efforts even if his original story had been an inaccurate one. He cheerfully identified the dead men, thus giving rise to the suspicion that perhaps he had been one of their group himself. In such a way was the first success of the Malayan Emergency achieved, without days of searching or weeks of patrolling as was to become the pattern later. The Company Commander summed it up: 'Good fresh information coupled with good luck on our side, had given us our success'. He should also have added, 'And excellent shooting by Major Neill!'

The Gurkha battalions were learning their trade as jungle fighters against an enemy armed with real bullets. In such circumstances young soldiers had to learn quickly. The Gurkha patrols and detachments stood up to their opponents and played a big part in blunting the initial onslaught that threatened to overrun Malaya until as late as 1951. Gradually the bandits found themselves forced to move their bases out of the rubber estates and into the jungle. As

24. *Corporal Rambahadur Limbu who won the VC in Sarawak in 1966* (p. 171)

25. *Men of the 7th Duke of Edinburgh's Own Gurkha Rifles laying a wreath on the memorial to Lord Kitchener in Saint Paul's Cathedral*

26. *A Gurkha Rifleman keeping watch over the Communist half of the strategic Border village of Sha Tan Kok, Hong Kong*

27. *Men of the 7th Gurkha Rifles mount guard at Buckingham Palace, December, 1971.*

an illustration of this phase, the story of B Company, 1/2nd Goorkhas who fought two main actions in the Labis area, one in January, 1950, and the other, a year later, in May, 1951, is worth recounting.

Initially, the January operation got off to a bad start. Major Richardson, the Company Commander, received his orders from another British officer over an indifferent telephone line, with the instructions being given in Gurkhali for security reasons. He understood, correctly, that there was a large party of enemy in the area north of Labis and the boundaries of such an area were clearly given. His task, too, was clear-cut – to move in under cover of darkness, locate and kill as many of the enemy as possible. What was misunderstood was the road by which the Company should enter. As events turned out, if the Company Commander had understood the Adjutant's orders, then his men would not have contacted the bandits.

Two platoons accompanied the Company Commander with four of the six sections being commanded by riflemen; the majority of the soldiers were young and very raw. In the early hours of 22 January, 1950, the men moved into the over-grown rubber and awaited first light. As soon as it was light enough the platoons moved southwards in the general direction of Labis, but, after only five minutes, the leading soldiers of the right-hand platoon came under fire. Major Richardson ordered his left-hand platoon under the Company Sergeant-Major to go round the left flank and cut off the bandits, while he with No 4 Platoon charged straight in. As it happened 4 Platoon was slow in advancing and the British officer found himself accompanied by two young riflemen in the middle of the enemy, with the platoon well behind them. Fortunately, like Major Neill of the 2/2nd, Major Richardson was a good man with his gun and he killed three bandits, causing the rest to scatter. The bandits then tried to cross the paddy fields on the east of the high ground but came under heavy fire from both Gurkha platoons. Although the light was not good, and there was an early morning mist rising off the paddy fields, the company succeeded in killing twenty-five of the enemy, losing one of the young riflemen who had accompanied the Company Commander in the initial charge. Major Richardson subsequently stated that the success of the action was entirely due to the quick reaction and initiative of his CSM who, by taking the left hand platoon behind the enemy at speed, drove them into a foolhardy attempt to cross the paddy fields. His superiors thought that Major Richardson's assessment of his own part was far too modest and both he and his CSM received immediate awards for gallantry.

The second action by this Company was a very different affair. This time it had been reported that there were several parties of bandits, now called Communist Terrorists (CTs), hiding in overgrown rubber to the north of Labis. Major Richardson took his whole Company with him to search the area. On 21 May, in the early morning, B Company was spread out over as wide a front as possible, and advancing through overgrown rubber when, after about one and a half hours, the leading section of the left-hand platoon came under heavy automatic fire. The section commander led his men into the attack and drove a large party of bandits back up the hill. However, to their astonishment the CTs stood firm and pinned them down until the rest of the platoon came forward to help. The platoon commander then tried to manœuvre his sections round the south-west flank of the bandit force.

Meanwhile, the other two platoons and Company HQ rushed towards the sound of the firing, meeting a lot of frightened rubber tappers who were streaming away from the area as fast as they could go. Soon these platoons also came under heavy automatic fire but managed to close to about thirty yards before taking up firing positions from where they engaged the bandits, who could be seen darting back and forth among the trees. The youngest rifleman in the Company was hit and died in a few minutes, while the CTs continued to bring a very heavy volume of automatic fire, mostly from Thompson sub-machine-guns, onto the Gurkhas. It was clear to Major Richardson that his men were outnumbered and, moreover, that the CTs were showing no sign of breaking off the engagement. He therefore decided to create a diversion and taking a section from one of the platoons as well as his own headquarters, he worked around to the other flank of the enemy, closed right in, and then managed to rush them. Surprised by this unexpected attack, the bandits were not ready for No 5 Platoon when they came in at them with bayonets fixed; the bandits broke and retreated, although by this time another Gurkha soldier had been killed outright. Apart from one more short stand, the CTs continued to retreat until eventually their total casualties were seventeen killed, with a further fifteen wounded as later reported by a surrendered bandit. An action like this was very rare in the Malayan Emergency: it was not often that the terrorists were as well clothed or well armed and with apparently unlimited ammunition. Their morale and discipline enabled them to fight with courage and they stood their ground until the last moment. It is now believed that they were a picked body of men, acting as escort to Communist VIPs who were moving down to hold a meeting in the Labis area of Johore. Their stubborn defence ensured that the VIPs they were escorting were able to escape.

After 1951, the tide began to turn and it became more and more difficult to contact the CTs. Jungle operations became a test of endurance, a trial of patience, full of frustration, with the rewards for hours of patrolling and nights spent in ambush positions being few and far between. By this time, the statisticians calculated that it took a soldier an average of 700 hours patrolling before he even saw a bandit. It was therefore remarkable that each of the eight Gurkha battalions eliminated 200 or more Communist terrorists during many operations in which success was obtained after a fleeting contact with the elusive CTs. As the bandits withdrew further and further into the jungle, so did the Army become more and more dependent on the eyes of the Auster pilots to spot possible bandit camps in the deep jungle, or locate cultivations where the bandits grew vegetables for their survival.

In February, 1953, the 2/7th Gurkhas carried out a most successful operation, an operation which highlights the skill of an Auster pilot, the jungle craft and initiative of a young Gurkha NCO, and the merciless precision of Gurkhas in attack. The story of this operation is told in some detail as it was a classic example of anti-guerrilla operations in the Malayan Emergency.

It started with an Auster pilot, Capt Metcalf, seeing what he thought was a jungle clearing when on a routine flight from Seremban. He took a quick map fix and flew on, wisely resisting the temptation to fly once more over the area. After returning to his base, Metcalf worked out from the map a more accurate location of the possible camp but realised an immediate return to the area would certainly frighten any bandits away. He decided on a careful deception plan and for five mornings at dawn, he flew south from Seremban, passing about one mile east of the suspected camp area. On the sixth day he set off on the normal flight but this time his flight path was just east of the spur on which he thought the camp was located. He found that his original map fix was correct; as he flew over the clearing he noticed that it was about the size of a tennis court and rows of vegetables were clearly visible. The bandits had tried to camouflage the jungle 'garden' with cut saplings but the leaves had turned yellow and were dead. Each day freshly-cut saplings had been placed by the bandits as their first daily task but on that day they were late and it was to cost them their lives. Although flying at about 1,500 feet, Metcalf also saw what he thought to be the roof of an atap basha and armed with this information he made a definite report about the bandits to Brigade Headquarters.

It transpired that the camp was just inside the operational area 'owned' by the Gordon Highlanders. A plan was made in which A Company of the Gordon Highlanders was to approach the area from the south, drop off a platoon for ambushes to the east, and then use two platoons to assault the camp. From the north, C Company, 2/7th Gurkhas, under command of the Gordons, was to approach the enemy camp and lay as many ambushes as possible on the north flank. For the Gurkha company the chance of a contact with bandits served as a real tonic to the young Company Commander and his forty-three men who accompanied him into the jungle. For ten months they had had no contact in spite of patrolling and ambushing – watching and waiting – with two of the three platoons continually in the jungle or on its edges. Now it appeared their luck might change even though the role that had been cast for them appeared to be a subsidiary one.

Their move from Rompin was typical of the great care necessary to deceive the bandits and their supporters. Two platoons actually climbed on to the trucks but as many men as possible lay down so that any informer would think that one platoon only was going out on a routine task. A long and devious route was taken to the debussing point where the vehicles merely slowed down while the men jumped off and darted into the rubber estate. It was still very dark and raining heavily but the rain would wash their tracks away and this in itself helped the security of the operation. At first light, they moved south along the top of a ridge where movement was comparatively easy and set up a base about a mile away from the suspected enemy camp. By this time it was four o'clock in the afternoon and the Company Commander immediately sent out seven patrols, each of about three men, who moved on compass bearings five degrees apart. One unpaid lance-corporal, Rabilal Rai, with two riflemen, moved due south and after about 300 yards they heard the sound of voices. Creeping closer they saw two bandits washing and it was obvious that the camp was very close and probably on the hill to their right. Rabilal decided to circle to the left of the area and after a few yards they came to the vegetable 'garden' which they skirted. Sounds of more voices reached them so that Rabilal decided to go by himself to the edge of the terrorist camp; there he saw about a dozen bandits, all dressed in khaki uniform, carrying out various chores. Even then Rabilal did not think that his task was over and he moved slowly round the perimeter, trying to find out the bandit sentry posts. However, time was passing and by now he realised that he could not complete his full reconnaissance and get back to his Company Commander so he sent one man back with his report, suggesting that he would meet the Company at an RV so that an immediate attack could be launched.

The rifleman arrived at Company Headquarters at five-thirty pm, bringing the exciting news but posing a problem for Lt Thornton, the young Commander. There were two choices open to him: firstly, an immediate attack, in which case the Company would have to move fast and assault a target that was really intended for A Company of the Gordons. Everything would have to be rushed and there would be no time to brief the soldiers in any detail. The other alternative, to delay the attack until the next day, brought two dangers: firstly, the rifleman might have been spotted on his way back and secondly, and more likely, the footprints of the recce patrol would be noticed before darkness fell. It was a difficult decision to make but Thornton decided to delay the attack and, in this case, he was right. Many other company commanders during the Emergency faced similar situations and decided one way or the other: only with hindsight can each commander say whether he made the correct decision or not.

By delaying his attack Thornton now had time to contact the CO of the Gordons, who decided that C Company, 2/7th Gurkhas, would carry out the assault. Using Rabilal's detailed recce as a basis for his attack, the Company Commander made a simple but effective plan. He was sure that the enemy's first thought would be to escape so his small assault party consisted of himself and nine men only. The remainder of the Company were to move into 'cut off' positions. After a very detailed briefing, they left at first light next morning, and moved along the route taken by Rabilal's patrol. At a stream near the camp, the force split into two parties. The cordon party went off into their 'cut off' positions while those who were to assault moved to the top of the spur. They crawled up the hill for over an hour and reached a position about five yards in front of an enemy sentry – the post noted by Rabilal on the previous evening. By this time, Thornton judged the camp to be about a hundred yards to their left, and he and his men patiently waited for the sentry to move away on his 'beat'. However, the sentry remained where he was and kept on looking round and was obviously worried, so that with time going by there was no alternative but to kill him and then charge into the camp. Rabilal fired one shot and Lt Thornton and his men ran as hard as they could towards the camp. The area had been cleared but small trees had been put around its perimeter. A CT Bren gun opened up on them but luckily no one was hit. Then there was complete silence. In Thornton's mind came the thought: 'Another failure, again the enemy have got away', but he'd forgotten about his close cordon and suddenly all hell was let loose at the foot of the spur. The bandits had run into 'the stops' and, without recounting a shot by shot story, the outcome was that eight dead bodies were eventually recovered. There could have been nine as Thornton had let another terrorist come to within five yards before pulling the trigger of his American carbine – there was a loud click but the round was a dud. The bandit looked up, his face one of complete astonishment. For seconds they looked at each other before Thornton's orderly opened fire, though he did not hit the man. He was never seen again and in Thornton's words: 'Secretly I was glad he got away.'

The action over, many messages of congratulations arrived but one Thornton particularly liked was the one from A Company of the Gordons. 'Well done – we listened to the sound of your firing with envy.' Thornton's lasting impression of the attack was the complete silence of it all. No one shouted, it was clinical and businesslike. There were no heroics; just silent, determined competence by the Gurkha soldiers. His final words on this: 'One thing I was quite sure about – I would never like to have Gurkhas on the other side.'

Although the bandits in the Rompin area were not prepared to stand and fight, in one or two other areas they continued to carry out aggressive actions. For example, in June, 1953, in Johore, some twenty bandits carried out a reasonably successful road ambush on a rubber estate. A platoon of the 1/10th Gurkhas under Lt Dhojbir Limbu was sent to a neighbouring estate as it was considered to be on a likely escape route of the ambush party. Although fresh tracks were found, no signs of the enemy were seen for a day of two. Lt Dhojbir was ordered to follow the tracks and so began the long arduous chase which was to take his platoon from one side of the Pengerang peninsula to the other, through some twenty-five miles of jungle swamp. The bandits were wily opponents, splitting into groups three or four times each day and then collecting together at a distant RV. These tactics, and the extensive swamps, delayed the Gurkhas in their follow-up but Dhojbir urged his men on as he realized that the meagre signs left by the bandits would soon be washed away by the torrential jungle rain. Moreover, the platoon rations were running out so that he ordered his men to have but one meal a day and to keep following the bandits from dawn to dusk.

Just ahead of the Gurkhas, the bandits switched direction several times and only Dhojbir's inspired leadership and his tracking skill kept them within striking distance of an elusive enemy. On 8 July, the men had no food all day and all of them were extremely tired when, for the twenty-third time since the operation started, the bandit tracks were lost. The Gurkha officer realised that if they didn't close with the enemy that very day then they would lose them for ever as their rations had long been exhausted. He split his men into groups and with himself leading one group, sent them off to search for the bandits.

Dhojbir's patrol suddenly and unexpectedly bumped the main bandit camp, a camp that was situated on an island in the swamp, around which giant jungle trees had been felled to prevent it being charged. The bandit sentries and the Gurkhas saw each other at the same time and although heavily outnumbered by the CTs, Dhojbir's small group immediately attacked the enemy. A fierce fight ensued, the bandits bringing three machine-guns to bear on the small group of Gurkhas as well as hurling grenades at them. Led by Dhojbir, the small group got into the camp and killed two bandits before the others fled into the swamp, leaving behind a lot of food and ammunition as well as some weapons. One of the dead bandits was found to have a price of 75,000 dollars on his head, later being identified as a Political Commissar. It transpired subsequently that none of the bandits realised that they had been followed right across the peninsula and had been confident that their precautions were sufficient to deceive anyone. They had underestimated the toughness, perseverance and jungle skill of Lt Dhojbir and his platoon.

Operations in Malaya demanded a high standard of leadership at platoon and section level. Moreover, a junior rifleman could find himself on his own, having to use his initiative and to rely on his ability to shoot quickly and to shoot straight – as happened on 12 January, 1954 when Rifleman Birbahadur Rai of the 1/10th Gurkha Rifles displayed courage and excellent shooting which resulted in five terrorists being killed. His platoon was moving in two sections through an oil palm estate when, from the right flank and some fifty yards away, a terrorist opened fire from across a small stream. Birbahadur's section at once turned and charged whereupon the terrorist fired one more shot and fled into a swamp on the far side of the stream.

When the section came to the stream it so happened that Birbahadur reached a point with firm ground on either side and this enabled him to get across in advance of his comrades. In the long grass and now under fire from other terrorists he was, for a moment or two, alone. Nevertheless, he charged on and came face to face with a bandit, aiming a Sten-gun at him from a range of about thirty yards. Birbahadur fired and the man fell dead. Enemy fire still continued to be directed at him but he went on. He next encountered two terrorists armed with pistols, both of whom he shot. A fourth terrorist came from behind a tree and fired two shots but missed. Birbahadur swung round and dropped him. Finally, some thirty yards on, he came up with a fifth terrorist who was firing a carbine in his direction. He managed to shoot him as well. Thus, in a matter of a few minutes, Rifleman Birbahadur Rai personally accounted for five terrorists. Although under fire for most of the time and although he never knew how many bandits were in his immediate area, he never hesitated. Behind him on either flank the rest of his section were hampered by more difficult ground and, although they wounded at least four bandits, found themselves in a supporting role to Birbahadur Rai. Birbahadur was put in for an immediate MM but this was upgraded to a DCM by higher headquarters, an appropriate decoration for such spontaneous gallantry.

By 1954, a more regular pattern of life had been established as it became vital that units should have an opportunity to rest, to re-administer themselves in one central place, and to carry out a modicum of training. An annual cycle included about ten months on operations in scattered company bases, and two months on 'R & R' (Rest and Re-training). The tempo of re-training was often at such a high level that officers and men looked forward to their return to

158

the neutral jungle, longing to be away from Adjutants, the RSM, fatigues, telephones and paper work. At each of the battalion bases were some 200 Gurkha wives, whose husbands could pay but fleeting visits between jungle operations. Life for the wives, British and Gurkha, was not easy during the early years of the Emergency but the majority bore the sudden partings, the complete absence of news when the husbands were in the jungle, and a degree of discomfort in somewhat primitive camps, with cheerfulness and stoicism. Their contribution to the final victory was no small one because when officers and men were back at the battalion base, the wives were there to greet them and to share the fleeting interlude of 'normal' living.

While the infantry battalions were battling with the Communists, the Brigade of Gurkhas had begun to raise other units. Regiments of Gurkha Engineers and Signals were formed and sent out on operational duty from the early days of the Emergency. Later in 1958, the Gurkha Army Service Corps was raised, again as a component part of the Brigade of Gurkhas. A short account of the three Gurkha Corps is contained in Chapter 11.

When the Communist terrorists found that their cultivations were being spotted by Auster pilots like Capt Metcalf then it became a struggle for them to survive and to exist in the remote areas. More and more Communist terrorists decided to surrender as the outlook got bleaker. The hard core of the Malayan Communist party tried to think of alternative tactics and in many parts of the Central and North Malaya they decided to use aboriginal tribes like the Sakai to grow and bring them food or provide early warning about the movement of the Security Forces in the deep jungle. The Government retaliated by building jungle 'forts' in some of the aboriginal settlements. The 'forts' served a dual purpose; firstly, protection was given by police, often augmented by an army sub-unit so that the CTs could not impose their will on the Sakai tribes, and secondly, in an attempt to win over the aborigines to the Government side, medical aid posts and shops were opened in the forts. Slowly such measures began to bear fruit and the local tribes started to bring information about CT parties.

Near one of these forts, Fort Brooke, C Company of the 1/6th Gurkhas under Major Harkasing Rai set out on 2 January, 1956 to investigate such a report. There were reputed to be fifty terrorists nearby and Harkasing and his men set out to track them down. Temporary resting places were found but it was clear that these had been used four or five nights previously and that the CTs had moved towards the west. The Company then performed a most remarkable feat of tracking. Major Harkasing realised that he was on the trail of a well-trained party, led by a high ranking Communist who obviously enforced strict discipline on the march and at their night stops. The CTs covered their tracks well and on several occasions the Gurkha patrols lost the tracks, and had to cast around up to about 600 yards before finding a small clue which showed in which direction the CTs had moved. It took perseverance and it demanded patience and self discipline; it also required a commander who had faith in the ability of his men to narrow the gap between the quarry and themselves. Led by Harkasing, C Company did this and by 9 January they knew they were within a day's march of the CTs.

At midday, the leading scout spotted a hut through the gloom of the dense jungle. He signalled the information back but as the leading men began to get into position they were fired on by a sentry, whereupon they rushed forward into the small camp. Its one occupant, an aborigine, was promptly killed but then the Gurkhas realised that fire was being directed at them from the main camp some 200 yards ahead. Quickly reforming, they charged into this camp and killed three more CTs. By this time the main body of the bandits had withdrawn in a disciplined manner across the nearby river and from there they directed heavy automatic fire onto Harkasing and his men. As the leading Gurkhas tried to cross the river, a particularly fearless Chinese bandit, armed with a tommy-gun, covered his comrades' withdrawal and forced C Company to deploy before he moved back. He was chased for over 1,000 yards up the far slopes of the valley. During the chase this brave man frequently turned and fired a few shots at his pursuers. He managed to escape in the end.

160

For a short time C Company lost contact with the CTs. A 'landing area' was cleared and a helicopter came in to take away the bodies of the dead bandits and a lot of valuable documents found in the camp. On 11 March C Company were on the move again, following two-day old tracks up to a knife-edge ridge 3,000 feet above the valley. Here they found that the CTs had split into two parties of equal strength, one going north and one south. C Company concentrated on the south-bound trail but found their already difficult task now well-nigh impossible. Having abandoned their packs in the previous camp, the bandits had thereafter moved with the wary stealth of hunted animals. They knew that they were being pursued: they slept in caves, leaving only the smallest traces of their stay. They crawled like insects along the faces of the cliffs, up crevices and down waterfalls and yet, carefully though they moved, they left some all but imperceptible sign of their passing. These were seen by the Gurkhas, expert hunters of game in their own country. And so the follow-up continued. Next day, a small patrol saw about fifteen CTs in a temporary camp. One rifleman was sent back to call up the Company Commander. When he arrived, only about ten minutes daylight remained so that he decided it was too late to attack. He ordered his men to lie where they were; there was to be no sound, no smoking, no cooking – the enemy were only a stone's throw away.

Next morning before dawn, C Company began to edge forward; moving inch by inch they crawled silently in an attempt to surround the camp when, just before light, a sentry challenged them. The whole company 'froze'. Minutes passed and the Communist sentry relaxed. By now it was light and Harkasing considered that the cordon was about half-way round the camp when the same sentry challenged again, but this time did not wait for any reply before he fired a long burst. Two Gurkha soldiers fell wounded and in a flash the CTs were up and away. In terror they scattered and split into groups of two or three men. Harkasing appreciated that they would now make for an area where they could contact local sympathisers and obtain food and help – for it was clear that they were in a bad way. He reported by radio to his Commanding Officer and accordingly other companies from the battalion were deployed in the north, to the south and in 'stop' positions on the jungle edge to the west. These companies had further contacts with the CTs benefitting from C Company's efforts. Later it transpired that the CT party had just begun building their new permanent camp when it was attacked on 9 January by C Company. Apart from suffering severe casualties, the gang had been split up so that it ceased to have any real influence in the aborigine settlements round Fort Brooke thereafter. Major Harkasing and his men had performed a most remarkable feat of tracking and for his leadership in this operation Harkasing Rai was awarded a bar to his MC.

The impression must not be given that the first ten years of service in the British Army – which coincided with the Emergency in Malaya – were spent solely in Malaya at grips with the terrorists. Usually two or three battalions were stationed in Hong Kong where in a tour of about two years, soldiering was of a more conventional nature and welcome for the first few months as a necessary break from operations. Then the successes of rival battalions serving in Malaya caused feelings of nostalgia and a longing for the realities of active service to overshadow the artificiality of life in Hong Kong. Nevertheless, the time spent in Hong Kong was a welcome break from the monotonous Malayan climate. The cold winters in the New Territories reminded Gurkhas of their native land and undoubtedly had beneficial effects on the health of their wives and children in the unit family lines.

The Emergency finally ended in 1958. Peace in Malaya meant many things in the Brigade of Gurkhas. To the married officers and men in brought an end to a series of partings with wives and children; to those who disliked conventional soldiering it heralded drill parades, spit and polish, ceremonial occasions and test exercises run by senior commanders, so that a nostalgic yearning for the good old days was not slow in appearing. But it was the first real peace for the older British and Gurkha officers since 1939. A respite from the years of 'jungle bashing' was both welcome and essential as without any doubt the whole Brigade had become parochial in outlook. However, the period of peace in South-East

Asia was not to be a long one for the British Army and, in particular, its Brigade of Gurkhas.

After 1958 for four years the British Army was not actually engaged anywhere in South-East Asia. However, the Major General Brigade of Gurkhas, Major-General Walter Walker, was convinced that another crisis would occur without warning – and his Gurkha battalions were trained to be ready to go anywhere at the drop of a hat. Such an opportunity was to arise in December, 1962.

The film '*The Longest Day*' was showing in Singapore on the night of Friday, 7 December, 1962, and as this was the end of the first day of the 1/2nd Goorkhas' Annual Administration Inspection, it seemed appropriate for some of the officers to go and see the film. Meanwhile Headquarters 99 Brigade had a Mess Guest Night at which one of the guests was the CO of a British battalion earmarked to go to Brunei in the event of trouble there. Shortly after the meal had finished, an operational code word was received from Army Headquarters which was passed down the table to the CO. 'That's yours, isn't it?' 'But my battalion is training on the west coast of Malaya,' he replied. He dashed off to see how many of his men were in Singapore but their numbers were insufficient. 'Better pass the task to the 1/2nd Goorkhas who should be "on the ball" because of their Inspection' said Brigade Headquarters. In such a way was the 1/2nd selected to quell the insurrection that had suddenly arisen in the British Protectorate of Brunei.

On the night of 6/7 December a revolt had broken out in Brunei and military assistance was requested. At five o'clock on the morning of 8 December, the CO of the 1/2nd was aroused from his sleep; shortly afterwards he briefed his officers. Many of them thought that this alarm was part of their Administrative Inspection, but then the telephone began ringing in earnest. Serious riots had broken out during the previous day in Brunei Town and an armed insurrection under the rebel leader, Azahari, threatened to take over control of the State. The Battalion was to move at once but for the rest of Singapore, it was still an ordinary, happy Saturday morning. The four vehicles sent under the RQMS to collect ammunition from an Ordnance depot were told to come back to Monday morning. The RAF had no planes available for the Battalion to play with; they were all up country on bombing practice but were expected to be back by four o'clock in the afternoon. The GHQ map storeman had gone to a beach and no one knew which. Transport to take the Battalion to the airfield would be available, once the school children had been taken home at one o'clock. Some but not all of these problems were overcome. Those at the top wanted the Battalion to move 'at once' but the speed of such a move depended on the availability of aircraft. Eventually, a small HQ and two rifle companies were able to take off from Singapore in the late afternoon, with the possibility of the remainder of the unit following during the next day.

The 'Initial Force Commander' (the Battalion Second-in-Command) was presented with a gloomy picture by the Commissioner of Police and the Deputy High Commissioner on his arrival at Brunei airport. Police stations had been attacked in Brunei Town itself, in Seria and at Kuala Belait, over seventy miles away. Armed rebels had tried to burst a way into the Sultan's Istana, while there were reports of another large force, reputed to be sailing down river to Brunei Town from Limbang, with the intention of attacking Government installations in the town. In Seria the police reported that European hostages had been seized from the oilfield; they feared that the rebels would attack their police station once more; shielded by these hostages. All told it was a difficult situation and it was clear to the Force Commander that more troops would be required in a hurry. However, he had to do as best he could with the two companies that were arriving in dribs and drabs at Brunei; although none of them had maps of the town and the equipment with them was meant to be used against hostile crowds rather than against a rebel force armed with an assortment of modern weapons and shotguns.

Before midnight mobile Gurkha patrols were sent out into Brunei Town, in addition to a platoon moving to the Istana to guard the Sultan. For C and D Companies the day had been both long and real but their excitement was only just beginning. At about midnight an urgent request for help was received from Seria, the Shell oilfield about seventy miles away from Brunei Town. Another attack on the police station was expected and C Company Commander was told to move to Seria as quickly as possible. His HQ moved in a Land Rover, with two platoons clambering into four PWD vehicles which had been hurriedly requisitioned for the journey. They brushed aside one or two half-hearted attempts at road blocks but when they reached the small market town of Tutong, half way to Seria, heavy fire was directed on the convoy from one or two buildings in the town. This fire was returned with heartiness by the soldiers in the PWD vehicles but unbeknown to them the driver of the Land Rover was hit and the vehicle crashed into a monsoon ditch. Having passed through Tutong the convoy met another party of rebels near a bridge and duly put them to flight. Meanwhile the small HQ party had taken up a position in an open fish market where they spent a most uncomfortable night, two of their number being wounded. After dawn they were found by the rest of the Company who had returned to look for them; thereafter the rebels were driven out of the town and its immediate surroundings by the tired but angry Gurkhas of C Company.

In Brunei itself during the early hours of 9 December, D Company in the vicinity of the police station near the centre of the town, had one or two brushes with the enemy and suffered a few casualties, including a young British officer who subsequently died. Without street maps and operating against rebels in and among the buildings around the 'Padang' was extremely difficult and all the Company could do to make its location known to the police was to flash the headlights of their leading vehicle. After dawn broke, it was much easier and they then cleared the buildings east toward the river and took many prisoners. All told, neither company had had an easy time but they had acted decisively which in itself was to prove a big blow to the rebels' hopes.

The rest of the Battalion arrived during the morning of 9 December and by now the gravity of the situation had been fully appreciated back in Singapore. Three more British units were put on immediate 'stand by' and subsequently flown in so that battalions could be given specific areas of operation. The 1/2nd retained Brunei Town and Tutong as their responsibility although companies at times operated in other parts of the State. For three weeks the men of the 2nd Goorkhas operated by day and night against the rebels, seeking them out in the jungle, killing a few but bringing the majority of them back into captivity. The Battalion's bag exceeded 800 prisoners. That the rebellion was both short-lived and ineffective was due in no small measure to the determination and speed shown by the two companies that landed on the evening of 8 December. Within the small State of Brunei peace soon reigned but the spark of revolt flared across the border into Sabah and Sarawak. President Sukarno was only too pleased to exploit an opportunity to seize Borneo. Military 'confrontation' between Indonesia and the newly-founded Confederation of Malaysia began in early 1963. As the months went by, it developed into one of the strangest wars that the British Army has ever fought.

The term 'war' has been used advisedly, as naval ships and fighter planes patrolled the seas and skies while artillery and regular infantry units were being deployed along the border by both sides. The clashes that took place along the 1,000 mile border between Indonesia and Borneo were invariably between regular units in which modern weapons were used.

The number of troops involved, however, was, to a great extent, limited by the nature of the terrain and the logistic problems that had to be resolved before large bodies of men could attempt anything of an ambitious nature. The threat came from across the border, and the small Malaysian Army looked to Great Britain and the Commonwealth for a large measure of help. Nevertheless, the soil the allies of Malaysia defended was no longer a part of the British Empire. 'Confrontation', an undeclared war between Indonesia and Great Britain with her Commonwealth partners, became a costly affair, the economics of which were to unseat President Sukarno.

By mid–1963, although the Indonesians were not yet very active, it was known that they were preparing parties for incursions across the border in order to take the initiative in turning the people of Sarawak against the Confederation of Malaysia which was then being formed. In the large Third Division of Sarawak an invading force had mauled a patrol of the 2/6th Gurkhas killing one British officer and inflicting casualties on the patrol. At this juncture, the 1/2nd took over the responsibility for the whole Division, about the size of Wales. Not only were distances considerable but the unmapped terrain itself posed many problems; it was mountainous, and intersected by numerous fast-flowing rivers which were often impassable. To watch and guard the many routes into Third Division was well beyond the capabilities of one battalion so that men from local Iban tribes were enlisted as Border Scouts under command of the Battalion. These Border Scouts carried out a short training course in the use of rifles or shotguns. Many of them were excellent trackers and boatmen but their value lay in a detailed knowledge of their villages and immediate surroundings rather than in their ability to fight. One of the Border Scout outposts in the 1/2nd's area was a place called Long Jawai.

Long Jawai was the last village in Sarawak before the border, about twenty miles away, with a corresponding village on the Indonesian side, Long Nawang, containing a similar large settlement of the same tribe of people. To such people the international border, established by their old colonial masters the Dutch and British, meant nothing at all and they continued to trade with each other, having no feelings about the formation of Malaysia or the disruptive intentions of Dr Sukarno in Djakarta.

The small isolated detachment which lived in Long Jawai consisted of twenty-one Border Scouts, two radio operators and five Gurkha soldiers under the command of a Gurkha corporal. The detachment headquarters with its radio sets was in a hut close to the village long house. The villagers had given very little assistance in preparing a defensive position on the small hillock nearby, although by the morning of 27 September some four or five slit trenches had been dug. Life at Long Jawai had been dull; no information was coming in at all, the locals were not being helpful and were generally apathetic.

On the morning of 28 September the men of the small detachment were sleeping in their partially-constructed positions on the hillock. At about half-past five the Gurkha rifleman on sentry duty heard movement near his post. Every man stood to. Shortly afterwards three or four shots were fired nearby. The detachment commander alerted the radio operators in their signal hut and donning earphones, they tried to establish communications with the Company headquarters. As the detachment commander arrived back on the hillock about first light, the whole area was blasted by mortar bombs, machine-guns and heavy small-arms fire from the area of a half-prepared landing zone to the west. In the half light a party of enemy charged the signal hut from the north and killed the operators as they sat at theirs sets, unable to hear the enemy approach because of their earphones. All hope of communication with the outside world had gone.

Soon after this the Border Scouts, having fought well up to now, started slipping away; they had not been trained to fight so who could blame them? One by one they went down the side of the hill to the stream and round to the enemy position to surrender. However, the last one, having seen his comrades being disarmed and bound decided to return to the Gurkhas and risk death by their side.

By now it was daylight and the small detachment kept up an effective fire against a hundred-man fighting force. The Gurkha machine-gunner was hit, his side torn open by a machine-gun bullet. Another Gurkha rifleman was killed outright by a mortar bomb which exploded in a tree above him. By eight o'clock there were only three effective men left, with two wounded who were in great pain, and one Border Scout in so state to fight. They had fought for two hours under continuous heavy mortar and small arms fire while their own ammunition was down to a very few rounds per man. The corporal decided to withdraw his party. One of the riflemen was delirious and begged to be left behind lest he should hamper their withdrawal. His request was ignored and slowly the three Gurkhas and the one Border Scout dragged the two semi-conscious men off the position. It was to take them two hours to get down to the stream to the south and thence into the jungle on the other side. Fortunately for them, the enemy had suffered sufficient casualties to deter them from physically assaulting the position during the withdrawal, but at about eleven o'clock they began to attack the hillock and kept on firing in its immediate area until nightfall.

Without food or medical supplies the small party spent the night in pouring rain, keeping the wounded men as warm as they could. Then, having made them as comfortable as possible, the corporal and his companions left for the nearest village, many miles away. Living off roots, they had a long and hazardous journey as it was four days before they reached the outpost of Belaga, weak and exhausted but with weapons spotlessly clean and able to give a first-hand account of the battle.

In the meantime the enemy had tied up all the Border Scouts who had surrendered, plundered the village and returned upstream towards the border. In a camp nearby they then murdered ten of the Border Scouts.

For the 1/2nd Goorkhas the next few days were hectic. Most of the Battalion was deployed, some following up, some ambushing and all covering a wide area by helicopter, by boat or on foot. The considerable effort made eventually paid dividends. On 1 October, a Gurkha officer and his platoon from C Company ambushed two enemy boats carrying some thirty men. The ambush was admirably executed and there were few, if any, survivors when both boats capsized in the middle of a fast flowing river. Anyone who escaped the withering fire from the platoon would have had little chance of reaching the bank. The arms and equipment recovered included weapons lost at Long Jawai and the police radio which the Indonesians had taken out of the signal hut near the village.

The relieving troops found that Long Jawai had been completely ransacked and 'smelt of death'. The two wounded Gurkhas had managed to get down the hill, more dead than alive, but they survived a harrowing ordeal. A more accurate picture of the enemy force emerged; it had consisted of about one hundred soldiers with nearly the same number of porters. The enemy commander was one Major Muljono who had been a guerrilla fighter all his life. He had fought against the Japanese, then the Dutch, had caused

President Sukarno repeated trouble in the fifties, and had attended many jungle warfare training schools, including the British one at Kota Tinggi in Malaya. It was not known how many of his force died before they eventually crossed the border; five graves were found during the rest of the follow up a further five were killed. One important result was that the Indonesians were reluctant to make any further deep incursions for over two years. They had expected that such invasions would win wholehearted support from the people of Sarawak. On finding that quite the contrary was the case, and that deep incursions exacted a heavy toll in men and effort, then they changed their tactics to harassment along the border.

The Indonesians set up a series of bases near the border, mainly in West Sarawak where the country was less mountainous and more friendly. From these bases it was easy for their patrols to slip across the border, to carry out acts of aggression, sabotage, or, as often as not, to murder a Border Scout in order to discourage other Ibans from enlisting. It was difficult to combat these tactics and inevitably the number of battalions near the border had to be increased. The exploits of any one Gurkha battalion during 1964 to 1966 would fill a chapter. The 2/2nd Goorkhas fought several brilliant actions, deploying companies supported by artillery and mortar fire. So did the 2/10th. One of their most striking successes was achieved at Serikan on 21 November, 1965. The force involved comprised their C Company and platoons from Support Company, with supporting fire being given by light and medium guns of the Royal Artillery.

The Indonesians occupied a strong position on top of a high, sheer-sided hill which could only be approached along a knife-edged ridge. By superb field-craft, the leading men reached a point, barely twenty yards from the enemy position, in complete silence. Then a machine-gun opened up on them, wounding one of L/Cpl Rambahadur Limbu's support group. Rambahadur rushed forward and killed the Indonesian machine-gunner.

This, however, caused the enemy to direct heavy fire against Rambahadur's group and two of his men were hit, both falling in an exposed position. Having put his men in a better fire position, Rambahadur then tried to rescue his men. His first attempt at crawling forward failed under accurate fire. Rambahadur decided that speed alone might give him a measure of protection so by a series of rushes, he reached one of the wounded men; covered by fire from his own comrades, the young NCO carried him to a position of safety. The Indonesians were ready for his next attempt but Rambahadur did not hesitate for long. After one short rush, he was pinned down for some minutes by intense fire but, once more, he dashed forward to hurl himself by the side of the second wounded rifleman. Picking him up, he doubled back through a hail of enemy bullets and, by some miracle, arrived unscathed.

For his gallantry, Rambahadur Limbu of the 10th Gurkhas was awarded the Victoria Cross; the supreme award for valour given to this junior NCO was a Royal tribute to the gallantry of all the Gurkhas who served in Borneo.

At Serikan, the hour-long battle resulted in a defeat for the Indonesians who retreated from their position, losing some twenty-five men at a cost to the attacking force of three killed and two wounded.

Gradually the British and Commonwealth Forces began to dominate the border area and the Indonesians had to move their camps back and the forays into Sarawak and Sabah became less daring and frequent. One major incursion was to take place during the last few weeks of the 'Confrontation'.

In June, 1966, the 1/7th were dispersed along the border in central Sarawak, occupying company bases at altitudes of some 2,500 feet in terrain that was rugged and mountainous. Opposite the company base at Ba Kelalan was the known enemy stronghold of Long Bawang. Reports indicated that a tough leader, Lt Sumbi, was training about one hundred volunteers in jungle warfare and he had boasted that, one day, he and his band of men would cross the border and march to Brunei Bay.

Rumours persisted so that the British company commander at Ba Kelalan, Major Jenkins of the 1/7th, opened a log entitled 'The Sumbi Saga'. Meanwhile the CO of the Battalion took these rumours seriously and precautions were taken; incursion routes were studied and patrolled, helicopter landing sites were constructed, and a general air of expectancy existed as Intelligence reports continued to come in from across the border. Then, on 23 July, a report reached Ba Kelalan; Sumbi, accompanied by some fifty men, had moved out of Bawang for 'an unknown destination'.

This was what the 1/7th were waiting for; platoons were deployed and a gigantic search operation was put into effect. The CO of the 1/7th considered the most likely place of entry was across the jungle-covered ridge line between Ba Kelalan and Long Samado. He concentrated his troops in that area and intensive patrolling was carried out along the most probable incursion routes. On 31 July a small patrol of the Gurkha Parachute Company reported finding four- or five-day old tracks of about thirty men, four miles north of Ba Kelalan. The patrol commander's suspicions were roused when he found a label from a coffee tin; this was an unusual item to find in the jungle and his report sparked off a lot of activity. The chase went on, day after day, week after week, and was continued without respite into October.

In the meantime, the report from the Parachute Company patrol gave the CO much more positive information on which to act. Further patrols found fairly new resting places not very far away and established the strength of Lt Sumbi's party to be about fifty men. More and more patrols moved across the extensive mountainous area until, on 3 August, the first contact was made in which one Gurkha rifleman received a minor head wound whilst charging towards the enemy. Sumbi's men fled, leaving blood stains in the area. Later interrogations were to reveal that Sumbi himself was completely surprised and confused by this encounter – being nearly twelve miles inside Sarawak, in thick jungle, he had assumed that his party had moved without being detected. As a result of this encounter, the enemy group split and this fact, plus the onset of heavy rain, made the subsequent follow-up even more difficult. Tracks were found, followed, lost, found again and then the whole process repeated and repeated. False trails were examined and rejected, platoons withdrawn for rest and re-rationing, fresh platoons inserted; days of exhilaration, nights of frustration, days without any information, then a surrender, further information and on with the chase once more.

The search for Sumbi's party eventually centred around Bukit Pagon (6,070 feet high) astride the Sarawak and Brunei border. On 20 August two platoons were winched into the remote mountainous area to the east of the mountain, while a third platoon walked in from the west, accompanied by two captured prisoners from Sumbi's incursion group. These prisoners showed where they had last seen their friends and after two weeks of cliff-hanging, river crossing and slow tracking, twenty-four enemy were killed or captured, with a few deciding to surrender. Sumbi himself was captured on the morning of 3 September. It was fitting that the company commander, Major Alan Jenkins was able to be there to close the final chapter of his log. In all, forty-six of the original fifty enemy were accounted for by the 1/7th – the remaining four being captured by the Royal Brunei Malay Regiment shortly after the 7th Gurkhas had departed for Sarawak. The aims and aspirations of Lt Sumbi and his incursion group were utterly destroyed, coinciding with the end of 'Confrontation'.

Messages of praise and congratulation poured in as the Gurkha battalions moved away from Borneo back to their peacetime bases in Malaya, Singapore and Hong Kong. At the same time, however, rumours began to appear in the Press, that a large scale reduction of the Brigade of Gurkhas was soon to be announced. In a time of changing defence commitments and reorganization of the British Armed Forces, it was inevitable that the future size and composition of the Brigade would be examined and weighed against other factors outside the scope of this book. Subsequently, the official announcement arrived which stated that the Brigade would reduce from some 14,000 to 6,000 by the end of 1971. This sad news was accepted by all ranks with a spirit of understanding and with remarkably little bitterness. Nevertheless, it was heartrending for the British officers to say farewell to so many loyal and experienced soldiers when they returned to the hills of Nepal as unit by unit contracted in size. The hero of 'Op Metcalf', Rabilal Rai, stood as

Captain Rabilal Rai, DCM in front of Lt. Col. J. M. C. Thornton, M.C., his old company commander and now his CO. Tears were in Thornton's eyes as he tried to break the news to his old friend that he, Rabilal Rai, would have to go on redundancy. Words would not come but Rabilal said: 'Don't worry, Sahib. I know what you have got to say and I know that it is as hard for you as it is for me. You have your duty to do – as I have tried to do mine.' In such a way did one Gurkha officer receive the news that he was going on redundancy; unfortunately there were many other fine Gurkha officers and men in the eight battalions and in the three Gurkha Corps who had to be sent back to be reluctant civilians after years of loyal service.

The planning of 'the rundown' was carried out at all levels with the greatest possible care. The efficiency of each battalion, and of each squadron in the Gurkha Corps, had to be maintained at a high level while, at the same time, the best possible compensatory terms were sought for each and every soldier declared redundant. On the original plan, by the end of 1971 the four regiments were to have amalgamated and been reduced to a single battlion each. However after the change of British Government in 1970, the decision was made to retain the Brigade of Gurkhas at five battalions so that the two battalions of the 2nd Goorkhas did not have to amalgamate as planned. Nevertheless, both battalions had reduced in strength and the change of decision meant that Gurkha officers and soldiers from the other three regiments were asked to transfer to the Second Goorkhas during 1971 in order to build up their numbers once more. In spite of the rundown, followed by the transfers, the morale of all units in the Brigade remained at a remarkably high level. Business went on as usual. In illustration of this statement, when 'the rundown' had barely started and was at a stage where commanding officers dearly wanted to give their personal attention to detailed arrangements, serious trouble started on the border between the New Territories of Hong Kong and Red China. Before many weeks had passed four Gurkha battalions were engaged in keeping the peace, outstaring the Red Guards and, as always, ready for anything. In these operations the 6th, 7th and

10th Gurkhas all played a notable part, whether conducting Internal Security duties in the urban areas or along the border where the situation became extremely tense. Junior British officers and their Gurkha soldiers in these three regiments were subjected to deliberate provocation and were forced to listen to a constant and steady flow of propaganda while trying to maintain an air of calm and good humour in the face of insults and planned incidents. It was a wearisome task which continued day and night, week after week, while back in Hong Kong life went on under normal conditions. Few tourists realized that the glitter and bustle of Hong Kong was like another world to the Gurkha riflemen who stood on lonely vigil at the border posts.

By 1970 the 'heat' had been taken out of the Anglo-Chinese frontier problem. Relations between China and Hong Kong improved and the scowls of the sentries on the other side of the border changed to smiles. This did not mean that the units of the Brigade went back to their peacetime bases. After 1975 the trickle of illegal immigrants seeking a new future in Hong Kong increased dramatically. By 1978, it was no longer possible for a single battalion to attempt to apprehend the scores of people who were prepared to risk life and limb in a bid to escape the Chinese brand of Communism. The climax was reached in mid–1979 when nearly 90,000 were arrested – and by that time five battalions were deployed in an attempt to stop the deluge. Without their vigilance the already crowded Colony would have been swamped by the flood of refugees. Nevertheless, the presence of British and Gurkha troops could only act as a deterrent: they could never stop everyone while the Chinese, on their side of the border, had yet to produce a political system attractive to all its peoples.

Chapter 11

THE QUEEN'S GURKHA ENGINEERS

THE first Gurkha infantrymen attached to the Royal Engineers, assembled in October 1948 at Kluang, Malaya, to become 67 Field Squadron RE. For nearly two years the future, or otherwise, of the Gurkha sappers very much depended on the prowess of that Squadron because there were many critics, both in and outside the Brigade, who affirmed that it was a mistake to turn first class infantry soldiers into second class sappers. However their enthusiasm and ability to learn so convinced the Royal Engineers and HQ Brigade of Gurkhas that a second squadron, 68, was raised two years later.

Not long afterwards, both Squadrons were moved in some haste to Hong Kong to replace two infantry battalions, suddenly posted to Korea. Quickly learning their trade, they helped alter the face of the Colony by building new roads, constructing Bailey bridges and completing a wide variety of projects. In June 1952 came the first batch of recruits, directly enlisted into the Regiment as sappers, from the very first day of their service in the Army. Two years later the Regiment moved to Malaya to join 17 Gurkha Infantry Division and provide operational engineer support at a time when the Emergency was at its height. The Regiment's base was to be at Sungei Besi, near Kuala Lumpur, where it was to remain until 1960.

Once on operational duty, both Squadrons tackled and completed a myriad of tasks so it is not possible to mention more than one or two in this account. In 1955 the whole Regiment was involved in a major road project from Rompin to Gemas. Apart from reducing the distance between the two towns from 70 to 13 miles – hence speeding up the movement of the Security Forces in the area – a series of bridges had to be constructed, the longest of which was 342 feet and 17 feet above the river. The bridge was ceremonially opened on 6th September by the GOC 17 Division (Major General R. N. Anderson) who named it 'The Gurkha Bridge': in truth the Regiment had won its colours by this feat. Three months later the Regiment became The Gurkha Engineers and as such, a component part of the Brigade of Gurkhas: this recognised their development as sappers; at the same time the Regiment felt some remorse at having to lose their original title of Royal Engineers. Justice was done when, twenty-two years later, in April 1977 Her Majesty the Queen graciously approved the title of 'The Queen's Gurkha Engineers', in official recognition of their achievements and, in particular, on operational service in Malaya and Borneo.

Before the Emergency in Malaya ended in 1960, the Gurkha sappers continued to grapple with a wide variety of projects throughout Malaya, one of the most ambitious being an 18 mile road in Kedah which included 35 bridges and culverts. In appreciation of that achievement, the Sultan of Kedah presented a ceremonial Kris to the Regiment on behalf of his people.

After the Malayan Emergency had ended in 1960, the Regiment, with some sadness, moved from Sungei Besi to Kluang but before that move was completed, a third squadron, 69 Independent Field, was raised. That it made such an encouraging start was in no small way due to a draft of first class NCOs and men who were posted in from the experienced 67 Squadron. However, the three Squadrons were not to be in Malaya together for long, because in 1962, 68 was sent back to Tidworth in the United Kingdom to form part of the newly raised 51 Brigade. Here their performance on exercises was carefully scrutinised by those who still doubted whether Gurkhas could become first class engineers: such doubts were quickly quelled by the Gurkha Sappers' enthusiasm and skill, demonstrated in a variety of ways on exercises, both in the United Kingdom and elsewhere. 68 Squadron even hit the headlines of the U.K. Press when 23 of their Gurkha soldiers became ill after cooking and eating what they believed to be mushrooms!

As it transpired, there was to be only a short interval between the end of the Emergency and another bout of operational soldiering, this time in Brunei and subsequently, in Borneo. In early December 1962, the Brunei Revolt broke out which led to 69 Squadron being deployed to that State to help the Security Forces quell the insurrection. There its primary tasks were road repair and maintenance as well as providing operational mobility on the waterways which included manning longboats, and the construction of airstrips. When the Confrontation with Indonesia began in Borneo, 68 Gurkha Independent Squadron was recalled from the UK to help their fellow Gurkha sappers carry out a variety of tasks. From 1963 until 1966 the three Squadrons played a most significant part in the counterinsurgency campaign by the construction of roads and operational camps, opening up waterways and manning small craft; airstrips and helicopter landing zones were hacked out of the jungle in the hinterland. During the Confrontation, like the infantry units, the Gurkha Engineers played an important part in helping with community projects, thus winning the hearts and minds of the local population. By that time, their Pipes and Drums was well established with a reputation for technical musical proficiency as well as being trained as combat engineers, which included driving and medical qualifications. Without doubt the Confrontation was to present the Gurkha Engineers with the most challenging role in their short history in the British Army. The wide variety of tasks carried out tested their skill and ability to improvise under the most difficult of conditions in the jungle. Of more long term significance was the part they played in opening up and developing the hinterland by constructing eight airstrips, suitable for medium and short range transport aircraft and building many miles of roads and tracks, together with village resettlement schemes.

After the Confrontation was over, 67 Squadron was posted to Brunei where it was stationed in Seria as part of the garrison. There they combined engineer training with welcome assistance to the local community, carrying out the sort of projects that had proved so beneficial during the Confrontation. Meanwhile, in Hong Kong, by 1967 the Internal Security situation had deteriorated until large scale riots broke out in that year. In the Sha Tau Kok border area booby traps had to be dealt with by both 67 and 69 Squadrons. 69 Squadron was also engaged in constructing a mammoth fence, approximately 18 miles in length, which stretched from Sha Tau Kok to Lok La Chau. Other engineer work included the construction of fire positions, bunkers and emplacements while motorable tracks were opened up so that the infantry could be administered while stationed at various points along the Sino-Hong Kong border.

While all this was taking place, the large scale rundown of the Brigade of Gurkhas began in the same year and the sappers had to take their share which meant that 69 Squadron – which had only come into being in 1961 – was formally disbanded on 17 August 1968. Another major change was that, in 1969, the Gurkha Engineers left Kluang in Malaya on a permanent move to the Colony. Prior to leaving Kluang, a major monsoon resulted in widespread flooding during which the Regiment helped with rescue operations and damage repair – its final task in Malaya. Once the move to Hong Kong had been completed, the field squadrons lost their 'independent' titles and the Commander of the Gurkha Engineers became CRE so that all engineers, serving in the Colony, came under the one headquarters.

During the next few years, the Squadrons from Hong Kong, and occasionally troops from the Squadrons, found themselves deployed in various part of the Far East, which included Fiji, The Solomon Islands, New Hebrides, Australia, as well as carrying out many tasks in Brunei. Community relation projects in the Colony itself also took up much time and helped to cement an excellent relationship with the civilian population.

During 1979, the massive influx of illegal immigrants from China into Hong Kong reached its ceiling and by the end of May it became apparent that much more had to be done in order to stem the tide. Although by that time four infantry battalions had been deployed along the Sino-Hong Kong border, the situation worsened which led to an extra battalion being flown out from the UK to help close the gaps. For the sappers this meant, amongst other tasks, reinforcing the main fence and refurbishing it as well as building watchtowers in the Mai Po marshes and clearing new sites, suitable for company bases at various points along the border.

With the illegal immigrants also attempting to come in by sea, a Boat Troop was formed which was trained initially by a team of Royal Marines. The Boat Troop played a vital operational role and even when the situation improved, they continued to operate well into the 1990s. However, there were one or two unfortunate casualties, including the loss of a sapper from 67 Squadron who was knocked overboard when a civilian craft hit his boat. Despite an intensive search his body was never found.

Fluctuations in the fortunes of the whole of the Brigade of Gurkhas meant that, once again, 69 Squadron was reformed in early 1981 after 13 years of disbandment. Soon afterwards, that Squadron moved back to the UK, where it operated in the same way as any Royal Engineer field squadron. This entailed carrying out a wide variety of combat engineering skills, including a six months' tour in The Falklands Islands. There 69 Squadron was involved in the difficult and often dangerous task of trying to make the island a safer place to live in after the Argentinian occupation. While clearing away mines and missiles, which had been used indiscriminately, a corporal was killed in an accident: that unfortunate death apart, it was a most successful tour which certainly enhanced 69 Squadron's reputation. Later the Squadron was to move to Belize on a six months' tour to gain further operational experience and subsequently one troop went to Kenya to operate under the command of 9 Para Squadron.

Meanwhile, those sappers based in Hong Kong continued to carry out projects in the early 80s, the most ambitious being on Lantau Island. Indeed, the Lantau bridge project continued to dominate the lives of all the Colony sappers during 1985: it was an ambitious project which provided a major challenge as well as providing valuable training for all types of tradesmen. The completion target was met and the bridge was duly opened by Commander British Forces at the end of December 1985, with the end result being something about which the Regiment could be proud.

By this time, 69 Squadron, based in Chatham, had so won the hearts of the local people that in recognition of their efforts, Rochester City Council granted them the Freedom of the City. The vagaries of the English winter in 1987 saw them fully involved in disaster relief around the Medway towns and the isolated Isle of Sheppey and this, too, enhanced their reputation in the UK. The Squadron also won the Minor Unit shooting competition at Bisley, a feat they were to repeat in later years.

While the level of illegal immigrants into Hong Kong dropped dramatically, so did the influx of Vietnamese boat people by sea begin to pose great problems, not only to the government but to 67 Squadron, in particular. At short notice it had to deploy to prepare Erskine Training Camp so it could be used to house the boat people who continued to arrive in droves – despite energetic efforts to deter them. In 1990, a year later, operations against illegal immigrants and smugglers began to take a higher profile once more; by this time, the smugglers were becoming more professional and could be extremely dangerous when confronted.

At work or during their recreational pursuits, the Gurkha Engineers continued to live up to the high traditions of the Royal Engineers and the Brigade of Gurkhas. For example, their footballers won the Nepal Cup on more occasions than the rest of the Brigade would like to remember! As an individual sportsman, Sapper Jhapatsing Bhujel not only won the Hong Kong lightweight boxing title but was so skilled that he was selected to join the Army squad in Aldershot.

'Options for Change' has hit the Gurkha Engineers badly – like the rest of the Brigade – as it entailed a large scale rundown for the once proud Gurkha Engineer Regiment until only a single Field squadron remains. In April 1993, 69 Squadron lost its independent title and became part of 36 Engineer Regiment at Chatham.

THE QUEEN'S GURKHA SIGNALS

By the time the Malayan Emergency began in June 1948, a decision had been taken to form the 17th Gurkha Division with its signal units being composed of Gurkha soldiers. The original idea was to post in trained signallers from the eight infantry battalions but the exigencies of the Emergency meant that the units could not spare these men from operations until well into 1949. As a consequence, 110 of the 1948 recruits were posted to X Brigade Signal Squadron, eventually to become The Gurkha Signals Training and Holding Unit. Prior to the beginning of their specialist training, these recruits spent three months at the Gurkha School of Education, during which they concentrated on learning English as well as basic maths and map reading. Only in late 1950 were they adjudged ready to begin operational duty: on the 18th of December 48 Gurkha Brigade Signal Squadron came into being and shortly after moved to Pahang to join the Brigade on its counterinsurgency operations in that State.

Initially these men were titled 'Gurkha Royal Signals' and wore the Royal Corps of Signals cap badge. Nevertheless, it was not long before there were some innovations in dress and thanks to the energetic efforts of Major L. H. M. Gregory, a Pipe band was formed, soon to be affiliated to the 51st Highland Division Signals as well as inheriting their tartan. Thus began the formative years of the Gurkha Signals from 1951–1954 during which many changes were effected. By 1954, HQ Gurkha Signals had three squadrons out on operational duty, with 26, 63 and 99 Gurkha Infantry Brigades so that when the MGBG (Major General L. E. C. M. Perowne) presented the new cap badge to the Regiment in September 1954, it was a fully operational signal regiment in every respect, under the command of Lieutenant Colonel L. H. M. Gregory – who had done so much to bring the Gurkha Signals into becoming an integral part of the Brigade of Gurkhas.

Changes of location occurred at fairly frequent intervals to fit in with operational moves. A most significant date in the Gurkha Signals' history occurred when the Royal Title was dropped and the Regiment became a full member of the Brigade of Gurkhas on 26 September 1954: in such a way did the Regiment, alone among signal units, appear in the Army List within the Corps of Infantry. By this time, officers and men of the Gurkha Signals had played a significant part in the Emergency operations. As well as manning radio and signals communications for 24 hours a day, all ranks carried out their share of HQ defence duties as well as acting as armed escorts to convoys on roads, always liable to be ambushed by the Communist Terrorists. HF radio was invariably prone to atmospheric interference especially at dawn and dusk, the most crucial times when operating in the jungle: resolving this entailed much patience and resolution on the part of the operators. When the Communist Terrorist offensive spirit was dampened and the pendulum swung towards the Security Forces, the use of the helicopter became paramount when seeking out the terrorists in their jungle hideouts. This enabled the Gurkha Signals to become air portable when new techniques had to be devised and learnt.

On 21 April 1956, HRH The Princess Royal presented her Pipe Banner to the Pipes and Drums of the Regiment, Royal recognition of the exploits of the Regiment during its six years of operations in Malaya. This presentation parade preceded by a few weeks a long-term move from Kuala Lumpur into the delightful Sikamat Camp in Seremban, a camp that was to be the home of the Gurkha Signals for eleven years until 1971, when they left Malaya for the last time and moved to the Colony of Hong Kong.

In Seremban the Gurkha Signals enjoyed a close association with the local community and many lasting friendships were made. In return, the Regiment's football team received vociferous support from the Chinese and Malayan inhabitants in their quest for the Brigade's Nepal Cup: this coveted trophy was won for the first time in 1959, the first of six successes by the Gurkha Signals during the years that followed.

After the Malayan Emergency officially ended in 1960, 17 Gurkha Division was disbanded although the Regiment still retained its original title of 17 Gurkha Signal Regiment. In line with other Royal Corps of Signals sub units, the squadrons in the Regiment were re-numbered to become 246 Squadron (in Hong Kong with 48 Gurkha Infantry Brigade) while 247 and 248 Squadrons continued to serve in Malaya. 247 Squadron was not to remain there for long, however, because in 1962, they left Malaya for the colder climate of Tidworth in the UK where they became part of HQ 51 Gurkha Brigade.

247 Squadron, like their fellow Gurkhas in 1/6 GR, 68 Gurkha Engineer Squadron and 31 Squadron GTR, fully appreciated that their technical skills and general behaviour would be under close scrutiny, on exercises and in barracks, while forming part of the first Gurkha contingent ever to serve in the UK. They rose to the occasion and participated, both in the UK and in BAOR, on a series of testing exercises with all ranks responding to the challenge. In February 1963 the Squadron moved to Hubbelrath, West Germany, to train with 4 Guards Brigade, an association that the tall Guardsmen and the short stocky Gurkhas enjoyed to the full.

However, the war clouds over Borneo and Brunei, in particular, meant that 248 Squadron was to be on operational duty for nearly four years where 247 eventually joined them. As part of HQ 99 Brigade, 248 Squadron went to Brunei in December 1962, the prelude to the Confrontation with Indonesia: the Squadron remained there with its HQ, for most of the time, based in Kuching. When 247 Squadron, as part of 51 Brigade, left the UK for Borneo, their HQ was established in Brunei Town itself. Both Squadrons faced daunting tasks as their respective operational areas were huge, thus testing their signallers in a wide variety of skills. The establishment of Radio Relay and VHF re-broadcast stations on the summits of certain key hills alleviated the problem of communications over such great distances. Nevertheless, it took much time and effort to establish such stations which thereafter were accessible by helicopter alone. After landing zones had been hacked and the stations established, the detachments there working on those lonely sites had to rely on helicopters for re-supply and occasionally if the weather permitted, from air drops. The living conditions were invariably uncomfortable, cold and damp and often in the clouds but despite that, detachments helped to establish and maintain excellent communications that were the key to all major operations carried out in their respective brigade areas.

One of the most interesting units to be formed during the Confrontation was the Gurkha Independent Parachute Company which was raised in April 1963: soon afterwards its role was changed to that of an SAS-type company, capable of providing a number of long-range patrols. The Gurkha Signals was asked to form a troop of highly qualified signallers to support the Parachute Company and its patrols: volunteers were quickly forthcoming and these men soon obtained the necessary parachute qualifications. It was not long before the troop reached its maximum strength of 40 soldiers. The signallers played a significant part in the exploits of the Gurkha Parachute Company and became expert at long range signalling: after the peace treaty was signed with Indonesia, they returned to their parent Gurkha Signal Squadrons, proud to be wearing their parachute badges, won during the Confrontation.

The Rundown of the Brigade of Gurkhas, which began in 1966, meant that the Gurkha Signals contracted until it led to the disbandment of 17 Gurkha Signal Regiment itself. This coincided with the end of the Regiment's stay in Malaysia when Hong Kong became its long term home, with a signal troop from 248 Squadron being based in Seria, soon to be known as the Brunei Signal Troop. From 1970 onwards 246 and 248 were the only squadrons left in the Regiment. But if Hong Kong may have appeared to be a peaceful posting, in the late 60s the Cultural Revolution in China spilled over the border into the Colony so that postings there became anything but quiet. 246 Squadron was soon to be fully involved in providing communications with the extra infantry units, deployed in the border area. In addition, they opened a Gurkha Broadcasting Station which was to be a great success especially at a time when the Chinese were pumping propaganda across the border by all means possible. In time, the Broadcasting Station was taken over by the British Forces Service, operating from Borneo Lines in Sek Kong.

Although in theory the period 1971 to 1994 was a peaceful one, numerous Brigade and Regimental exercises over the years meant that the Gurkha Signals did not lose the skills that they had learnt during the Emergency and later perfected in the Confrontation in Borneo. As it was, some of their officers and men did go to war on two occasions, firstly, in 1982 and then in 1991.

As far as peacetime activities were concerned, an important one was the Regiment's contribution to the Annapurna South Face Expedition in 1971, led by Chris Bonnington. From the Gurkha Signals went Captain Kelvin Kent, supported by a Lieutenant QGO and a signalman, who later became Major (QGO) Gambahadur Butuja. Much support was given in establishing the base camp and thereafter maintaining communications between the camp itself, Pokhara and the climbing team throughout the expedition. In later years the Regiment was to support other expeditions to Everest, Nuptse and later in 1992, the British Army's attempt to climb the west ridge of Everest itself. The Regiment was represented on all these, supplying much needed communication skills under conditions that were invariably difficult and arduous.

Within the Colony itself, perhaps the most important change for the Regiment was to become responsible for all Far East and Defence communication network circuits to the UK, Brunei and Nepal. Of more significance to all ranks of the Regiment, in 1977 was the occasion when, as part of the Queen's Silver Jubilee celebrations, the Regiment regained its Royal title, along with the Gurkha Engineers, and became the Queen's Gurkha Signals. This event was celebrated in true style with picnics, cocktail parties and family barbecues, as well as a formal re-badging parade, held on 21st September 1977 at Gun Club Hill Barracks.

Like the Gurkha Engineers, the Regiment was involved when hordes of Vietnamese boat people descended upon the Colony: indeed, hundreds were encamped on the runway of RAF Sek Kong outside the Regiment's Sergeants' Mess, visitors that could not be disregarded!

During the 1980s, a series of exercise in the Colony and in other parts of the Far East, as well as Europe, ensured that the technical skills of the Gurkha Signal Regiment were honed and kept up-to-date. A 'red letter day' for the Regiment was 1st June 1990 when 250

Gurkha Signal Squadron reformed as part of 30 Signal Regiment in Blandford. As an integral part of 30 Signal Regiment, 250 Squadron provided signals capabilities outside the UK and over the past few years, has seen service in Namibia, Saudia Arabia, Kuwait, Iraq, Turkey, Bosnia and Croatia. This was new ground for the Brigade of Gurkhas because 250 Squadron was the first Gurkha unit to move to the UK on a permanent posting and integrate with a British unit – in preparation for 'Options for Change' and the rundown of the regiments themselves.

As a consequence, in August 1990, when 30 Signals Regiment deployed to Saudia Arabia as part of the Allied response to Saddam Hussain's aggression against Kuwait, within two weeks elements of 250 Squadron also moved to the Gulf area where Sergeant Padambahadur Rai had the honour of being the first Gurkha in the Gulf, when he arrived on 13th October 1990. Many more of the Squadron followed as detachments were established in various places, some of whom served long enough there to be replaced on roulement and then sent back. In addition, a dozen signallers, as radio operators, deployed with 28 Squadron Gurkha Transport Regiment, who were providing ambulance support for 1 UK Division. The war was resolved with few casualties, but the Gurkha Signals, once more, had shown that they possessed all the necessary skills and could more than hold their own with the best Royal Corps of Signals units.

Options for change will reduce the Gurkha Signals Regiment to the equivalent of one squadron only. Small though it may be, it is certain that it will live up to the tradition of the Gurkha Signals Regiment established in peace and on operations since its inception some 45 years ago.

THE QUEEN'S OWN GURKHA TRANSPORT REGIMENT

The Gurkha Army Service Corps (GASC), the original name of the present Queen' Own Gurkha Transport Regiment, was formed on 1 July 1958 in Singapore and Malaya and from its inception was an integral part of the Brigade of Gurkhas.

The formation of the Regiment, under command of Headquarters Royal Army Service Corps, 17 Gurkha Division/Overseas Commonwealth Land Forces, was beset by many unusual problems. Not least the Gurkha soldiers had little or no experience of vehicles, or driving, or RASC operating procedures and few spoke English. In addition, the British Command Training Team, although widely experienced in mechanical transport and Corps procedures, knew nothing of the Brigade customs and did not speak Gurkhali. However, the other units in the Brigade of Gurkhas gave the new Regiment every possible assistance to get off to a good start. The RASC British Officers, posted in to fill company appointments, were sent on a Gurkhali Language Course, held at the Brigade of Gurkhas' Depot at Sungei Patani in North Malaya.

Queen's Gurkha Officers (QGOs) and senior ranks, transferred into the raising cadres for 28 MT Company Gurkha ASC and 30 Infantry Brigade Group Company Gurkha ASC, arrived at the RASC School Nee Soon in Singapore during August 1958 where they began training immediately. This phase was completed by December 1958 when they, in turn, became instructors for the Junior NCOs who, by then, had reported to the School.

The first recruits were received from the Brigade of Gurkhas Depot in November 1959. This batch consisted of fifty four men, recruited directly from Nepal into the Regiment as well as a further forty from Boys Company then training at the Depot. The soldiers recruited were selected from both East and West Nepal and this custom persists today because the Regiment contains men from all parts of the Mountain Kingdom.

In July 1960, 28 and 39 Companies completed their initial training: 28 Company then sailed to Hong Kong on the troopship 'Nevasa', arriving on 10 September to replace 8 Company RASC. 30 Company remained in Malaya as the MT Company of 63 Gurkha Infantry Brigade and was soon deployed in direct support of operations against the Communist Terrorists, towards the close of the Malayan Emergency.

In May 1960 the raising cadres of 31 and 34 Companies Gurkha ASC were formed and moved from Nee Soon. 31 Company went to join its newly formed Composite Platoon in Buller Lines, Kluang while 34 Company moved to Batu Pahat where, initially, it shared accommodation and facilities with 28 Company.

Headquarters Gurkha ASC itself was formed on 1 July 1960 by the redesignation of Headquarters RASC 17 Gurkha Division/ Overseas Commonwealth Land Forces. The affiliation of the Gurkha Army Service Corps to the Royal Army Service Corps was graciously approved by Her Majesty The Queen in December 1959. During the same year, Her Majesty The Queen also approved the Regiment's badge and Regimental buttons. The Commander of the Regiment presented these badges and buttons to the Malaya and Singapore-based companies on parades held during December 1961. 28 Company in Hong Kong also received its badges at the same time. The Regimental black Malacca cane, with silver knob embraced with the Regimental badge and silver ferrile, was taken into use by all officers on 1 June 1961.

On arrival in Hong Kong, 28 Company settled into Whitfield Barracks (now Kowloon Park) alongside Nathan Road. For its MT role, the Company had three platoons, each equipped with the standard complement of 20 × 3 ton task vehicles plus 2 × 3 ton in reserve. The Company also had a heavy section of 10 ton vehicles and a section of two tank transporters with trailers. The transporters and their short, stocky drivers, provided an awe-inspiring sight along the narrow roads of the New Territories while they carried out their annual major task of rotating the Colony's stockpile of Centurion tanks between Sek Kong and Kowloon.

30 Company in Kluang began training as an infantry brigade group company with standard platoons and an additional composite platoon. However, it was not long before one and a half platoons were moved to the Brigade Depot to assist with driver training. Even this redeployment proved short-lived because, in March 1961, the Regiment was advised that 30 Company would be moving to the UK in early 1962 to support 51 Gurkha Infantry Brigade (Air Portable). Once there, 30 Company flourished as a

part of the United Kingdom Strategic Reserve: moreover, the Gurkha soldiers enjoyed the benefits of better accommodation, rations, scales of equipment as well as higher rates of pay. The tour was to be curtailed when the Indonesian Confrontation in Borneo and the impending return of 51 Brigade to the Far East, led to the Company packing its equipment and returning vehicles, before travelling back to Nee Soon Camp on Singapore Island during February and March 1964.

In December 1962, 31 Company was moved into North Borneo as a part of 99 Gurkha Infantry Brigade Group. Nearly all the units that deployed on this operation did so through Labuan Island. The Resupply Points, manned by 31 Company, stretched from the Labuan airfield all the way to the mainland capital of Brunei Town. In addition, an RASC Maritime Fleet and RASC Air Despatch Section were in support of this logistic operation, the sheer scale of which soon necessitated reinforcements from 28 and 34 Companies.

Although the Brunei Revolt was short-lived, units in the State continued to be operational so that 31 Company did not withdraw from Brunei to regroup and retrain until November 1963. The Company had upheld, with great credit, the Regiment's name in that operational theatre for over 12 months.

The Indonesian Confrontation dominated the Regiment's activities from 1963 to 1966. 31 Company's return from Brunei was but a short respite as, on 6 January 1964, they were off again, this time to join 30 Company, already deployed in the East Malaysian theatre at Kuching in support of 99 Gurkha Infantry Brigade. During the Confrontation companies and composite platoons of the Regiment relieved each other on a trickle basis. All ranks were operational in either East or West Malaysia and many were to serve in both before peace was declared in 1966. The Gurkha Service Corps came of age during the Borneo Confrontation, demonstrating to the Army that they were well trained and efficient while performing their specialist role.

As a result of the Macleod Reorganisation, in 1965, the RASC became the Royal Corps of Transport (RCT). It was intended that the Regiment would be renamed on the same date in July 1965 until it was discovered that Headquarters, Far East Land Forces had failed to seek the necessary approval of Her Majesty The Queen. All arrangements, therefore, had to be postponed and the Regiment was eventually redesignated on 1 November 1965, the Gurkha ASC becoming the Gurkha Transport Regiment (GTR).

At the end of 1966, the Regiment was at its peak with a strength of 1268, including the Nepal Leave increment and men on Extra Regimental Employment (ERE). Regrettably the Rundown, during that period forecast many cuts for units in the Brigade of Gurkhas so that the Regiment was directed to reduce its numbers to 806 by December 1969. Although redundancy hung over the Brigade like a dark shadow, normal life in the Regiment continued in Kowloon, Nee Soon and Kluang.

After the completion of the Defence Review in 1968, a period of consolidation followed. 31 Squadron joined its sister squadron in Hong Kong during 1971 and the last remnant of 34 Squadron, the Gurkha All Arms Training Wing, was absorbed by 31 Squadron and redesignated the Gurkha MT School.

After being fully established in Hong Kong, the Regiment continued to prosper in a peace time environment. In 1975, one British officer and nineteen soldiers from the GTR left Hong Kong for a tour of duty with the Korean Honour Guard. The Regiment was the first Corps unit to undertake such a duty in Korea and periodically continued to provide soldiers for the Korean Honour Guard duty in the years that followed as did the other two Gurkha Corps and the infantry battalions.

On the 1 September 1976 the Regiment welcomed 29 Squadron and 415 Maritime Troop RCT into the fold. Hong Kong Military Service Corps (HKMSC) soldiers now became a part of the Regiment and were destined to play a significant role in Regimental duties in Hong Kong and abroad in the years that followed. In the latter part of the year the APC Troop was born. Initial training was carried out at the Gurkha Mechanical Transport School in Sek Kong and it was not long before IS training, employing the APC Troop with infantry battalions, was underway.

During the next few years the Regiment continued to carry out a wide variety of Hong Kong Garrison duties, as well as participating on IS exercises, undertaking overseas commitments as well as filling a growing number of ERE appointments in the UK. Detachments at RMA Sandhurst, the Infantry Tactical Wing Brecon and the Royal Engineers Training Depot at Chatham were but examples of the places the soldiers found gainful and varied employment and every attempt was made to provide them with a greater depth of military experience worldwide. Overseas exercises for Infantry battalions invariably included a detachment of GTR drivers to assist with transport and to participate in general.

In the latter part of 1990 the Regiment was called to arms with the prospect of a squadron deploying to the Gulf as part of Operation GRANBY. On 6 December 1990, 214 all ranks of 28 (Ambulance) Squadron GTR moved to Church Crookham to begin pre-deployment training and take on their specialist ambulances. 28 Squadron was the major part of the Gurkha Ambulance Group in support of 4 and 7 Armoured Brigades in the Gulf War. All ranks of the Squadron performed extremely well in a role that was completely new to them, thereby demonstrating once more that the GTR was capable of operating in any theatre of war.

No sooner had all of the soldiers safely returned to Hong Kong from the Gulf when the Regiment was tasked to send a squadron to complete a United Nations commitment in Cyprus. Although a strain on manning and routine Hong Kong tasks, the GTR met the challenge. The contingent, representing the United Nations Force in Cyprus (UNFICYP) from July 1991 to January 1992, resurrected the name of 34 Transport Squadron GTR for that particular operational tour.

More recently the Regiment has been blessed with positive news despite the bleak future for the Brigade with amalgamations and further bouts of redundancy looming. On 30 August 1992 Her Majesty was pleased to grant the Gurkha Transport Regiment with a Royal Warrant. The name of the Regiment was to be the Queen's Own Gurkha Transport Regiment, thus bringing them into line with all other Brigade of Gurkhas' Regiments.

In 1992 came the confirmation that 28 Squadron was to be

redeployed to the UK. This move was a part of the 'Options for Change' and thereby secured a place for the GTR in the British Army, albeit as a single squadron only. As a consequence, 28 Squadron joined 10 Regiment RLC on 15 November 1993 where, in 1994, it is training with its heavy lift vehicle as a part of 3 (UK) Armoured Division. With less than forty years history behind the GTR, 28 Squadron will carry, with pride, the reputation and hopes of the Queen's Own Gurkhas Transport Regiment into the future.

Chapter 12

WHEN the newsletters of the four infantry regiments are studied, it can be seen that the years between 1971 and 1994 held a wide variety of tasks for all units. At regular intervals some of these were carried out, in turn, by one or other of the regiments. Perhaps the most momentous of these was the long-waited opportunity to serve a two-year tour in the UK, with the 7th Gurkha Rifles being the first to go. The news was greeted with relief because the British officers and their Gurkha soldiers did not wish to serve forever within the Colony of Hong Kong. Following the Seventh Gurkhas, the other infantry battalions completed similar tours in Church Crookham and this roster continues to this day: Gurkha soldiers in and around Aldershot and Fleet are now a familiar sight and they have become very popular locally. Each of the resident Gurkha battalions in the UK has carried out Public Duties in London, organised and run Bisley, as well as providing men for the Demonstration Company at the Royal Military Academy. To add to the Brigade's renown, 10 GR in 1973 won the major Unit Championship at Bisley and that victory has been repeated on several occasions by one or other of the Battalions: sadly, the rundown of the Army under 'Options for Change' has meant that the Bisley Championship has been curtailed as far as the Regular Army is concerned.

Back to Hong Kong then which, by 1971, had become the home base of the Brigade, with 10 GR being the last unit to leave Malaya in late 1970, to join the other units then serving in the Colony.

While it would be quite wrong, and inaccurate, to state that the officers and men of the Brigade settled down to a regular humdrum pattern of life under peacetime conditions, there were duties and commitments that had to be carried out annually. Ceremonial occasions in the Colony were frequent in addition to the provision of Guards of Honour in Korea; internal security training in conjunction with the Hong Kong Police, annual military exercises in the hills of the New Territories; these and others found a place in every unit's diary from 1971 onwards. When describing these regular commitments, it would be difficult to single out one particular year as, in the main, they varied but little.

One assignment that was to occupy the attention of the Brigade units more and more was the ever-increasing stream of illegal immigrants from China who were seeking a new future in Hong Kong. After 1975 the trickle threatened to turn into a deluge as scores of people were prepared to risk life and limb in a bid to escape from the Chinese brand of Communism. The challenge that faced the Gurkha battalions was to deter and, if that failed, to apprehend the illegal immigrants as they sought shelter in the Colony. In the early days, Border duty was usually for two weeks duration, every two months, duties that became 'very dull after three days'. However, the situation continued to deteriorate until by 1980 there were twelve companies deployed from Castle Peak, along the land frontier, to inclusive of the Saikung Peninsular. A 10 GR newsletter commented: 'Up to five hundred IIs were being caught in a 24 hour period, the majority at night and across the land frontier. On the two coastal flanks, individuals had improvised floating aids, junks, which might arrive with up to 150 people aboard. Despite the number of troops deployed, many IIs would avoid capture and once they were clear of the Border could apply for an identity card – a touch base policy'. Fortunately this policy was cancelled in October 1980 so that an II remained an II wherever he or she reached within the Colony and there is no doubt that this change of policy was a major factor in the dramatic drop in numbers when captures then averaged 200 a month.

As already mentioned in the history of the QGE, obstacles along the length of the land border included a 10 foot high fence with rolls of dannert wire on the top: this fence was illuminated by lights which could be independently operated, while in some areas there was a sensory system which triggered an alarm when anyone touched the fence. By 1980, operations on the Border were for six weeks at a time and increasingly with all creature comforts. However, there was a detrimental effect on the soldiers' training for war especially as they were operating against a generally passive 'enemy'. Platoons did not operate as such because they were broken down into 'four-man bricks' so that patrol discipline was inevitably more relaxed than would have been tolerated on 'real' active service. Following their Border duty, each unit had to carry out extensive training to eradicate those habits and teach the correct operating procedures – although there were some benefits as junior NCOs and senior riflemen had to use their initiative when operating in four-men bricks as well as being able to use the correct voice procedures when speaking on the radio. The humanitarian aspect was keenly felt by the Gurkha soldiers and their compassion in dealing with the unfortunate IIs was in direct contrast to the attitude shown by members of their own race. Irrespective of which battalion carried out border duties – and when – there is little doubt that all ranks greatly enhanced the reputation of the Brigade under very trying circumstances.

One trouble spot that Brigade units never expected to visit was Cyprus where 10 GR, based at Church Crookham, carried out an emergency tour between August 1974 and February 1975. War clouds threatened Cyprus when an attempted Greek National Guard coup against President Makarios failed. This occurred on the 13th July and the President narrowly escaped assassination before fleeing the Island. Eight days later, Turkish troops invaded, landing at Kyrenia on the north coast and after a week of bitter fighting linked up through the Kyrenia Mountains with airborne troops northwest of Nicosia, when a cease-fire was arranged between the Turks and the defending Greek National guard. While the battle raged, 10 GR in the UK was warned for an emergency air move although at the time organising and running Bisley was still their responsibility. Major Michael Allen, OC B Company, briefed his men about the situation which by then was so confused that it was not surprising that at the end of his briefing a junior rifleman asked: 'But who is my enemy?'. As Major Allen was to say, 'We never really solved that to his satisfaction!'.

The move to Cyprus was carried out with great speed and efficiency by the Battalion and they arrived on the Island during the uneasy cease-fire which followed the initial Turkish landings. On 14th August, the peace talks in Geneva having broken down, the Turks resumed their advance and moved south to Nicosia and then southwest to Famagusta. The Canadian contingent of the UN successfully prevented the international airport from falling into Turkish hands which then became a UN Protected place. It was not long before 10 GR was involved with the Turkish Army and only firm but tactful handling prevented several dangerous situations from developing because, in general, the Turks were in an ugly mood. Civilian refugees from both communities moved one way or the other like flotsam, fleeing before the violence. The Battalion's two roles were necessarily passive; firstly, to defend the territorial integrity of the Eastern Sovereign Base Area and protect British personnel and installations and, secondly, to assist refugees irrespective of their nationality. In carrying out these tasks the unit was extremely stretched; indeed, it was a Signal Officer's nightmare but as the 10 GR account states, 'The RSO (Captain Rupert Litherland) kept communications going'. By Monday 19th August the hostilities had officially ended but the air of tension continued since Turkish intentions remained uncertain. Internal security mainly involved controlling large numbers of refugees which taxed the administrative elements to the limit. 'All were grateful for the aid and safety we offered them and the response was amazing when our Pipes and Drums under Pipe Major Bhairamani Rai provided a break in the monotony and uncertainty of their daily lives'. The Gurkhas were adept in their role of handling refugees and had a most quietening and reassuring effect on British, Greeks, Turks, Armenians, Cypriots and a host of foreign nationals alike.

Once the border line had been established and agreed the situation and tension eased somewhat. Occasionally a fire fight would break out: indeed, on 29th October one did so which lasted almost $1\frac{1}{2}$ hours until a local cease-fire was arranged. President Makarios returned to the Island on 7th December, landing at Akrotiri to a rapturous welcome with large parades being held in Nicosia while, generally, all the rallies organised were peaceful. Another incident occurred when the former acting President, Clerides, visited a refugee camp. During his visit, Turkish soldiers captured an old Greek shepherd and occupied the escarpment overlooking the camp. Some two thousand angry refugees advanced towards the Turks who adopted firing positions. It was a tricky situation but one that was extremely well handled by Major Mike Allen: a platoon of his B Company, supported by two armoured cars from B Squadron 1RTR, quickly and courageously interposed themselves between the Greek refugees and the Turks.

By skilful use of the ground, the Gurkhas were able to dominate the Turks who by now were reinforced to company strength and a potentially dangerous situation was defused. For his part in this incident, Lieutenant (QGO) Gajurmani Rai received The Queen's Commendation.

There were other incidents and even on the last day or two of their tour, 10 GR had to 'stand to' ready for action. At midday on 24th February the 1st Battalion The Devonshire and Dorset Regiment relieved the 10th Gurkha Rifles who left the Island, knowing well that they had carried out a difficult role superbly. The CO, Lieutenant Colonel C. J. Pike, DSO received the OBE for his leadership and in a letter from the GOC NEARELF, Major General C. W. B. Purdon, CBE, MC was to write:
'I thought that you would wish to know how highly I think of your splendid regiment. I am very grateful indeed to Chris Pike and his grand Battalion for all they have done for us in Cyprus during their highly successful tour'. He went on to give more detail ending with the words, 'We will miss 10 GR greatly, they have set the highest standard'.

Another overseas commitment that the infantry battalions of the Brigade, in turn, were to carry out during this period was a six month tour in Belize. This small Central American country, formally the Colony of British Honduras, had long been under the threat of a territorial claim by neighbouring Guatemala and therefore needed the guarantee of a British garrison, even after achieving independence on 21st September 1981. Belize with a population of only about 150,000, and a struggling economy, could not form sufficient defence forces of its own to protect lengthy land borders of about 240 miles.

The main duty of the Gurkha battalions, when they carried out their six month tours, consisted of maintaining the integrity of the land border with Guatemala by manning some static OPs and carrying out much jungle patrolling on foot. In addition, they helped to train the small Belize Defence Force. Usually, each battalion found itself based in four main operating camps, with one training camp and an adventure training centre on an offshore island. Some mobile patrols in land rovers also covered the less sensitive northern border which ran along that with Mexico. It was an ideal opportunity for all ranks to carry out occasional jungle exercises to test their readiness and revise routines as well as embarking on adventure training expeditions which tested individuals to the full. At various times there were 'scares' but no actual conflict ever occurred during a tour carried out in Belize by a Gurkha battalion.

After life in the UK, all units found that on arrival in Belize they were immediately critical of the gentle pace of life adopted by the locals. For example; one camp painter caused a few chuckles when he was asked how long a particular painting job would take. He replied; 'Don't rush de brush man'. Eventually he completed a good job in his own time! After a week or two, it was appreciated that, for the local population, it was a pleasant easy way of life and the effort to break out of it into a more sophisticated lifestyle hardly seemed worth the effort: besides, the hectic western world's lifestyle 'ain't no big deal man'. The tours in Belize will be much missed not only by the Brigade but the British Army as a whole as a means of keeping alive jungle-warfare techniques and training.

On October 19th 1981 came an event of great significance in the history of the Seventh Gurkha Rifles. The Colonel of the Regiment received the following message: 'I have the honour to report that the Army Board has agreed to the re-titling of the Gurkha

Reinforcement Battalion as the Second Battalion Seventh Duke of Edinburgh's Own Gurkha Rifles'. This move was brought about by the necessity to man and guard the Sino-Hong Kong Border but, as it transpired, the new Battalion was not to remain in being for many years. The first Commanding Officer, Lieutenant Colonel Evan Powell-Jones, had the considerable responsibility of welding together British officers, QGOs and men from all regiments of the Brigade as well as from 2/7 GR's sister unit, now retitled 1/7 GR. It was not long before the new Battalion had concentrated in Lyemun Barracks and shortly afterwards taken its turn as an operational unit on the Border. It is important to emphasis that 2/7 GR was very much a Brigade unit, being composed of men from East and West Nepal especially at the onset of its short history. It was fitting, too, that a young Gurkha 2/Lt, Bijaykumar Rawat, should arrive in the unit having just won the Sword of Honour at Sandhurst – the first Gurkha ever to have been awarded that coveted prize.

In 1982 fate decreed that the spotlight should again shine on the Seventh Gurkha Rifles when, with little warning, the First Battalion of that Regiment was summoned in haste to move to Southampton and embark on the Queen Elizabeth II. This took place on the 12th May as part of 5 Brigade which set sail for the Falklands – which had been invaded and occupied by the Argentinians, some five weeks before. Prior to leaving Church Crookham, the national press took a series of photographs of the Gurkha soldiers preparing for war, including ones that were much publicised showing the men sharpening their kukris and waving them around with mock ferocity. It was not long afterwards that stories about 'the wicked Gurkhas' appeared in the Argentinian newspapers and the fact that such a reputation was well known in advance by their adversaries played no small part in the bloodless victory the Battalion achieved after landing on the Falklands.

On the whole, life on the QE II was pleasant especially as there was no seasickness among the Gurkhas. One rifleman was to write: 'Such a ship had to be seen to be believed. Why, it was even larger than any building I have seen back home. . . . .Never have I slept in such beautiful surroundings or in such a big soft bed nor perhaps

I ever will again. If I was to go to war, then there is no better way to go'.

Initially 1/7th Gurkhas moved to Goose Green and spent many hours climbing in and out of helicopters to scour the East Falkland hills for pockets of enemy, believed to be hiding there. By good fortune they just missed the terrible fate that befell the Welsh Guardsmen at Bluff Cove. Then, for the next few days, it was a question of marching with full kit and extra burdens to carry during which, at one stage, they were spotted by the Argentinians and a fierce mortar barrage followed. A company second-in-command and three riflemen were wounded, although not seriously, and all had to be evacuated, eventually reaching the hospital ship,. 'Uganda'.

Meanwhile the Battalion waited for new orders, patiently remaining in reserve until 13th June when they were flown by helicopter to a point just south of the Two Sisters feature. It was here that they were given orders for their part in 5 Brigade's projected attack on Tumbledown and Mount William which was due to begin just after midnight on 14th June. In extremely difficult country, moving slowly in single file with illuminating shells of all kinds lighting up the sky and tracers crisscrossing the hills in front of them, the Battalion was nearing its start point when part of the column was hit by enemy gun fire. Fortunately, the soft nature of the ground saved countless lives and later it was found that only eight men of the Battalion had been hit. Thereafter there followed a long and frustrating wait for the order which would release them to pass through the Scots Guards and attack Mount William. It was at that stage that white flags were seen flying over Port Stanley – the war was over.

Not surprisingly the officers and men who had taken part in the night advance felt thoroughly dispirited, even cheated. It was not because they were thirsty for blood or the chance to prove the stories circulating among the Argentinians concerning the Gurkhas and their kukris. Rather was it having travelled so far they were not given the opportunity to show the world they could do as well as their British comrades on the Falklands – or even better! Nevertheless, the Battalion received a heartwarming reception back in the UK, especially from the people of Fleet who took the opportunity to express their appreciation, not only of the Battalion's part in the Falklands campaign but their excellent discipline and immaculate behaviour while stationed at Church Crookham. Fittingly, the Commanding Officer 1/7 GR, Lt. Col. D. P. de C. Morgan, was awarded the OBE for his leadership before and during the Campaign.

Other units have since followed 1/7 GR to the Falklands, in particular the Gurkha Engineers whose Troops in the islands have been engaged in the extremely dangerous task of clearing mine fields and dismantling booby traps, many of which had not been recorded or marked by the Argentinians.

The next major conflict in which the British Armed Forces were to be engaged was the Gulf War. On this occasion, however, the Brigade's representatives, in the main, came from the Corps as described in Chapter 11.

At the time of writing (May 1994) there are a few Gurkha soldiers serving in Bosnia (Signals and Transport) as well as several ex-soldiers, who, in the main, are driving for United Nations Aid Agencies. To date, however, no Gurkhas have served in Northern Ireland where the operational situation so confuses the average British soldier: the Gurkha soldier would find it an imponderable puzzle, coloured by virulent propaganda on the part of both factions so that wisely, the Ministry of Defence have used them elsewhere in the world.

During these autumn years, inevitably the decisions made by the politicians in Whitehall held the key to the future of the Brigade of Gurkhas and, of course, the British Army as a whole. As has been mentioned before, the heavy influx of illegal immigrants into the Colony of Hong Kong led to 2/7 GR being raised for the third time in the history of the Seventh Gurkha Rifles. That welcome reversal of fortune did not last long as the unit was disbanded after only six years. Shortly afterwards, the clouds of rundown hovered over the whole Brigade, stemming from the Government's 'Options for Change' which heralded several amalgamations as well as dramatic reductions throughout the whole Army. Unfortunately the Brigade was ordered to reduce its five infantry battalions to two only by the end of 1996, while, as mentioned in Chapter 11, the three Corps will have but one squadron each in the new order of battle.

All this has meant a heavy programme of redundancies, with a constant stream of Gurkha officers and men leaving the Army for Nepal, with their departure softened, to a certain extent, by pensions or gratuities. The task of selecting these officers and men has placed a grave burden on the senior officers who, despite the comings and goings, strive to maintain as high a standard of battle efficiency and discipline in the units under their command as would be expected under normal conditions. Moreover, when units contract, prior to a formal amalgamation, drafts and individuals have to be cross-posted with all the flux that involves: the task of officers knowing their men really well will continue to be a major headache until the two battalions of The Royal Gurkha Rifles finally settle down by the end of 1996.

That there has never been a heavy cloud of doom and gloom over the Brigade has been due to sound leadership at all levels plus the self-discipline and resilience of the Gurkha soldiers. As an aid to maintaining high morale throughout these difficult years, participation in a wide field of adventure training and recreational pursuits has continued in every unit and sub unit. In the eyes of the Gurkha soldiers themselves, there is little doubt that winning the Brigade soccer competition, The Nepal Cup, which has been competed for every year, is the most coveted trophy of all. 1/2 GR, closely followed by QGE, have had more victories than the other teams but all have tasted glory at one time or another.

Shooting at Bisley and especially the Major Unit Championship became a competition that attracted the close attention of all units in the Brigade, major and minor. From the 1970s onwards, the Major Unit Championship was usually won by one or other of the Gurkha Battalions. In addition, individual Gurkha marksmen began to win the Queen's Medal and that included a British officer, Major Richard Coleman, of the Second Gurkha Rifles. The annual victories of the Brigade's shooting teams at Bisley evoked some wry comments from British units, semi-seriously suggesting that the Gurkhas did nothing else but shoot! What cannot be disputed is that by the mid 1980s, every Gurkha infantry regiment had won the Major Unit Championship and the Queen's Medal at least once, and some of them several times. The Corps, too, have also done remarkably well in the non-infantry competition and teams from smaller Gurkha units have often won the Minor Units Championship. In 1981, the Brigade of Gurkhas, for the first time, won the coveted Methuen Cup, competed for by infantry Divisions and the larger Corps.

Mention must be made about the Brigade Khud race which has been held every year. Thanks to their origins in the world's highest mountain range, Gurkhas excel at running on steep slopes and especially down hill. The 'Khud Race', is a legacy of warfare on the North West Frontier of India, when advance and rear-guards had to move to and from high ground at full speed to cover the movements between columns. Although each year British units have competed in the Khud race with great courage, the race invariably results in a victory for a Gurkha battalion team, with the Eastern Regiments, 7 GR and 10 GR, tending to dominate the competition. Records have been established over the years and in 1985 the time taken for the 1300 foot climb and 1200 foot descent was 15 minutes and 12 seconds, a truly formidable achievement. Gurkha teams, from units stationed in the UK, have also achieved great renown in the arduous events held in Wales under the titles 'Welsh 1000' and 'Welsh 3000'. The latter is the British Army's most gruelling race, a course run in uniform with webbing equipment, starting on the summit of Snowdon and covering 24 miles including 14 peaks of over 3000 feet and finishing on Drum. More recently Gurkha runners have achieved equal renown while racing to the top and back of Mount Kinabhalu in Sabah. All these successes have demonstrated that the Gurkhas are supreme at this particular ability.

Climbing some of the mighty peaks in the Himalayas has attracted the attention of a handful of British officers and Gurkha soldiers over the years. In 1975, for example, Duncan Briggs and Cpl. Rinchu Wangdi Lepcha from 6 GR reached the summit of Annapurna South Peak. Likewise 7 GR produced some excellent mountaineers, inspired, no doubt, by the example of Mike Kefford (now Colonel) whose exploits culminated in him leading the British Services Expedition to Mount Everest in 1991.

As the truncated Brigade faces an uncertain long term future in the British Army, the young Gurkha riflemen serving today are well aware of the responsibilities that rest on their shoulders – whether they are serving in Church Crookham or in The Falklands: whether they are shooting at Bisley or fire fighting in Sussex, as 6 GR had to during 1975 when the firemen were called out on official strike. The Gurkhas have served the British Crown for 180 years. Their motto is 'Kaphar Hunnu Bhanda Mornu Ramro' – It is better to die than be a coward'. Such a motto has been quoted over the years by many old soldiers to their young sons as they set out from the mountain village in Nepal to enlist in the British Army.

The well remembered and much loved quotation from an officer who served in the First World War, Professor Sir Ralph Turner, MC, makes a fine end to this story of the four famous Gurkha Regiments and the three Gurkha Corps.

'As I write these last words, my thoughts return to you, my comrades, the stubborn and indomitable peasants of Nepal. Once more I see you in your bivouacs or about your fires, on forced march or in trenches, now shivering with wet and cold, now scorched by a pitiless and burning sun. Uncomplaining you endure hunger and thirst and wounds, and at the last, your unwavering lines disappear into the smoke and wrath of battle. Bravest of the brave, most generous of the generous, never had a country more faithful friends than you.'